THE 'NATIONS WITHIN'

THE
'NATIONS WITHIN'

Aboriginal – State

Relations in Canada,

the United States,

and New Zealand

Augie Fleras
and
Jean Leonard Elliott

Toronto   OXFORD UNIVERSITY PRESS   1992

Oxford University Press, 70 Wynford Drive, Don Mills, Ontario M3C 1J9

Toronto Oxford New York
Delhi Bombay Calcutta Madras Karachi Kuala Lumpur
Singapore Hong Kong Tokyo Nairobi Dar es Salaam
Cape Town Melbourne Auckland

Fleras, Augie, 1947-
   The 'nations within'

Includes bibliographical references and index
ISBN 0-19-540754-7

1. Native peoples – Canada – Government relations.
2. Native peoples – Canada – Politics and government.
3. Indians of North America – Government relations –
1934-   . 4. Indians of North America – Politics
and government. 5. Maori (New Zealand people) –
Government relations. 6. Maori (New Zealand people) –
Politics and government. I. Elliott, Jean Leonard,
1941-   . II. Title.

E92.F53 1992   323.1'197071   C92-093863-9

This book is printed on permanent (acid-free) paper. ∞

1 2 3 4 — 95 94 93 92

Printed in Canada by Metrolitho

TABLE OF CONTENTS

To W. Frank Bates
and Dorothy Bates (AF)

To Eula Thornton Elliott
and Henry G. Elliott (JLE)

ACKNOWLEDGEMENTS

We wish to express our appreciation to the Social Sciences and Humanities Research Council of Canada, for funding the New Zealand portion of our research; the University of Waterloo and Dalhousie University, for providing supportive environments; Professor Sally Weaver, for her boundless energy and information; and Richard Teleky and Phyllis Wilson at Oxford University Press, for making all stages of the production process run more smoothly than previously thought possible. Special thanks to Sally Livingston, for guiding the manuscript through to its completion in the present form, and to our families, for sharing our goal and making it their own.

The study of aboriginal politics in the 1990s lacks a much-needed comparative dimension. Our intent is to provide this dimension with respect to aboriginal–state relations in Canada and, to a lesser extent, in New Zealand and the United States. It should be stressed, though, that this book is not about aboriginal peoples *per se*; it does not delve into aboriginal language, culture, history, or personalities. As non-aboriginals, the authors are not equipped to speak about aboriginal groups as social or cultural entities. Pretending to possess the skills or expertise to deal with aboriginal experiences is tantamount to appropriating aboriginal voices at a time when the 'nations within' are in a position to articulate their own realities and visions of the future.

In the following pages we attempt to address the evolving status of aboriginal peoples as 'nations within' (Deloria, Jr, and Lytle, 1984). Our sociological perspective focuses on relationships and intergroup dynamics within a framework of government policy and administration. Particular attention is paid to group processes, especially the ways in which perception and collective definition shape political action and policy outcomes. Social structures, in turn, define the parameters and restrict the options of the participants in this political drama.

A sociological commitment to explore aboriginal–state relations as an interplay between structure and agency is central to our work. Groups not only act *within* the limitations set down by society; they also tend to act *upon* these limits in reworking the social order around them. The problem of agency and the relationship between action and structure is a perennial conundrum. However, we concur with others (e.g., Miller, 1989; Cornell, 1988) that aboriginal peoples, like all peoples, are shapers of history, not merely passive victims shaped by the cumulative historical forces of colonization and settlement that were unleashed against them. Recently aboriginal peoples have resumed the initiative to restore their collective status and group entitlements as 'nations within'. Our role as authors is to chronicle the nature and characteristics of this emergent paradigm shift in aboriginal–state relations. In charting the progress from colonial dependency to relative aboriginal autonomy, we survey the events and developments that precipitated this renewal in aboriginal relations with the state, as well as the logic and rationale behind it.

Primary attention is focused on the political situation in Canada, where innovative steps in redefining aboriginal–state relations have been proposed and implemented. But we have not limited ourselves to the Canadian experience. In the field of race relations, Schermerhorn (1970) has argued convincingly for comparative studies selecting societies with somewhat comparable histories. Canada, the United States, and New Zealand—liberal democracies supported by capitalist economies—are all settler societies in which most of the earliest immigrants, with the exception of the French in Canada, came from the British Isles. Although a more thorough study of the response of indigenous peoples to subjugation would include such diverse colonial powers as the Dutch, German, French, and Portuguese, such considerations are beyond the scope of our present undertaking.

The comparative method will guide our investigation of the 'nations within' and their relations with the larger societies of which they are a part. The unit of analysis is the larger society. In painting a picture with such broad brush strokes, the challenge is to avoid homogenization and excessive generalization. Yet the task of simplifying complex matters for the sake of clarity or space is daunting. In Canada alone there are at least 53 distinct aboriginal languages. Specific tribes will be highlighted whenever possible, but it will not be feasible to give even passing attention to all on an individual basis. Again, it is the primary task of the aboriginal writers and artists themselves to do this in-depth analysis.

The appeal of the comparative method lies in its ability to transcend the limitations inherent in theorizing about and analysing a single society. By investigating the effects of predominantly English-speaking invaders elsewhere, we are able to acquire a much fuller picture of group dynamics than would be possible had we limited ourselves to any one society. In this regard, Cornell's (1988) use of the comparative method in his study of aboriginal peoples in the United States is instructive. Fully aware of the danger of appearing to reduce unique identities to a bland and meaningless whole, Cornell (1988: vi) argues that 'critical commonalities' remain within the Indian experience that increasingly link native Americans with each other and to a common political trajectory.

In a similar vein, we see a need to extend the search for 'critical commonalities' beyond the confines of Canada to include the original peoples who comprise the 'nations within' of the United States and New Zealand. To what extent are aboriginal peoples experiencing a common political trajectory? How relevant is the discourse on nationhood, particularly in relation to race (or ethnicity) and class? Concepts such as 'nation', 'race', and 'class' are political ideas that arise from underlying economic and political structures. The dynamic interplay of these concepts contributes to our understanding of the 'nations within'. The term 'nation' implies a sovereign people with the right to self-government. The submergence of this nationhood within the confines of the larger nation-state is the reality behind the 'nations within' debate. It is the process of loss and retrieval of nationhood that is the underlying theme of our study.

Ideas of race, class, and nation have been examined most extensively in the literature on ethnic minorities, especially minority/majority interaction within a single state. While this literature is informative up to a point, it excludes the central fact of concern—the subjugated status of the 'nations within'. Those struggling to have their sovereignty reinstated go beyond the vocabulary of race, class, or ethnicity to adopt the vocabulary of nationhood, for, just as racial minorities have rejected efforts at assimilation to assert racial pride in their own distinctiveness, so too aboriginal groups have moved beyond the narrow view of themselves as a minority. In its place has evolved a commitment to dialogue on a nation-to-state basis with the larger society. The expectations of self-government and sovereignty are of a different magnitude than cries for 'equal opportunity' and 'fair play'. Liberal democracies have a long tradition of attempting to accommodate the latter, but are relatively inexperienced in responding to the agenda of aboriginal nationalism. The full political and social agenda has not been acknowledged by the central governing bodies.

The benefits of the comparative perspective cannot be stressed enough. We can no longer afford the luxury of standing back and passively observing global developments in aboriginal–state relations. While acknowledging our differences, what can we learn from each other? The recurrent patterns underlying the restructuring process in other countries such as New Zealand and the United States may enable us to recognize shared experiences and common aspirations. Our concern is especially critical and timely as each of the countries examined here is grappling with the implications of these new political realities for statehood and nation-building.

A final word on terminology is due. There is not one term that will accurately describe the indigenous peoples of Canada, the United States, and New Zealand in the way that they would wish. The term 'peoples', with its connotation of autonomy and self-determination, is widely endorsed by aboriginal groups, although often rejected by central authorities for precisely that reason. In Canada 'people of the first nations' is preferred by some; others embrace 'aboriginal people' or 'Native peoples'. In the United States the term 'Native American' is widely used but not universally accepted. Most commonly aboriginal peoples in North America have been known by the larger society as 'Indians'—a designation that stemmed from the original fifteenth-century voyages of discovery. While serviceable as an all-embracing

racial category, the term 'Indian' is not the preferred mode of self-identification among aboriginal peoples, and it will be used here only if the
historical or legal context warrants it.

In New Zealand the indigenous Polynesian population is composed
of numerous tribes, and anyone who ignores the politics of tribal
reality does so at his or her own peril. This diversity is reflected in their
preference for self-identification as *tangata whenua o aotearoa*; that is,
the original inhabitants of New Zealand. For our purposes, however,
we will rely on the administrative term 'Maori', with full awareness
that tribal, linguistic, cultural, and regional differences prevail.

ONE

Introduction: Aboriginal Peoples as Nations

Challenges await the investigator intent upon formulating a definition of aboriginal peoples that is distinct from other related concepts such as 'cultures' or 'ethnic groups'. It is an even more difficult task to distinguish accurately between those aboriginal peoples who are characterized as 'nations'—either by themselves or by others—and those who are not. Mindful of the diversity of opinions and definitions at hand (Burger, 1987), we will provide working definitions of aboriginal peoples and aboriginal nations as an intellectual starting point to spark further discussion, reflection, and, as necessary, revision.

In this book we will define 'aboriginal peoples' as the existing descendants of those who are commonly thought to be the original inhabitants of a territory, who now occupy an encapsulated status as subordinate members of a larger society, but who continue to identify with a cultural lifestyle at odds with that of the dominant sector. Aboriginal people assume the politically self-conscious stance of 'nation' when they go a step beyond identifying themselves as the 'original' occupants of a land who wish to preserve and protect their cultural heritage. This additional step consists in their assertion that they have a special relationship with the state based on a unique set of entitlements. These entitlements typically involve the inherent right to some form of self-government and an acknowledgement of sovereignty. Aboriginal national concerns are varied, but most tend toward the principle of self-determination at political, social, and cultural levels as part of a wider drive to redefine their relationship with state.

In the countries under study here—Canada, the United States, and New Zealand—considerable energies have been expended on both sides, aboriginal and government, in reclassifying aboriginal peoples as a distinctive social type, with a corresponding set of characteristics and powers that derive from acknowledgement of their status in society as 'nations within'. Our text is concerned primarily with exploring this dimension of aboriginality. It is our perception that the process of reclaiming a right to aboriginal status and forging a new relationship with central authorities is likely to define aboriginal politics for the remainder of the twentieth century, if not beyond.

Confrontation between aboriginal peoples and the state in the last two decades has tended to focus around issues pertaining to land and political status. Possession of land is crucial to the survival of aboriginal people as a nation: that is, as a people with the right to self-determination over matters of internal jurisdiction. Recognition of their sovereignty over their land is also essential if they are to secure, manage, and develop a sustainable economic base. Land is the economic bedrock for the renewal of aboriginal peoples as a distinct society or nation.

Aboriginal attitudes toward land are strikingly different from non-aboriginal, and these differences present untold difficulties. For aboriginal peoples, land possesses a sacred quality, rooted in an attachment to history, a sense of identity, and a perception of duty towards future generations. In this sense, land is not merely inherited from our ancestors: even more important, it is held in custody for our unborn children. Land and natural resources are not to be exploited and consumed in the pursuit of material gain; they must be protected and conserved. This collective reverence for land and spiritual rapport with it contrast sharply with the larger society's material conception of land as a commodity for individual ownership, consumption, and sale.

Aboriginal peoples were often overwhelmed by the technological and military power of the colonizers. Land, culture, and identity were subjected to prolonged pressure, while the loss of control over resources proved lethal in terms of status, economic health, and identity. The combination of population decline and resistance toward the colonizer pushed the aboriginal peoples to the margins of society, both socially and geographically. In some instances, land-for-cash transactions resulted in wholesale transfers of land ownership to the settlers while aboriginal populations were relegated to reserves under centralized control and administration. The diminution of numbers followed by deterioration of morale and motivation was further exacerbated by assimilationist pressures that sought to undermine the cultural basis of aboriginal authority and incorporate the indigenes into society as productive citizens.

But not all aboriginal peoples conceded the inevitability of colonial domination over their land and culture. Resistance took many forms, both passive and active, from conventional approaches through societally approved channels such as court challenges and petitions to civil disobedience and armed rebellion. In recent years, the intensity of the resistance has increased to the point where aboriginal peoples now constitute a distinctive force in world politics with a capacity to embarrass and exert leverage on national governments.

The success of their endeavours is reflected in the gradual decolonization of aboriginal–state relations. Relationships of domination and control have been replaced by patterns of interaction that claim to embrace the unique status of aboriginal peoples as 'nations within': that is, as a distinct societies with special claims and collective entitlements that derive from formal recognition as the indigenous occupants of the land.

Many complex factors account for this renewal in aboriginal assertiveness, including a reversal of the demographic collapse that was evident on a world-wide basis by the early twentieth century. The decline in aboriginal populations was such that for a few decades their disappearance was widely predicted. Aboriginal peoples were being 'naturally' extinguished through famine, disease, and cultural dislocation as well as by warfare. By 1930 the indigenous populations in North and South America had been reduced by almost 95 per cent, from a pre-contact total of almost 19 million to less than one million; most of this depopulation took place after 1800. Likewise in Polynesia, the population was reduced by approximately 80 per cent, or more than 1.25 million, following 1800 (Bodley, 1987: 23).

The invaders invoked certain myths to legitimize and justify the colonization, displacement, and exploitation of aboriginal peoples in the name of evolutionary progress and national development. Terms such as the 'vanishing American' were coined to describe the demographic plight of the American aboriginal. The situation was viewed with both alarm and ethnocentric complacency, as if the extinction of aboriginal peoples were the inevitable price of 'progress'. In the United States, 'manifest destiny' meant that the European invaders, as the true representatives of a 'higher' form of civilization, were divinely intended to settle the continent from coast to coast. Even the more liberal and progressive elements in society tended to blame the victims for their misfortune.

According to the racist assumptions of the day, the 'inferior peoples' had been given a chance to acculturate, but collectively they had demonstrated that they were unable to benefit from exposure to 'civilization'. Their dying was tragic, but could not be helped. This mode of thought had its origins in the social Darwinism that, like biological

Darwinism, maintained that competition between groups is 'natural', and that not all groups will survive; those that do survive are the 'fittest' and, by implication, the most deserving in an evolutionary sense. Since these evolutionary processes of competition, conflict, and survival were 'natural', they should be accepted as such. Any attempt to interfere with the evolutionary laws of nature would be self-defeating.

Currently, the aboriginal populations in New Zealand, the United States, and Canada are younger than the larger populations. In each case, a higher percentage is below 15 years of age, and mortality rates at all ages are high, with a life expectancy that is from 6 to 10 years below that of the general non-Native population (Farley, 1987: 405; Norris, 1990: 48). Aboriginal fertility tends to be double that found in the general population, but is declining in comparison with previous decades. Despite this growth rate, it is thought that in the United States aboriginal peoples, for the most part, have not replenished their numbers to pre-contact levels (Dobyns, 1966), although in Canada the pre-contact level was surpassed in 1960 (Norris, 1990: 34). Demographic recovery in New Zealand more closely parallels the situation in Canada than in the United States. The current growth rates have contributed to the increasing need for economic incorporation into the larger society and have given demographic strength to the political arguments for greater autonomy and self-determination.

Like their counterparts in North America, the New Zealand Maori have struggled for years to establish conditions conducive to ensuring control over land and resources, language and culture, and political and social institutions. In New Zealand and elsewhere, state policies and programs that once were routinely accepted have lost their legitimacy when juxtaposed with aboriginal demands for redefinition of their relational status within society. New visions and diverse arrangements have been proposed as practical expressions of this demand for nationhood status.

While the specifics vary from one context to the next, aboriginal peoples share a number of social and economic features that stem directly from their status as encapsulated populations under colonialist rule (Stea and Wisner, 1984; Paine, 1985). No matter what economic index is cited—income, employment, education—aboriginal peoples, in a statistical sense, tend to occupy the bottom-most rung of the socio-economic ladder. Incomes are well below those of the general workforce. Unemployment rates are disproportionately high, with aboriginal peoples often constituting a reserve pool of cheap, menial labour for the dominant sector. Advancement and career opportunities tend to be non-existent for all but a few, as pervasive discriminatory barriers—subtle, if not blatant—deny full access, representation, and equal protection under the law. Formal levels of education from primary to tertiary lag behind those in the larger society, reinforcing the vicious cycle of poverty–restricted opportunities–impoverishment.

The grinding physical poverty that is often part and parcel of aboriginal status is sufficient cause for concern. No less worrisome are dislocations in the social sphere of family, kinship, and group relations. Aboriginal peoples confront psychological disorientation and spiritual destruction as a result of sustained assimilation pressures that have in some cases involved relocation. Loss of culture and control over life have in some instances led to chronic problems over personal identity, group integrity, and social solidarity. To overcome the disabling effects of cultural, social, and psychological abuse, aboriginal peoples have taken steps towards radical reassessment of the past and progressive reappraisal of the present.

Fortified in part by the ascendancy of concern for human rights in such world bodies as the United Nations, aboriginal nations have organized to resist further encroachment by central or corporate authorities. Efforts to block government and corporate entry onto aboriginal lands, from the rain forests of South America to James Bay in northern Quebec, have been instrumental in galvanizing consciousness and mobilizing protest among aboriginals and their non-aboriginal supporters.

The structural similarities between encapsulated peoples as 'nations within' have been reflected in decolonizing relations of dependency and exploitation in exchange for status based on inalienable or inherent rights. The focal point of these struggles is twofold. Inextricably related to the restructuring of interaction with the state on a government-to-government basis is, first, the ownership of land as a springboard for nationhood and, second, aboriginally-controlled social and economic development (Burger, 1987). *The 'Nations Within'* attempts to illustrate this process of redefinition and restructuring as it concerns the aboriginal nations encapsulated within Canada, the United States, and New Zealand.

To what extent might it be premature or inaccurate to speak of a paradigm shift in aboriginal–government relations? That much of the government's rhetoric of reform betrays a continuing commitment to the status quo is something to which aboriginal peoples have become accustomed through decades of neglect, broken promises, and exploitation. Does the so-called new aboriginal agenda in fact perpetuate relations of control and domination, merely rephrasing the terms in such a way as to create the impression of a renewal in aboriginal status? The arguments for and against such a determination will be examined in the following pages.

Much is at stake in the restructuring process, as political and private interests would prefer to continue a benign colonialist arrangement that ensures control over the aboriginal agenda and access to aboriginal resources. Aboriginal sectors, by contrast, want a decolonization of their relationship with the state, with access to the tools required for charting a new course based on freedom and self-determination in political, economic, and cultural matters. Arguing from first principles, they claim such self-determination to be their inherent right as founding nations. It is clear that, in the struggle between competing groups for power, status, and entitlements, aboriginal–state relations are a contested site. We argue that a comparative study of the aboriginal peoples encapsulated in three nation-states will increase our understanding of the historical processes whereby aboriginal peoples become aboriginal nations, and will increase our awareness of the range of options and choices confronting us throughout that process—collectively and individually, aboriginal and non-aboriginal alike.

We begin our study with an in-depth examination of the aboriginal nations within Canada, focusing in turn upon Indians, Métis, and Inuit—the three groups named and accorded aboriginal rights in the Canadian Constitution. The national situation of the aboriginal peoples who currently live under the jurisdiction of the United States is explored in the following section. Finally, shifting our focus to the South Pacific, the final section examines the Maori with respect to the entitlements they claim to Aotearoa (New Zealand). We conclude by comparing the historical processes affecting aboriginal nations in all three societies, the paradigms of aboriginal–state relations represented, and the future trajectories that appear to be indicated.

PART I

ABORIGINAL NATIONS WITHIN CANADA

T W O

'Unfinished Business': Reconstructing Aboriginal–State Relations

I am not
what they portray me.
I am civilized.
I am trying
To fit in this century.

Pray
meet me halfway —
I am today's Indian.
  —Rita Joe, from *Poems of Rita Joe* (Halifax: Abanaki, 1978); quoted in Petrone (1990).

Where do we begin to interpret and assess the aboriginal situation in Canada? The challenge of sorting out these issues cannot be lightly discounted. On the one hand, Canada remains the only country in the world in which constitutionally entrenched aboriginal and treaty rights serve as the basis for framing aboriginal–state relations. Following the government's aborted effort to abolish aboriginal status in 1969, aboriginal issues have catapulted into the forefront of debate over restructuring Canadian society. Aboriginal peoples have wrested increased control over land, their lives, and the laws that govern them, while central authorities continue to search for innovative ways to address the evolving concerns of Canada's first nations. Empowerment is the key, and practical actions are now driving aboriginal aspirations that only recently seemed beyond reach.

Yet Canada's treatment of its aboriginal peoples has been called a 'national tragedy' and an 'international disgrace', with ominous parallels to the white supremacist regime in South Africa (DuCharme, 1986; Angus, 1990). There is some evidence to back up this assertion: reports of federal neglect, long-standing bureaucratic oppression, rejection of meaningful dialogue, and disempowerment of aboriginal communities are testimony to second-class treatment. Aboriginal peoples as a group continue to lag far behind mainstream Canadians in terms of socio-economic status and attainment (Frideres, 1988). Levels of unemployment, undereducation, violent death, imprisonment, and ill health outstrip those of other Canadians in virtually all age brackets. Perhaps only the geographical isolation of aboriginal peoples in scattered pockets of misery accounts for the public's indifference towards what should otherwise evoke national outrage and mass demonstrations.

Two decades of intense protest and substantial reform have left aboriginal–state relations at a critical juncture (Frideres, 1991). Paradoxes abound, and grievances mount over failure to resolve certain contradictions in renegotiating aboriginal relations with the Canadian state. Consider these incongruencies. First, aboriginal peoples remain economically dependent on federal authorities for a variety of services and activities; at the same time they are embarking on a quest for self-determination through self-government within the parameters of Canada's constitutional framework. Second, to establish a workable system for negotiation and compromise, the national agenda has shifted towards finding a common ground on which to address aboriginal interests in a culturally appropriate manner; yet this effort is increasingly fraught with danger and deception as ostensibly positive initiatives (such as community self-government negotiations) are double-edged in both their immediate and their long-term effects. Third, aboriginal activism for renewal and reform is escalating, and is subject to increasingly intense media publicity—much of it reflecting a popular view of aboriginal peoples as (a) a 'social problem', (b) 'having problems' that cost the Canadian taxpayer, and (c) 'creating problems' that threaten Canada's social fabric.

The circulation of this misinformation is unfortunate. As long as the historical and cultural bases of aboriginal grievances and aspirations are misinterpreted, the potential for conflict remains even at a time of general public openness to aboriginal concerns (McMillan, 1988; Ponting, 1988). Public sympathy and support notwithstanding, Canadians as a whole remain abysmally unaware of what aboriginal peoples want, why they want it, and how they propose to attain their goals (Ponting, 1988). They are equally confused, and often misled, as to what Ottawa and the provinces have done, are doing, and intend to do in addressing aboriginal issues.

This section will examine the restructuring of aboriginal relations with the Canadian state in terms of the historical evolution from colony and colonialist dependency to limited aboriginal autonomy and nationhood. Particular attention is directed to the politics of aboriginal renewal as manifested in official policy and administration. Central to our interests is the shift in the state agenda, from a preoccupation with the 'Indian problem' (as exemplified in the White Paper of 1969) to the current focus on aboriginal peoples as distinct self-governing societies with the right to determine their future on a government-to-government basis. Acknowledging the causes, rationale, and impact of this shift in status and relations is critical. At a time when the national agenda is being shaped to a profound degree by aboriginal demands for restoration of their 'nations within' status, the stakes are too high to risk misunderstanding.

We begin with an overview of the legal, socio-economic, and demographic status of aboriginal peoples. Chapter 3 also examines aboriginal aspirations in the social context of demands for citizen-plus status, self-determination through self-government, recognition of aboriginal and treaty rights, and settlement of outstanding land claims. Major conflicts between aboriginal peoples and Canadian society centre around control of resources, particularly where development concerns are high, and the precise nature of aboriginal self-governing rights *vis-à-vis* Canadian sovereignty (Feit, 1989). The following chapter looks at the policy changes that have shaped the relationship between aboriginal peoples and federal/provincial sectors. Briefly, government policy focused on eliminating the 'Indian problem' by way of assimilation and controlled culture change (Miller, 1989). Assimilationist strategies based on the practices of segregation, wardship, and protection (1867-1945) gave way to integration and a commitment to formal equality (1945-73), which in turn were followed by the contemporary focus on limited aboriginal autonomy (from 1973 on). A collective effort to move aboriginal status away from the legacy of the colonial past, to a position nominally commensurate with aboriginal aspirations for 'nations within' status, lies at the core of the restructuring process (Fleras, 1990). But state responses to aboriginal assertions are subject to federal pressures to 'manage aboriginality' without relinquishing control of the national agenda. As a consequence of this pragmatism, aboriginal–state relations have *not* undergone as substantial a restructuring as the rhetoric would have us believe. Rather, assimilationist pressures continue to permeate the federal agenda, albeit less obtrusively than in the past. The resultant reality gap between aboriginal expectations and government actions suggests that the so-called 'Indian problem' is indeed formidable, and impervious to facile solutions.

Chapter 5 explores the politics of aboriginal renewal and reform at the level of self-government. Much of the debate over aboriginal self-government revolves around its underlying rationale, nature and scope, jurisdictions, and financial arrangements. Central to our understanding is the contentious claim of an *inherent* right to a constitutionally defined and distinct order of self-government within Canada's federalist constitutional framework. The chapter concludes that federal definitions of self-government are largely self-serving, designed to absorb aboriginal demands without risking any substantial change to the status quo. A closer examination of the First Ministers Conferences on Aboriginal Constitutional Matters between 1983 and 1987 reveals the highly political nature of aboriginal self-government as a policy issue.

The administrative dimension of aboriginal policy is explored in Chapter 6, which examines the role of the Department of Indian Affairs and Northern Development (DIAND), particularly the Indian and Inuit Affairs Program, in light of its mandate under the Indian Acts of 1876 and 1951; its latent functions for the control and domination of aboriginal clients; recent initiatives for revising organizational objectives, style, and goals; and ambiguities in the formal sorting out of aboriginal issues within a bureaucratic framework. That the Department is still beset by multiple mandates and competing agendas, to the detriment of its clients, points to a fundamental incompatibility between the principles of bureaucracy and aboriginality.

Chapter 7 looks at current trends and developments, with emphasis on the political implications of the 1990 Oka crisis and its aftermath for the restructuring of aboriginal–state relations. Aboriginal initiatives for renewal and reform are couched in the symbolic politics of images, protest, and polemics. Proposals for a New Zealand-style system of aboriginal electoral districts in Canada are but one intriguing example of the politics of symbols. As one way of integrating aboriginal peoples into a national political framework, the concept of guaranteed parliamentary representation possesses a certain appeal, in spite of obvious drawbacks in the post-Oka era. Finally, political initiatives and public opinions are analysed and assessed in light of the agenda-shattering confrontation at Oka. The inner logic of Oka is reflective of long-standing concerns and grievances, both of the Mohawks and of aboriginal peoples in general. No less important are the challenges, highlighted by Oka, inherent in the process of reconstituting aboriginal–state relations. Whether Oka will symbolize a turning point in the struggle to redefine aboriginal–state interaction remains to be seen.

THREE

The Social Context

ABORIGINAL STATUS

Demographic Features

Aboriginal peoples comprise an extremely diverse constituency, with numerous tribes (Ojibwa, Cree, Dogrib, Mohawk, and so on), unique histories and cultural systems, and varying legal divisions. Although all Native Indians are defined as aboriginal for constitutional purposes, the term 'aboriginal' itself encompasses status Indians (who are registered under the Indian Act), non-status Indians (who lost, or never had, formal status under the Indian Act), Métis (of mixed Indian and non-Indian relationships), and Inuit (aboriginal peoples of the north). In the 1986 census, a total of 712,000 reported themselves to be members of an aboriginal group or descendants of the original occupants of the land, representing 2.8 per cent of Canada's population (possibly 3 per cent if reserves and settlements that were not enumerated properly are included), up from 1.4 per cent in 1941 (Norris, 1990). Population increases are likely to accelerate in the future: the aboriginal population is growing more quickly than the general population, with birth rates about twice the general rate (30 per 1000 versus 15 per 1000). Mortality rates more consistent with those of the general population will continue to swell the overall numbers.

Widely dispersed geographically, aboriginal groups differ in size, degree of urbanization, settlement patterns, and socio-economic status

(see Norris, 1990). With respect to demography, for example, the aboriginal share of the population varies across Canada, with a high of 58
per cent in the Northwest Territories, followed by lesser proportions in
the Yukon and the western provinces. In absolute numbers, aboriginal
peoples are most heavily concentrated in Ontario, where nearly 25 per
cent of the total aboriginal population lives; British Columbia and
Alberta follow. The urban-rural distribution of aboriginal peoples is
also distinctive. Only 23 per cent of Canadians in 1986 were classed as
rural, compared with 53 per cent (up to 59 per cent including those
incompletely enumerated) of single-origin aboriginal peoples who
reside on reserves or settlements. Those who live off reserves and in
urban areas tend to be more transient: that is, they change cities and
dwellings more often than the general population. Finally, the aboriginal population is younger in age structure than the population as a
whole, with an average age of 23 in 1986 versus 34 in the general population: nearly 68 per cent are under 30, compared with 47 per cent of
all Canadians.

Legal Distinctions

The term 'aboriginal' refers to the descendants of the original inhabitants of Canada, and includes six recognized culture areas as well as
ten linguistic groups (DIAND, 1985; Canada, 1991). Today aboriginal
peoples enjoy the rights and privileges of citizenship available to all
Canadians; this was not the case in the past, when restrictions were
imposed on everything from federal voting to consumption of alcohol,
both off and on the reserve. As well as full equality under the Charter
of Rights and Freedoms, aboriginal peoples possess additional, albeit
unspecified, rights as set out in the Constitution Act of 1982. The
Indian Act of 1951 also confers special benefits, subsidies, and exemptions, especially for those who live on reserves. Responsibility for
'Indians' and 'lands reserved for Indians' was assigned to federal
authorities under the British North America Act (now called the Constitution Act) of 1867. As wards under the stewardship of the federal
government, status Indians were governed by separate legislation (the
Indian Act of 1876), and occupied a different legal status from all Canadians (McMillan, 1988). Reflecting divisions and distinctions within
the Indian Act, the Métis and non-status Indians were not formally
recognized by Ottawa until 1982, when both were accorded constitutional status as aboriginal peoples with unspecified rights, claims, and
entitlements.

Aboriginal peoples are legally classified into four categories. Status
Indians are the most numerous, with a population of just over 500,000
(nearly 2 per cent of Canada's total population), of whom 86 per cent

are located west of Quebec and in the two territories (Canada, 1991). They also possess the resources and organization to command a relatively high profile as the 'official' voice of aboriginal peoples in Canadian politics. Membership is defined by (a) admittance to a general registry, (b) affiliation with one of 596 bands (although membership is not automatic), and (c) jurisdiction under the Indian Act. Status Indians are legally permitted residence on one of 2,272 reserves ranging in population up to 16,000 at the Six Nations Reserve near Brantford, Ontario. Federal authorities provide services (health, justice, education, and welfare) on the reserves, in addition to funding for cultural programs, band government, and economic development. Status Indians are also entitled to certain benefits such as subsidized housing on reserves. In addition, as part of Canada's constitutional and statutory obligations (DIAND, 1990d), they are exempt from federal or provincial taxes on income earned on reserves. Up to 40 per cent of the band population at any given time lives off the reserves, reflecting high rates of out-migration since the 1960s—much of it actively fostered by the government. Nationally, status Indians are represented by the Assembly of First Nations, whose mandate to monitor federal policy and to lobby on behalf of aboriginal interests has given it an extremely high profile in constitutional affairs.

The second category consists of non-status Indians, whose numbers are unknown but may stand at approximately 75,000 (up to 750,000 by some estimates). Reinstatement of nearly 55,000 non-status Indians since passage of Bill C-31 in 1985 has wreaked havoc with specific figures. In legal terms, non-status Indians and their descendants have opted out of the Indian Act and are no longer governed by its provisions or privileges. In some cases, non-status Indians never possessed legal status because their ancestors were never included in any treaty arrangement. In many cases, however, status was voluntarily relinquished. Through enfranchisement, aboriginal persons (and their families, or entire bands by majority vote) could surrender status, assume full citizenship rights, and acquire the right to vote and own property (McMillan, 1988).

At present, non-status Indians are formally defined as aboriginal under the provisions of the 1982 Constitution Act. But classifying both status and non-status Indians under a single constitutional category has not diminished misunderstanding, as intergroup competition for access to limited federal resources has increased. The move to reinstate the reserve entitlements of aboriginal women (and their children) who lost Indian status because of marriage to non-aboriginals (see p. 19 below) has also drawn attention to issues pertaining to band self-determination, resource allocation, and community factionalism. Since

1968, the grievances and goals of non-status Indians have been represented at the national level by the Native Council of Canada.

The third category, the Métis, is also amorphous. Comprising the offspring of mixed aboriginal–European unions (and their descendants), the Métis population stands at 128,640 according to the 1986 census (Norris, 1990), although estimates can range up to 400,000 by other head counts. Many Métis dwell in relatively remote settlements throughout the Prairie provinces; in Alberta settlements they collectively exercise rights of land ownership and self-government (Martin, 1989). Although formally excluded from the Indian Act (like non-status Indians), Métis are officially regarded as aboriginal peoples with a corresponding right to make certain claims upon the Canadian state. Recent government land transfers ('comprehensive land-claims settlements') involving Métis and non-status Indians have offered these groups full or partial control of much of Canada's northern land mass. The Alberta government has also recognized Métis rights to self-government with control over institutions of relevance to them and a Métis homeland for the future (Martin, 1989). Nevertheless, confusion remains as to who qualifies as Métis, and what rights they are constitutionally entitled to. In 1983 the Métis broke away from the Native Council of Canada and formed the Métis National Council to represent their varied interests.

The Inuit constitute the fourth and final category. The 33,465 Inuit (based on the 1986 census) enjoy a special status and relationship with the federal government even though they have no special treaty arrangements and are not included under the Indian Act (Canada, 1991). They differ from other aboriginal peoples in having immigrated relatively recently into Canada, and share genetic similarities with Asian populations such as the Siberian Chukchi (McMillan, 1988). Formerly nomadic peoples who were relocated into permanent settlements during the 1950s and 1960s, the Inuit are seeking a new and comprehensive social contract with Canada that will integrate them as sovereign nations. The proposed establishment of Nunavut as a self-determining territory for the Eastern Inuit is but one example of northern efforts to avoid repetition of errors that have lead to aboriginal disempowerment in the south. A variety of Inuit organizations—the first being the Inuit Tapirisat, formed in 1970—serve to advance regional interests at the national level (Frideres, 1988). Nonetheless, there is evidence that the future for the Inuit may be bleak given the rapid social changes and cultural clashes that are inevitable as the affluent Canadian south continues its relentless march northwards (Irwin, 1989). We will examine the Métis and Inuit as 'nations within' in more detail in Chapter 8. The analysis that follows is relevant for the most part to status Indians.

Socio-economic Status

If there is any single issue on which Canada cannot hold its head high in the international community, any single area in which we can be accused of falling down on our obligations, it is in the area of *aboriginal relations* (emphasis added).
— Max Yalden, Chief Canadian Human Rights Commissioner,
Annual Report (1989).

Colonialist domination has exerted an overwhelmingly negative effect on aboriginal peoples (Bienvenue, 1985). In some cases, government policies deliberately undermined the viability of aboriginal communities in the never-ending quest to eliminate the 'Indian problem' once and for all. In others, however, this decline came about through less obtrusive yet equally powerful measures pertaining to education, bureaucracy, and missionary endeavours. The colonialist legacy has been nothing short of calamitous. Despite considerable federal outlays during the 1970s and 1980s, aboriginal peoples as a group dwell at the bottom of the socio-economic ladder in terms of education, income, employment, and health (Frideres, 1988). Many live in conditions that conjure up images of rural backwaters and underdeveloped populations in faraway Third World countries (Comeau and Santin, 1990). Housing is inadequate on many reserves, failing to meet basic standards for amenities and structure. Fewer than 50 per cent of Native homes have sewer or water connections; another 50 per cent can be described as overcrowded (DuCharme, 1986).

Economic indicators are equally deplorable. Unemployment rates are three times the average among non-Native Canadians. Fully 45 per cent of registered aboriginal individuals in 1985 depended on some form of social assistance—nearly two-and-a-half times the Canadian average (Comeau and Santin, 1990). On certain reserves, up to 95 per cent of the population subsists on welfare or unemployment benefits. Alcohol/substance abuse and broken families are all too common, and leave youth permanently scarred. Income levels are well below average both on and off the reserve, with family incomes of about $9300—less than half the national average.

Educational parity remains a long way off. Despite federal commitment to aboriginal control over education as part of the devolutionary policy of the early 1970s, both Ottawa and the provinces continue to dominate the curriculum and control the purse-strings. Government expenditures of $6.3-billion since then have had minimal impact as modest gains have been offset by comparable improvements in the general population, leaving the education gap relatively intact (Comeau and Santin, 1990). Only a small proportion of aboriginal students (about 25 per cent, according to 1986 census data) finish high school, compared with about 50 per cent of the non-aboriginal student body (DIAND, 1990a). Some experts contend that an aboriginal youth is three times more likely to land in jail than to graduate from secondary school (Comeau and Santin, 1990). Few ever make it to university (non-aboriginals are three times more likely to attend, and seven times more likely to graduate). Recent government restrictions on post-secondary spending are bound to put a damper on further improvements.

Of course, not all aboriginal people are destined to fail. Bands such as the Sechelt in British Columbia and the Blood in Alberta have been successful in matching resources with resourcefulness for community benefit. There are individuals who possess secure and satisfying jobs with comfortable suburban homes and exceptionally enriched lifestyles. They, however, are the exceptions.

The material poverty of aboriginal communities is worrisome in its own right. No less distressing is the spiritual and cognitive upheaval brought about by relentless exposure to assimilationist pressures. The attempted Canadianization of aboriginal peoples has taken numerous forms, including the routine placement of aboriginal children in residential schools where many were subjected to physical and sexual abuse. Other evidence that has recently come to light suggests that parents may also be victimizing their own children. The combination of structural constraints and negative experiences has robbed many aboriginals of any positive self-concept, leading to self-fulfilling cycles of despair and decay (Shkilnyk, 1985a). The deterioration of aboriginal cultural values has compounded the difficulties of identity and adjustment. In addition, numerous aboriginal languages are currently under threat because of pressure from the schools and mass media (Fleras, 1987b). Local efforts to stem the loss of language and culture among aboriginal youth have shown promise (Hall, 1986a), but the situation is still critical (Shkilnyk, 1986).

The psychological damage is equally noticeable, deriving in part from a sense of powerlessness, suspension between competing cultural systems, and internalization of white racism. Mortality rates are up to four times the national average, while life expectancies are about ten years below those in the general population (Norris, 1990). Infant mortality rates range nearly 60 per cent higher than the national average. Violent deaths and suicides are also out of proportion when compared with those in the general population; while the national average for incidents of violent crime hovers around 998 per 100,000, in the Northwest Territories the rate stands at 4,445 per 100,000, and 2,901 per 100,000 in the Yukon (*Maclean's*, 1990a). With a suicide rate six times the national average for certain age groups, Canada's aboriginal peoples currently represent one of the most self-destructive groups in the world.

Finally, aboriginal involvement with the criminal justice system is out of all proportion. Nearly 70 per cent of status Indians have been incarcerated in a correctional centre at some point by the age of 25 (DuCharme, 1986). Natives comprise 40 per cent of the inmates in western Canada's prisons, but only about 12 per cent of the Prairie population. With such frightening statistics, who can be surprised by repeated allegations of police brutality and cultural insensitivity by the criminal justice system in general (La Prairie, 1988; Aboriginal Justice Inquiry, 1991)?

Urban Aboriginals

Once regarded as tools of colonialism and subjugation, reserves are now perceived as central to aboriginal identity, self-determination, and self-government (Comeau and Santin, 1990). They provide spiritual assistance and sociocultural refuge for aboriginal persons, despite high levels of unemployment and impoverished living conditions. Yet nearly 40 per cent of the aboriginal population, according to 1986 census data, prefer to live off reserves—twice as many as in the early 1970s (McMillan, 1988). Prairie cities such as Regina and Winnipeg are characterized by high aboriginal concentrations (about 20 per cent of the total population). Toronto alone has 65,000 urban aboriginals, making it the largest 'reserve' in Canada.

Reasons for migration are numerous, but often reflect an interplay of 'push' factors such as lack of resources, opportunity, or excitement and 'pull' forces related to employment, education, and lifestyle. Structural (band size, proximity to urban centres), social (housing, employment), and cultural (socialization) factors are also important influences on the decision to leave—or return (Frideres, 1988). For some the move to cities is positive. Off-reserve aboriginals, for instance, have higher average incomes than those on reserves ($11,000 versus $9,300 in 1986), but these are still well below the national average of just over $18,000 (Comeau and Santin, 1990). For others, life off the reserve is beset with arrested economic opportunities, derelict living conditions, substance abuse, discrimination and lack of cultural awareness, and unhappy brushes with the law. These are the core conditions confronting urban aboriginals, and are perceived by many as symptomatic of broader economic and social forces beyond their control (Maidman, 1981).

Dual residence may be common among aboriginal migrants (see Dosman, 1972). During winter, the availability of welfare and heated accommodation makes life bearable in the city; then in summer there is an exodus back to the reserve to be with relatives and to supplement livelihoods with hunting and fishing (Comeau and Santin, 1990). The government for its part offers little in the way of services to off-reserve aboriginals, citing jurisdictional problems with the provinces as a stumbling-block. Established government institutions are ill equipped (in terms of both resources and needs assessment) to provide adequate culturally-sensitive services to aboriginal clients (Maidman, 1981). Many aboriginal-run voluntary agencies have been established to address issues pertaining to identity or adaptation, but the gap between supply and demand increases.

Aboriginal Women

The plight of aboriginal women is attracting increasing exposure. Formal studies and personal testimonies alike indicate that aboriginal women rank among the most severely disadvantaged in Canada (DIAND, 1979; Silman, 1987; see also Allen, 1986, and Witt, 1984, for similar assessments in the United States). Economically, they are worse off than both non-aboriginal women and aboriginal men in terms of income levels and employment options. Social hardships are numerous, including abuse by male family members, sexual assault and rape, inadequate housing, squalid living conditions, unhealthy child-raising environments, and alcohol and drug abuse. Depression and self-hatred among aboriginal women is reflected in high rates of suicide, alcohol dependency, and neglect of children. In 1986, nearly 6.4 per cent of status Indian children were in protective care, compared with only 1 per cent of the general child population (Comeau and Santin, 1990). Stereotypes from the past such as 'squaw', 'drudge', or 'prostitute' are an ongoing problem (Witt, 1984; also LaRocque, 1975, 1990).

Negative images make it difficult to recognize the positive contributions of aboriginal women to community life and social change. Historical and social factors work against adequate recognition. For those without status because of marriage with non-aboriginal males, penalties included deprivation of Indian rights, ostracism from involvement in band life, and exclusion from housing and jobs. Not even the repeal of the offending passage, section 12(1)(b), of the Indian Act in 1985 has eased the barriers for some women. In abolishing the discriminatory sections of the Indian Act that had stripped any Indian woman of status upon marriage to a non-Indian, Bill C-31 reinstated all non-status Indians who had lost status for financial, educational, or career reasons. It also eliminated those sections dealing with enfranchisement in general, making it impossible (and unnecessary) to gain or lose status through marriage. To ensure band control over membership and resources, only women who had lost status because of marriage became eligible to join the band or to partake of reserve land or benefits. Although children of reinstated women were also entitled to band resources, they stand to lose this status unless they marry into 'status'. Finally, aboriginal women's efforts to end blatant forms of discrimination have met with resistance on the grounds that tampering with the status quo could jeopardize special Indian status as set out in the Indian Act (Silman, 1987). Insistence by aboriginal women that the equality provisions of the Charter be written into any collective self-governing arrangement has also been a subject of disagreement (Platiel, 1992b).

In light of these grim statistics, it cannot come as a shock that Canada's treatment of aboriginal peoples is widely regarded as a blot on an otherwise enviable human-rights record. As Prime Minister Brian Mulroney observed, on launching a new Royal Commission on Canada's treatment of its aboriginal peoples: 'Anyone with an eye to see who has ever walked across an Indian reserve knows these are Third World conditions' (quoted in *Toronto Star*, 1991g). There are no simple answers or clearly defined villains or events that would account for the marginal status of aboriginal peoples (Comeau and Santin, 1990). The causes are complex and diverse, reflecting for the most part an interplay of various forces, historical events, and clashing visions. What we have is not really an 'Indian problem' or a 'white problem', but more accurately a white–aboriginal problem involving the interaction of mutually opposed sectors with different amounts of power and distinctive views of reality. The dominant sector seeks to enhance its position by imposing its definition of reality on society. The subordinate sector reacts by resisting and exploring alternative channels for the acquisition of power, status, and resources (Elliott and Fleras, 1991). Racism and discrimination, both blatant and systemic, have contributed to the subordination of aboriginal people through policies and programs that perpetuate the status quo. Inequities are amplified by the clash of competing cultures —one based on the rational pursuit of profit and the corresponding values of progress, competition, consumerism, and individualism; the other on values that reflect a commitment to harmony (social, spiritual, and environmental), co-operation and consensus, and tradition. Together with the imposition of an alien political and economic system, this cultural conflict has pushed aboriginal peoples to the margins of Canadian society.

In all fairness to central authorities, the socio-economic status of aboriginal peoples has improved recently, and the declining gaps in areas such as infant mortality and educational levels are promising. Yet we must continue to question whether government policies reflect an accurate reading of contemporary aboriginal aspirations. How real is the commitment to reform? Are policies rooted in a fundamental commitment to 'business as usual' once the rhetoric of reform is stripped away? It stands to reason that aboriginal groups are anxious to replace unproductive government solutions with proposals that hold out more promise for a progressive future.

ABORIGINAL CONCERNS AND ASPIRATIONS

> We are talking about the capacity to live as a nation, to act as a nation, and to deal with other nations on a nation-to-nation level, and this is quite different than what the Indian Act offers right now.
> —Conrad Sioui, Regional Chief, Quebec and Labrador (quoted in
> *Kitchener-Waterloo Record*, 23 Nov. 1990).

The aspirations of Canada's aboriginal peoples focus on 'citizen-plus' status, self-government, aboriginal and treaty rights, and settlement of land claims (Royal Commission, 1992; Native Council of Canada, 1992a, b). These goals are the cutting edge of a new paradigm in aboriginal policy and administration that threatens to overhaul conventional wisdom about the place of aboriginal peoples in Canada. In eschewing the colonialist-assimilationist mentality of the past, what aboriginal leaders propose is an innovative arrangement based on recognition of aboriginal peoples as 'nations within' the Canadian state, with an inherent right to self-determination through self-government. Although a holistic relationship exists among these proposals, since none can be fulfilled without the others, for convenience we will examine them individually, as if they were relatively independent.

'Citizen-Plus' Status

Aboriginal peoples are anxious to possess the same rights that most Canadian citizens take for granted. They want to live in a just and equal society where (a) they can set down roots and make a contribution to society at large, (b) they are not victimized by racism or discriminatory barriers that preclude meaningful involvement, (c) the rights of individuals are protected against unwarranted state interference and bureaucratic meddling, and (d) their culture, language, and identity can flourish as legitimate components of Canadian society. These concerns and demands are no different from those espoused by all Canadians, and reflect the right of all Canadian citizens to be the same as well as different.

Like all Canadians, aboriginal peoples demand the right to equal institutional access, as well as removal of the discriminatory barriers that deny equitable treatment. Consider, for example, the criminal justice system. While jails across Canada are teeming with aboriginal people—out of all proportion to their share of the population—public inquiries in Nova Scotia (the Donald Marshall case) and Manitoba (the Helen Betty Osborne and J.J. Harper cases) have exposed the criminal justice system—from the police to the courts—as racist, culturally insensitive, and hypocritical ('double standards'). Aboriginal difficulties with the law stem from breakdowns in intercultural communication, variable experiences with law enforcement and the courts, different expectations of the criminal justice system, and a dearth of aboriginal police officers as role models (RCMP, 1989). Various proposals have been put forward to ensure some measure of equality for aboriginals as citizens. Foremost among these are suggestions for indigenizing the criminal justice system (see p. 120 below). Under such an arrangement, aboriginal cultural values and personnel would be incorporated at all levels, from policing and sentencing to incarceration and release. The key here is the notion of aboriginal control over select aspects of the criminal processing system through establishment of parallel institutions. The emphasis would be on superimposition of community-based aboriginal styles of social control, especially in the areas of offender rehabilitation and victim restitution.

The protection and promotion of aboriginal cultures is another central concern. Language issues are particularly high on the priority list. Evidence suggests that, with the exception of Cree, Ojibway, and Inuktitut, most of the 53 aboriginal languages are perilously close to extinction (Shkilnyk, 1986). The solution as far as aboriginal leaders are concerned is placement of aboriginal languages on the same footing as official languages (*Toronto Star*, 1991a). Conferral of official status is seen as a way of freeing up the resources required to avert the demise of Canada's linguistic diversity. Concerted community efforts at language renewal, from preschool onwards, will also enhance the likelihood of survival (Hall, 1986a).

In addition, aboriginal peoples have clearly articulated a demand for rights over and above those of citizenship in general. Conferral of citizenship and equality rights, they argue, does not address the special problems that aboriginal peoples face with respect to assimilation and the destruction of their land base, culture, and identity. Citizenship upholds the rights of individuals but ignores the collective concerns of aboriginal peoples as a 'distinct society'. Nor do citizen rights acknowledge the unique status of aboriginal peoples as the original inhabitants with founding-nations status. 'Citizen-plus' status, coupled with the entitlements that would flow from such recognition, is seen as the minimum necessary to prevent further decline. The individual equality provisions of the Charter, according to Georges Erasmus (1992), are foreign to aboriginal people unless balanced by collective rights. For this reason, section 25 of the Constitution Act of 1982 claims to protect collective aboriginal rights (especially those recognized by the Royal Proclamation of 1763 and various land-claims settlements) from the individual equality provisions of the Charter of Rights (McMillan, 1988).

In short, aboriginal peoples want to be treated the same as all citizens. But equal citizenship is insufficient either to initiate a substantial change in the socio-economic status or to fulfil the political ambitions of the 'nations within'. Since aboriginal concerns and demands transcend conventional definitions and orthodox solutions, what is required is special recognition of specific needs and concerns. Under citizen-plus status, aboriginal people would enjoy the benefits and privileges of Canadian citizenship, but not at the expense of their collective rights and group entitlements, or their land and lifestyle.

Central authorities in Canada rarely dispute the assertion of citizen-plus status. A wide variety of state policies and programs with respect to land, culture, and development issues have formally acknowledged this claim. The entrenchment of aboriginality within the Constitution, in addition to ongoing case-by-case discussions regarding land rights and self-governing arrangements, is proof of this commitment. What remains to be negotiated, however, is the nature and scope of citizen-plus status with regard to the nationhood debate.

Self-Determination Through Self-Government

We are the founding nations of Canada and we will not allow the lie of two founding nations [English and French] to continue.
—Ovide Mercredi, Grand Chief of the Assembly of First Nations; quoted in *Globe and Mail*, 27 Aug. 1991.

Aboriginal peoples have long asserted a right to self-determination on the grounds that their survival as distinct societies is contingent on aboriginal control over social and cultural development (see also Steinlien, 1989). On the assumption that self-determination constitutes an inherent aboriginal right, they are determined to exercise control over those political, cultural, economic, and social issues of concern to them. Self-determination is seen as essential not only to break the cycle of deprivation, dependency, and underachievement, but also to permit aboriginal people to conduct various internal affairs according to their own priorities and values.

Central to this goal of self-determination is the conviction that aboriginal peoples constitute a social collectivity with an inalienable duty as custodians to bequeath land and culture to future generations (Dacks, 1990). Stewardship of this historical legacy cannot be properly fulfilled under existing political arrangements, especially since liberal democracies are often oblivious to aboriginal grievances and aspirations. Nor can existing government agendas, with their emphasis on individual rights, offer protection from assimilationist threats to collective survival. Only self-governing structures are perceived as having the potential to restore aboriginal peoples to their rightful place as the founding occupants of Canada.

Aboriginal discourse on self-determination is frequently rooted in the idea of inherent aboriginal self-government rights—a concept so elusive that most calls for clarification have generated more heat than light (Little Bear et al., 1984). Prior to European contact, aboriginal peoples were organized in politically autonomous structures with sovereign control over their territories. European colonization and settlement eroded this autonomy and transferred substantial control over land and lives to the Minister of Indian Affairs (DIAND, 1985). Band councils were given by-law powers under the Indian Act, with some discretion over spending and allocation. But conflicts with traditional (often hereditary) chiefs and cultural values often undermined the credibility of federally-imposed governing structures.

Although recent initiatives have explored the merits of restoring aboriginal self-governing powers, defining self-government has been problematic. That there is little in the way of consensus even among aboriginal leaders reflects in part a desire to be flexible, adaptable and non-dogmatic. In rejecting a singular definition of self-government, Assembly of First Nations Grand Chief Ovide Mercredi acknowledges that aboriginal societies are too diverse to operate under a single set of rules (Newman, 1991). The bottom line is *power*: the concept of self-government implies aboriginal rather than external authority over jurisdictions and institutions of relevance to aboriginal peoples. As Mercredi states: 'Self-government means having the authority to control our own lives and to manage the day-to-day affairs of our people without having to ask to do so. It also means having the necessary financial resources to carry out these plans' (*Toronto Star*, 27 Oct. 1991). Beyond those parameters, however, self-governing structures are expected to evolve over time in accordance with local needs and regional aspirations.

This lack of detail regarding self-government may be viewed as an asset rather than a weakness. Nevertheless, general patterns in function, structure, and jurisdiction can be detected. The overall function of self-government would be to promote (a) greater self-determination and social justice, (b) economic development to abolish poverty through local development and equitable distribution of wealth, (c) protection of aboriginal language, culture, and identity, and (d) development of the social vigour required to tackle problems related to health, housing, alienation, and empowerment. With respect to structure, self-governing units would constitute a *unique and distinct order of government* alongside federal and provincial levels, with corresponding control over matters of relevance to aboriginal communities. As befitting a distinct and founding people, these powers would not be delegated by federal authority; nor would they be created by Canadian law. Rather, they would reflect an inherent, pre-existing aboriginal right that is said to derive from the Creator and remain untouched by treaty or conquest. This excerpt from a booklet published by a BC aboriginal group highlights the fundamental principles involved:

1. Sovereignty including Aboriginal Title and Rights is a gift of the Creator to the people of the First Nations. This sovereignty has never been given up. It is on the basis of the sovereignty of the First Nations that the relationship with Canada must be elaborated and enhanced.

2. The right of self-determination of the First Nations is recognized in international law and in covenants on international human rights and political rights. The First Nations will not allow the question of their self-determination to become a domestic issue for Canada to resolve, and they will not abandon or compromise their international standing.

3. The relationship of each First Nation to Canada is a nation-to-nation relationship, requiring the free and informed consent of each First Nation to all aspects of the relationship. First Nations may turn to other international situations such as those of states like Monaco and San Marino, for guidance and a model. The details of the relationship and the manner in which consent is given by a First Nation can be the subject of treaties and agreements (Sto:lo, 1984: 31).

The concept of an 'inherent right' to self-government is critical in promoting aboriginal peoples as a distinct and founding nation, for it acknowledges that they were sovereign and self-governing prior to European contact, that they were treated as independent nations by the first colonists, and that they have never lost that pre-existing right to self-determination. Thus 'inherent rights' are empowering. But they are not synonymous with separation or secession from Canada. Ovide Mercredi is careful to place inherent self-governing rights within a Canadian framework: 'What we are looking for is inclusion. We're trying to end exclusion. . . . Our whole constitutional strategy is based on that—to belong, to be accepted, to be respected' (in Bryden, 1991). Yet federal authorities are uneasy, seeing inherent rights as a threat to Canada's unity and survival as a sovereign state (*Globe and Mail*, 2 Nov. 1991). A 'negotiated' level of self-government along municipal lines is preferred, to avoid creating a patchwork of independent aboriginal nations outside Canadian law and the protections it offers for individual rights and private property interests. Whichever scenario is accepted—'inherent' or 'negotiated' self-government—it will entail costly and time-consuming arrangements regarding powers, financing, jurisdiction, and constitutional guarantees.

Jurisdictional matters under self-governing structures are expected to vary from band to band. Apart from a general commitment to deny dependency and promote development, they are likely to include (a) control over the delivery of social services such as policing, education, and health and welfare ('institutional autonomy'); (b) control over resources and use of land for economic regeneration; (c) control over the means to protect and promote distinct cultural values and languages; (d) control over band membership and entitlements; and (e) control over federal expenditures according to aboriginal priorities rather than those of the government or bureaucracy. These jurisdictions would have to be negotiated with federal and provincial authorities even if the concept of inherent self-government is accepted.

Significant social, political, economic, and cultural benefits are expected to follow from a self-governing arrangement (Ponting, 1986). In the case of the economy, decisions regarding investment, marketing, industrial location, and royalty fees would lie with aboriginal groups. Aboriginal groups are not against economic development *per se*, but are anxious to control the pace, scope, and benefits of resource extraction.

Case Study: Reclaiming Destiny, Restoring Control
As noted above, self-government in the final analysis consists of aboriginal people's right to manage their own affairs, in the process moving away from the colonializing mentality of the Indian Act, with its emphasis on forced dependence and underdevelopment. Instead, aboriginal communities would exercise control over the design and delivery of various programs related to education, child and health care, employment and the local economy, and politics and government. To some extent, aboriginal peoples have already assumed limited control in these areas as part of a broader effort to deal with problems that afflict their communities, as well as to secure a place for themselves in Canadian society. Capitalizing on DIAND's commitment to devolution, aboriginal band councils now control and administer the vast bulk of monies spent on Department programs in a wide range of areas, from economic renewal to aboriginal language retention.

The restructuring process is clearly manifest at the institutional level. In a series of articles that appeared in the *Toronto Star*, Dan Smith (1991), the current holder of the Atkinson Fellowship in Public Policy, points out the growing number of aboriginal successes in taking over a variety of formerly government-run services for aboriginal communities. Consider the following examples, taken in part from Smith (1991). From the first aboriginal–run school established by the Saddle Creek Cree in northeastern Alberta, there are now 324 such schools throughout Canada, leaving only 43 reserve schools under the administrative control of DIAND. This is a far cry from the past, when—fearing that outside contact would harm aboriginal youth—the government segregated the large majority of aboriginal pupils into residential schools under federal supervision on reserve lands (DIAND, 1991g). From 1950 on, a series of joint school agreements endorsed the principle of integrating students into the provincial school systems. The creation of aboriginal-run schools continues this shift towards aboriginal control over education.

With respect to criminal justice, several groups including the Bloods of Alberta and the Six Nations in southern Ontario have attempted to sever the depressing cycle in which aboriginal offenders are repeatedly incarcerated by an alien and alienating system. In its place they have advocated a restructuring of aboriginal criminal justice procedures to (a) incorporate aboriginal cultural and community-based values, (b) create aboriginal-based institutions and agencies, from police to jails, and (c) promote reconciliation and rehabilitation rather than incarceration. Still, the healing process remains a formidable challenge.

The care and protection of children is another jurisdiction increasingly taken over by local aboriginal communities. In just over a decade, up to 37 aboriginal-controlled agencies (at last count) have sprung up across Canada with the objective of sheltering children and resolving home conflicts under extended-family arrangements. In the economic sphere, there is no shortage of success stories highlighting aboriginal entrepreneurial skills in everything from resource extraction (e.g., logging) to aboriginal-owned and -controlled businesses, to sophisticated computer-training programs. Another concept that has come a long way in a short time is that of aboriginal-controlled health care. Not only are aboriginal groups taking charge of local health programs and community clinics previously under DIAND administration, but broader moves to take control of the entire health-care system are also evident, as reflected in the creation of Canada's first aboriginal-run hospital at the Kahnawake Mohawk reserve near Montreal in 1986.

Finally, in areas related to government, aboriginal communities are looking to establish a form of local self-rule that is sensitive to community needs and aspirations, and consistent both with local levels of development and with geographic location. Political control has been invested in various institutions, ranging from non-elected hereditary chiefs to regional tribal councils in which several bands may form a coalition to pool resources for improving the delivery of government services. In some cases, local communities are seeking to modify the existing band council system in hopes of expanding the collective basis of decision-making.

There is little doubt that impressive developments have occurred in restoring aboriginal control over programs and institutions of relevance in making a claim for self-government. But not all communities have been able to share equally in this restructuring. As Smith (1991) notes, small reserves and those that lack either a reliable resource base or access to markets and investments continue to depend on DIAND for delivery of services. Métis and non-status Indians are often excluded from any fundamental restructuring, since they lack the economic levers to take control of their destiny. Escaping the suffocating confines of the Indian Act has not been easy, moreover, and in many cases provincial laws and stringent operating standards make it difficult to design and implement aboriginal alternatives in child and health care. In addition, there are deep-seated suspicions of 'hidden agendas' in the decision by DIAND to transfer programs and funding as part of its commitment to self-government and devolution. The Department is seen by many as merely fobbing off its responsibilities to aboriginal communities without providing the resources, training, and expertise needed to sustain programs and institutions. Finally, it has been difficult to shake the suspicion that Ottawa's endorsement of aboriginal self-government amounts to little more than a willingness to remove Indian Act restrictions on the authority of elected band councils.

The federal government's commitment to restructuring seems enlightened, but so far its approach to politically-negotiated self-government has been extremely cautious. Since the Sechelt Band Act of 1986 (see p. 61 below), the only negotiations to produce a self-governing agreement have been those with the tiny, oil-rich Sawridge Cree band of northern Alberta (Smith, 1991). The fact that, as of late 1991, even that agreement has not yet been approved by Parliament does not augur well for the future.

Is self-government the panacea for aboriginal problems? Not everyone thinks so. Some dismiss federal proposals for self-governing structures as little more than ploys to transform reserves into quasi-municipalities along lines of wardship reminiscent of South Africa's homelands. The danger of disempowerment through isolation of bands from the broader sources of power in society is also of concern (Hall, 1990). Self-government may not suit the interests of those on remote reserves where the land base and resources are inadequate for self-sufficiency. Off-reserve populations may also pose a problem, as it is difficult to envision models of self-government for urban Indians without any collective land base for economic development (McMillan, 1988). Turning the concept into reality will be a challenge in provinces such as Ontario, where the vast majority of aboriginal peoples (approximately 140,000 of 200,000) live away from the reserve (*Globe and Mail*, 1991h). As well, there is no guarantee that grassroots support for self-government is as extensive as aboriginal leaders maintain, especially in the face of pressing social conditions and cultural priorities (Gibbins and Ponting, 1986).

Ultimately, debates over self-government are concerned with the restructuring of aboriginal status in society. They also serve as a symbol heralding the end of colonization. But the implementation of self-governing structures has proceeded at glacial speed, and the vision of self-government held by many aboriginal leaders is at some variance with that of federal authorities. Nevertheless, as the Sechelt of British Columbia and the Cree-Naskapi of Northern Quebec have shown, aboriginal communities are already moving away from the indirect rule imposed by the Indian Act and exploring innovative styles of self-government within broadly defined constraints. (The politics of self-government will be examined in Chapter 5.)

Aboriginal and Treaty Rights

The third component of aboriginal aspirations concerns the recognition, definition, and constitutional entrenchment of aboriginal and treaty rights. Section 35 of the Constitution 'recognized and affirmed' existing aboriginal and treaty rights, whereas section 25 was inserted to protect these rights from any adverse effects resulting from inclusion under the Charter of Rights and Freedoms (Royal Commission, 1992). Confusion is widespread in this area, however, and has contributed to misunderstanding and resentment.

Aboriginal Rights and the Principle of Aboriginality
Bewildered by the concept of aboriginal rights and the placement of aboriginality on the national agenda, many non-aboriginal Canadians fail to comprehend the necessity of redefining aboriginal peoples' status in society and their relationship with the Canadian state. There is confusion over whether aboriginal rights flow from inherent and unextinguished aboriginal sovereignty, from existing aboriginal and treaty rights such as those set out in the Constitution, or from federal and provincial governments (Asch, 1989; Hawkes, 1989). In addition to these questions about the source of aboriginal rights ('inherent', 'treaty-based', or 'delegated') there are concerns about the scope of such rights (do they include an inherent right to self-government? fishing rights? etc.); whether these rights have been or can be extinguished; and how aboriginal rights relate to the constitutional and charter framework of Canada (see Burns, 1991). Such confusion makes it difficult for all Canadians to respond intelligently to aboriginal grievances.

The principle of aboriginality may be defined in essentially political terms, as a statement of power that acknowledges the special status of the original occupants of a territory and aims at restoring rights and entitlements that flow from recognition of this unique relationship with the state (Weaver, 1984). The key issues associated with aboriginal rights pertain to separate political jurisdiction and establishment of a land base. This politicized view of aboriginality has several implications. There is a sense in which aboriginal people retain their original, inherent sovereignty, because the Canadian Constitution does not necessarily apply to them, because they are exempt from federal/provincial laws, and because of treaties that are viewed as nation-to-nation agreements specifying separate jurisdictions. Programs and policies that apply to other Canadian minority groups are dismissed as inapplicable—even counterproductive—to aboriginal ambitions. Any move towards integration as one ethnic component in a Canadian multicultural mosaic is rejected as diminishing entitlement as 'first among equals'. What has been proposed instead is recognition of the aboriginal people's 'priority' status as a founding nation of Canada—a status not unlike that of the French in Quebec. In rejecting an ethnic or immigrant dimension, aboriginal people prefer to define themselves as a 'sovereign' entity within the federal state, with collective rights guaranteed by virtue of their ancestral occupation and arising from first principles.

Within the restructuring process, aboriginality is inextricably tied to inherent self-government rights. Aboriginality provides the 'theory' for redefining aboriginal–state relations; self-government is the practical expression of this 'theory'. Self-government implies self-determination with regard to relevant agendas, especially at the level of institutions and decision-making powers. The principle of aboriginality legitimizes the restoration of this sovereignty over internal affairs. One model is that of the 'domestic dependent nations' in the United States, whose sovereign status minimizes federal/state interference in internal tribal matters. Claims to sovereignty are defended either by appeals to natural law or on spiritual grounds (Ahenakew, 1985). As the original occupants whose inalienable rights have never been extinguished by treaty or superseded by conquest, aboriginal people defend their claims against the state as intrinsic and basic rather than contingent on government largesse or political decree.

The concept of aboriginal rights was put to the test in 1984, when Ronald Sparrow, a member of BC's Musqueam Indian Band, was charged under the federal Fisheries Act with using an illegally-sized drift net. Sparrow defended himself by claiming his aboriginal right to fish as guaranteed in section 35(I) of the Constitution, which 'recognized and affirmed . . . existing aboriginal and treaty rights'. In 1990 the Supreme Court of Canada accepted his defence (that the net restriction was invalid because it denied his aboriginal rights) and quashed the original conviction. In ruling that governments must have a valid legislative objective before compromising aboriginal (hunting and fishing) rights, the Supreme Court circumscribed an earlier principle of parliamentary paramountcy with powers to extinguish rights at will (Platiel, 1992a).

The impact of this landmark decision cannot be lightly dismissed (Usher, 1991). First, the court confirmed that aboriginal rights (in this case, the right to fish) cannot be extinguished by federal or provincial laws (e.g., the Fisheries Act), but can only be regulated by them. Second, it confirmed that the federal government has a responsibility to uphold its special trust relationship with aboriginal people by dealing with them in a generous and honourable manner; the government is thus required to ensure that its policies are consistent with the spirit of this ruling (Canada, 1991). Third, in cases where aboriginal rights are infringed by federal or provincial statute, the burden of justifying such infringement rests with the Crown. Legislators must ensure that (a) the legislative objectives are valid for purposes of conservation and resource management; (b) the legislation is consistent with the government's fiduciary responsibilities; and (c) aboriginal groups have been consulted (Usher, 1991).

Treaty Rights and Land Claims
Equally important is the enforcement of the federal treaty obligations that are a central component of many aboriginal claims and grievances (Canada, 1982). Many aboriginal peoples look on the treaties as 'living' agreements that specify the special legal status of aboriginal nations and constitute the basis for meaningful political dialogue (Coolican, 1985). Treaties are regarded as semi-sacred, binding documents according to which land and resources were transferred to central authorities in exchange for guarantees of protection, control over aboriginal land and resources, and various goods and services. Treaties provide Canada with a basis in international law for the territory it claims as sovereign; they also entitle non-aboriginal people to settle on this land and possess private property (Native Council of Canada, 1992). The notion of federal trusteeship and the obligations associated with this fiduciary relationship remain intact at present. The 1990 Supreme Court ruling in the Sparrow case confirmed Ottawa's obligation to discharge its trust responsibilities in a manner that protects and advances aboriginal interests.

With the 1763 Royal Proclamation, the British entered into the first of many treaty engagements with aboriginal peoples. The Royal Proclamation established the principle of exclusive Crown acquisition of aboriginal lands. Subsequent treaties focused more on peace and friendship, but by mid-nineteenth century the emphasis had shifted to land surrenders involving a one-time payment and occasionally a reserve and guaranteed access to fishing and hunting (McMillan, 1988). Following Confederation, thirteen 'numbered' treaties were signed between 1871 and 1929 encompassing much of Canada west of the Quebec-Ontario border. The signing of a treaty was viewed by authorities and agents as marking the surrender of aboriginal land in exchange for certain concessions (Gibbins and Ponting, 1986). Treaty terms stipulated that, in return for vast tracts of land, the government would set aside reserve land for the local aboriginal population on a per capita basis (Wagner, 1991) and grant special privileges (such as annuities, uniforms, and medals) for the chiefs, cash, and services in perpetuity. Aboriginal leaders are adamant that treaty benefits and services (such as free government services and tax exemptions) are neither a charitable handout nor a benevolent gesture on the part of an enlightened authority. Rather, these benefits derive from a legally binding exchange that aboriginal peoples have paid for time and again, not only through the expropriation of land and resources, but also through the loss of their language, culture, and identity.

It is commonly accepted that on many occasions the treaty process was fraudulent—at times, riddled with deceit. Differences appeared between what the aboriginal groups thought they were signing (pacts of friendship and mutual assistance) and the actual detail and intent of the documents (primarily deeds of sale) (McMillan, 1988). Federal authorities have long taken the brunt of criticism, in large measure for not living up to treaty obligations, either through calculation or through too-literal (and too-legalistic) interpretation of the treaty provisions. Historically, Ottawa has opted for a rigid, narrow, and literal interpretation. For example, because post-secondary education is not mentioned in the treaties, the government argues that it is not obligated to fund university education—that it does so only at its pleasure, as a matter of largesse, not as an aboriginal right (Comeau and Santin, 1990). For aboriginal peoples, on the other hand, the preferred reading is broad, and must be adapted to meet the emerging realities and evolving needs of the modern world.

Land-Claims Settlements

First of all that God created us Indians in this territory in a good many tribes. So are the white men, brown men and coloured people in their own territories in Europe and in Africa, and therefore we claim that we are the real ownership of this territory. That our title and rights are sacred in which is called aboriginal title. From time immemorial various tribes of Indians exclusively possessed, occupied and used exercised sovereignty over the territory now forming the Province of British Columbia. When the white men came into our country we treated them as good as friends and brothers as they came along. *Sir James Douglas, the first governor, made a verbal promise* to us Indians on his first surveying the lands. He said, for which I survey as Indian lands it really belongs to the Indians only. That no white man shall intrude in your lands, and for all the outside of your lands, H.M. Queen Victoria will take and call to the white people, and that land shall be owned as a lasting fruit tree to the Indians. Her majesty will take the said fruits and give it to the Indians as their lasting support. *And the second governor, Seymour by name, he also had a verbal promise in his speech. He said her Majesty the Queen will divide the revenues in three parts. One third shall remain for the Crown, one third will be spent to the public for roads and other things, and one third shall go to the Indians, the owners of the land for their lasting support and benefit* and that we shall hold just as much privilege as a white man, and that we must treat the white man the best way possible, and that we shall be treated the same way as if we were brothers. Now for this last many years standing we have been expecting to receive those good promises in the name of Queen Victoria, but it yet has never come, because the latest governor of the province has concealed it and buried it and worked all kinds of schemes around it to keep it hidden. All us Indians claim that the Provincial Government has no rights whatever to claim a reversionary interest in our reserves, and that no other but the Indians has a clear claim to it. Therefore we ask to obtain a permanent and secure title to the present Indian reserves we are at present time living on, as well as to all the lands which Sir James Douglas surveyed as Indian lands.

> — Excerpt from Royal Commission meeting; statement signed by Chief John Leon, per Andrew Phillip, 10 Jan. 1915; reprinted in Sto:lo (1984).

Aboriginal peoples have repeatedly claimed a special relationship with the land as integral to their cultural distinctiveness and unique aboriginal status (DIAND, 1990e). Reaffirmation of this relationship through settlement of both comprehensive and specific land claims is central to aboriginal objectives. Since a crucial court decision in 1973 (see p. 44 below) the Canadian government has also made it a policy priority to negotiate comprehensive settlements in areas where aboriginal title to land has never been extinguished by either treaty or due process (McMillan, 1988; Miller, 1989). With the entrenchment of existing aboriginal rights in the 1982 Constitution—which made Canada one of the few countries to legally address the notion of legitimate tenure rights in land for indigenous populations (Wilmsen, 1989) —the government now purports to be fully committed to the 'fair' and 'equitable' resolution of aboriginal land claims based on rightful ownership and occupancy rights (DIAND, 1987).

Aboriginal interest in land-claims issues is not derived from some quixotic dream of establishing a traditional aboriginal homeland. Nor is it a manifestation of 'greed' for aboriginal people to reclaim ownership over what they regard as rightfully theirs. Resolution of land claims is imperative if a solid economic base is to be secured for future development and prosperity. Future economic development will require clearing away legal obstacles to commercial growth; clarifying aboriginal rights to hunting, fishing, and trapping; allocating a share of mineral and subsurface rights; and transferring funds to accelerate aboriginal economic projects (Simpson, 1990). Moreover, implementation of aboriginal self-governing structures is contingent on establishment of a sound financial footing—for example, by renting out lands at rates favourable to community interests. The key here is controlled resource extraction (in tandem with public or private interests) at a pace that reflects community priorities and developmental levels. Indeed, it is claimed, any fundamental changes in the status of aboriginal people can be achieved only by negotiating from a position of economic strength within a self-governing framework.

A distinction between specific and comprehensive claims is critical. Specific land claims are based on perceived violations by federal authorities of their lawful treaty obligations. Specific claims may also arise from problems in the administration of aboriginal land and other assets under the Indian Act. By early 1990, a total of 532 specific claims had been lodged with the federal authorities. Of these only 43 had been settled, while an additional 22 cases were in the settlement negotiation phase (DIAND, 1990d).

By contrast, comprehensive claims resemble modern-day treaties in that they are based on traditional occupancy and ongoing aboriginal use of lands (Canada, 1982; Cross Cultural Consulting, 1989). In 1986 the Minister of Indian Affairs, Bill McKnight, unveiled the Comprehensive Land Claims Policy, drawn in part from recommendations in the 1985 Coolican Report (reaffirming the principle of aboriginal title and treaty rights) and grounded in the process of claims resolution by direct negotiation. The objective of comprehensive land claims is to clarify aboriginal relationship with the land—that is, to establish certainty of ownership over land and resources—as a basis for cultural renewal, economic development, and political control (DIAND, 1991b). Federal agreement to negotiate (although not necessarily to accept the position of the claimant) rests on certain criteria. A claim for negotiation can commence only when the claimant group can demonstrate that it is an organized society with exclusive occupancy of a specific territory prior to European contact; that it has continued to use and occupy this land into the present; and that aboriginal title and rights remain intact and have not been dealt away by treaty or abrogated through lawful means.

Only three comprehensive land claims have been settled to date: the James Bay and Northern Quebec Agreement—the first comprehensive agreement in Canada that also specified a set of aboriginal rights to self-governance in the context of a modern nation-state (Feit, 1989)—in 1975; the Northeastern Quebec Agreement (sparked in large part by fears of a legal impasse for Quebec's hydro ambitions) in 1978; and the Inuvialiut Final Agreement in 1984. The latter conferred entitlement to 91,000 square kilometres of land in the Northwest Territories and Yukon on 2,500 Inuit, granted a one-time payment of $10-million as well as $152-million in financial compensation, and guaranteed rights over resource management (DIAND, 1991b). A fourth settlement appears imminent. On 15 July 1991 the Gwich'in Tribal Council and the governments in Ottawa and the Northwest Territories initialled a comprehensive land-claim settlement that, pending ratification, will restore Gwich'in rights to 22,000 square kilometres of land in the Mackenzie River delta in addition to 1,500 square kilometres in their traditional settlement area in the Yukon. A non-taxable payment of $75-million is also included, as well as rights to wildlife harvesting, a share in resource royalties, and representation on wildlife and environmental management boards (DIAND, 1991f).

Currently there are seven claims under review and negotiation, while another twenty are pending negotiation (Comprehensive Claims Branch, 1991). As well, several agreements in principle have been signed in recent years with the Dene/Métis (since rejected by the annual assembly), Yukon Indians, and Eastern Inuit (Angus, 1990). The terms of agreement are massive in scope. For example, in 1988 the federal government proposed to transfer 180,000 square kilometres of land, plus $500-million, to the 13,000 Dene and Métis of the Mackenzie River valley. Had this offer been accepted it would have been the largest North American land transfer since the American purchase of Alaska from Russia in 1867 (*Globe and Mail*, 3 Sept. 1988). Two additional agreements in principle proposed for ratification in the 1990s will transfer ownership of another 550,000 square kilometres, as well as a say ('co-management') in the development of another 2.5 million square kilometres. With these and earlier arrangements, northern aboriginal peoples will possess full or partial control of up to 40 per cent of Canada's land mass.

Land-claims settlements have attracted considerable publicity, especially in the north where the threat of uncontrolled development and irreparable damage to communities by outside forces is ever-present (Angus, 1990). The federal government's decision in 1986 to soften its insistence on extinguishment of aboriginal title as a precondition for land-claims settlement has accelerated the proceedings. Prior to 1986, the government demanded aboriginal renunciation of all rights to land and related rights following any settlement. But aboriginal groups objected to this 'blanket extinguishment', arguing that it violated constitutional recognition of existing aboriginal and treaty rights, including an intrinsic right to self-government as promulgated in the Royal Proclamation (DIAND, 1987; Clark, 1990). At present the government strategy is based on the need to settle the legal question of who controls the land, while postponing other political issues such as self-government and aboriginal control over resource development for later negotiations (Smith, 1986b).

This blueprint for revising state interaction with aboriginal peoples has much to offer. Yet aboriginal groups have experienced intense frustration with existing land-claims processes, and have exhorted government officials to honour such obligations not only on legal grounds, but also on the moral grounds of the government's historical trust responsibilities (First Nations, 1990). The following case study, of the Gitksan-Wet'suwet'en land claim in British Columbia, is indicative of the politics that make finding a mutually acceptable solution so difficult.

Case Study: Aboriginal Land Claims in British Columbia
Despite positive initiatives by federal and provincial authorities, aboriginal peoples continue to be displeased by the seeming lack of progress in resolving outstanding issues pertaining to land, treaty rights, and aboriginal title. The situation in British Columbia is particularly turbulent and complex since much of the province—from its land mass to its coastal and inland waterways—is subject to comprehensive land claims by aboriginal groups (Cassidy and Dale, 1988; Tennant, 1990). Prior to the arrival of Europeans in BC, aboriginal societies lived as distinct and self-sufficient peoples; each had its own language, economy, and political structure, although they were broadly alike in cultural values relating to tradition, community, spirituality, and harmony with nature (BC Claims Task Force, 1991; Sto:lo, 1984). In the eastern part of North America, the British Crown pursued a policy that recognized the continuation of aboriginal title, ownership, and authority over land. But the policy of signing treaties to acquire aboriginal land did not extend to BC, where the Crown gave trading rights to the Hudson's Bay Company and put it in charge of immigration and settlement and the purchase of aboriginal lands. Thus although the BC aboriginal population remains subject to federal control via the Indian Act, 85 per cent of the province's land mass is not covered by treaty (Hall, 1991a). Complications arise from the province's steadfast refusal to recognize aboriginal title in any of the seventeen claims currently filed in BC. Until recently, moreover, when the Premier's Council on Native Affairs was created to address various aboriginal issues, BC refused to enter into any comprehensive land-claims negotiations, contending that such claims neither exist nor have any legal basis. If title existed, both provincial and federal authorities have argued, it was extinguished when BC joined the Confederation, by acceptance of reserves in exchange for claims to aboriginal territory, or through assimilation and so-called loss of a distinctive way of life (Gitksan-Wet'suwet'en, 1987).

British Columbia's reluctance to deal with aboriginal claims reflected its unique circumstances. The province relies on the same rich resource base that aboriginal groups claim as theirs. While there was a willingness to open talks on the validity of aboriginal title rights as pre-existing prior to European arrival, the question remained as to whether these rights were extinguished upon British settlement and annexation, or if they continued to exist in the absence of a formal treaty transaction (Tennant, 1990). Did provincial legislation after 1867 (both in BC and elsewhere) have the power to extinguish aboriginal title rights to land unilaterally (*Globe and Mail*, 1991b)? A court decision involving the claims of Gitksan-Wet'suwet'en nation provided the answer.

• *The Gitksan-Wet'suwet'en Comprehensive Land Claim.*   The Gitksan-Wet'suwet'en claim is the most comprehensive yet to come before the BC courts. It challenged the ownership of and jurisdiction over 57,000 square kilometres of northwestern BC along the Upper Skeena and Bulkley Rivers. Although initiated in 1984 by the hereditary chiefs of the Gitksan-Wet'suwet'en peoples, the claim had already been accepted for negotiation by federal authorities in 1977 in response to a petition filed in 1908. When proceedings bogged down, the Gitksan-Wet'suwet'en took action to protect their land and resources from encroachment by logging operations and resource-based corporations such as the Aluminum Company of Canada (Cassidy and Dale, 1988).

In 1987, the Gitksan-Wet'suwet'en initiated legal action against the province for declaration of sovereignty over the disputed lands. The Tribal Council claimed sovereignty by virtue of long-standing use and traditional occupancy; since their rights had never been extinguished by treaty or conquest, they also argued that without specific federal action to extinguish aboriginal title, they remained the rightful owners (Tennant, 1990).

The ruling was delivered in early March 1991. Judge Allan McEachern stunned many observers when he bluntly denied the Gitksan-Wet'suwet'en claim for aboriginal title over 57,000 square kilometres of the BC interior: they had no claim to ownership of the disputed land, nor did they have any jurisdiction over the land they lived in. According to McEachern, European sovereignty over BC was established in 1858 when title to the province was vested in the British Crown. Because of the doctrine of extinguishment (aboriginal title to land was lost when the province declared sovereignty over Indian land), the Gitksan-Wet'suwet'en forfeited their aboriginal title. Any claim to aboriginal title existed at the 'pleasure of the Crown' and could be extinguished when convenient.

The fallout from this decision is far-reaching. For the aboriginal peoples of BC, the ruling sent out a negative message regarding the litigation route to settlement of aboriginal grievances. McEachern himself encouraged aboriginal groups to seek political rather than judicial solutions. The hopes of the Gitksan-Wet'suwet'en for self-governing powers outside provincial jurisdiction but within Canada were dashed. The court decision was seen as ethnocentric, culturally insensitive, and racist in consequence if not intent. As well, the ruling revealed the inherent bias within European law against aboriginal peoples and aspirations, which renders aboriginal interests subordinate to those of the province. Far from promoting an enlightened view of the new realities underlying aboriginal–state relations, they argued, the court decision reflected and reinforced a colonialist mentality.

In a similar case the Supreme Court of Canada ruled against the Teme-Augama Anish Nabai people of Temagami in northeastern Ontario, arguing that aboriginal title to land was surrendered to the province by treaty in 1850 and acceptance of treaty benefits (*Kitchener-Waterloo Record*, 1991d). It is too early to predict the long-term effects of this ruling on aboriginal aspirations and strategies. But the danger of spiralling violence cannot be ignored. As Paul Tennant (*Globe and Mail*, 16 March 1991) has observed, the recommendation that aboriginal peoples seek political redress for land grievances rather than judicial solutions could well increase the likelihood of open confrontation. Seeking solutions through competition for raw political power may escalate the risk of conflict by pitting the state and vested interests against a people determined to take control of their land and destiny.

Yet there are signs of progress towards securing a 'new relationship' based on recognition of the unique place of BC aboriginal peoples as a distinct society with self-determining rights over land, culture, and language (BC Claims Task Force, 1991). A BC Claims Task Force (Report, 1991) has recommended overhaul of the land-claims process and proposed the creation of an independent commission to monitor the proceedings (*Globe and Mail*, 1991e). As well as supporting an unlimited number of claims for concurrent negotiations, the Task Force has advised against the principle of extinguishing aboriginal rights that were not dealt with specifically by treaty as part of the land-claims process. While the cost of settling some thirty separate claims in BC is high, the Task Force went on to say, the cost of not settling could be equally prohibitive in terms of lost business investment because of economic uncertainty over unsettled claims. The recent election of a sympathetic NDP provincial government is likely to reshape the contours of the aboriginal agenda in BC.

FOUR

Aboriginal Policy: Principles and Practices

The great aim of our civilization has been to do away with the tribal system and assimilate the Indian people in all respects with the inhabitants of the Dominion, as speedily as they are fit for the change.
— Sir John A. Macdonald (1887); quoted in Miller (1989: 189)

ABORIGINAL POLICY: HISTORICAL PERSPECTIVES

The perception of aboriginal peoples as a 'problem' to be solved con- stitutes a central motif in the evolution of government aboriginal policy and administration. An initial period of co-operation and accommodation was followed by a long-standing commitment to eradicate the aboriginal problem through government intervention and controlled culture change (Miller, 1989). Strategies for attainment of this objective have varied, ranging from a commitment to *assimila- tion* by way of *segregation, wardship, and protection* between 1867 and 1945, through to the era of *integration and formal equality* encom- passing the post-war era to 1973. A preference for *limited aboriginal autonomy* has been in place since 1973, based in part on federal responses to aboriginal demands for self-determination across a broad range of political and economic fronts. Each of these eras defined the 'aboriginal problem' in a distinctive way, and attempted to solve it by means of policies and programs that were consistent with prevailing public and political opinion about the status of aboriginal people in Canadian society.

Symbiosis and Co-operation (Pre-Confederation)

The ancestors of Canada's aboriginal peoples arrived as far back as 50,000 years ago by way of the land bridge across the Bering Sea. Prior to the arrival of the first Europeans, aboriginal peoples were firmly established as hunters and foragers throughout much of Canada. Aboriginal tribes saw themselves as self-governing entities exercising sovereignty over specific territories. Initial contacts with French and British explorers, missionaries, and traders were reasonably co-operative and mutually beneficial. Relations were based on a principle of co-existence involving reciprocal trade, commercial partnerships, and practical accommodation. The necessity for military alliances meant that the aboriginal nations were treated diplomatically as powerful nations whose favour had to curried in pursuit of European goals (Miller, 1989). (For a more detailed discussion of this early period, in British North America, see Part II.)

The Royal Proclamation of 1763 reaffirmed the co-operative nature of early white–aboriginal relations. It sought to establish British sovereignty over the unexplored interior of the continent, as well as to forge military alliances with powerful tribes. It also recognized aboriginal peoples as 'nations' under the protection of the king. A series of treaties based on pacts of mutual assistance and friendship was a direct result of the Proclamation and its willingness to recognize aboriginal title to land under traditional use and occupancy. Whether or not the Proclamation confirmed the right to aboriginal self-government is at present subject to debate (Clark, 1990; Raphals, 1991).

Assimilation: Protection, Civilization, and Absorption (1867-1945)

> I want to get rid of the Indian problem. . . . Our objective is to continue until there is not a single Indian in Canada that has not been absorbed.
> — Duncan Campbell Scott, Superintendent-General of Indian Affairs, 1920; quoted in Miller (1989: 207).

This symbiotic relationship of co-operation and interdependence began to unravel by the turn of the nineteenth century, following military transfer of Indian control to civilian forces (Purich, 1986). Reciprocity and accommodation were replaced by a system of internal colonialism and conquest-oriented acculturation, reflecting the need for (a) political control of Native populations, (b) protection of British and French interests, and (c) removal of competition for scarce resources. Political events dictated this relational shift. After the 1812 War with United States, British colonizers no longer required aboriginal peoples as allies—or for that matter, as explorers or traders. Their value rapidly diminished, with the result that aboriginal tribes became stigmatized as obstacles to the progressive settlement of Canadian society. More-over, by refusing to relinquish their identity and assimilate into 'higher levels' of 'civilization', aboriginal peoples were dismissed as an inferior and unequal species whose rights could be trampled on with impunity (Porter III, 1988). Aboriginal lands were increasingly coveted by colonists intent on settlement and agriculture. Policy directives were formulated that dismissed aboriginal peoples as little more than imped-iments to be removed in the interests of progress and settlement (Miller, 1989).

A policy of assimilation evolved as part of this project to subdue and subordinate aboriginal peoples. From the early nineteenth century on, elimination of the 'Indian problem' was one of the colony's—later the Dominion's—foremost concerns. Authorities rejected extermination as a solution, but focused instead on a planned process of cultural change known as assimilation (Miller, 1989). Through assimilation, the dom-inant sector sought to undermine the cultural distinctiveness of abo-riginal tribal society; to subject the indigenes to the rules, values, and sanctions of Euro-Canadian society; and to absorb the de-culturated minority into the mainstream through a process of 'anglo-conformity' (Frideres, 1988). The means to achieve this outward compliance with Euro-Canadian society lay in the hands of missionaries, teachers, and law-makers.

Protection of aboriginal peoples was a key component of the assim-ilationist agenda (Tobias, 1976; Gibbins and Ponting, 1986). Federal authorities were anxious to protect aboriginal peoples both from their own noxious cultural habits and from the vices of the outside world. In an effort to shield aboriginal peoples from dealings with unscrupulous whites, laws were enacted that prohibited the consumption of liquor, the private sale of land, and economic transactions with Europeans without approval of the Indian Affairs Department. A similar logic underlay the introduction of the reserve system. Many were herded onto reserves for protection from lawless elements interested only in profit or amusement. Reserves offered protection from the ravages of alcohol, trade, and even indigenous practices such as the sun dance. They also served as 'holding pens' to facilitate the resocialization of these 'misguided heathens'. Here the 'industrious and peaceful habits' of civilization and Christianity were to be inculcated, not only to wean Natives from a state of barbarism but also to transform these 'wards' of the state into productive, self-reliant, and God-fearing citizens of the Dominion. To hasten the assimilation process, aboriginal communities were expected to adopt elected band councils under the supervision of a federal Indian agent.

This commitment to protect, convert, and civilize the aboriginal peoples reflected the paternalism that continues to permeate aboriginal policy and administration (Gibbins and Ponting, 1986). How do we evaluate the success or failure of these endeavours? The imposition of racist and evolutionary philosophies that disparaged them as inferior and helpless (Weaver, 1984) resulted in denial of self-governing rights, foreclosure of social and economic opportunities, and withering of language and cultural values. The reserve system failed to bring about the anticipated changes. The protection offered by reserves (and the Indian Act in general) served to reinforce the isolation and distance of aboriginal communities from the very society they were expected to join (McMillan, 1988). Even legislation ostensibly aimed at improving the lot of aboriginal communities achieved little. The Indian Act of 1876 denied aboriginal people's claims to political sovereignty, while imposing a system of indirect (elected band council) rule and pervasive segregation. Treaty agreements signed with the federal government resulted in sometimes fraudulent arrangements and illegal land transfers. The concept of guardianship reinforced the stereotype of aboriginal peoples as childlike and dependent, in need of protection by civilizing powers (Davies, 1985a; Ponting and Gibbins, 1980; Ponting, 1986). Even the protective measures inherent in the Indian Act could do little to blunt the impact of federal policies and programs. Nevertheless, efforts to solve the Indian 'problem' by imposing an assimilationist framework upon aboriginal–government relations prevailed well into the twentieth century.

Canadianization of Aboriginal Peoples: Integration and Formal Equality (1945-1973)

Canada's treatment of its aboriginal people came under scrutiny after the Second World War. Among the reasons were growing public resentment over the slow pace of directed culture change and economic development within aboriginal communities, increases in the aboriginal population, and shifts in intellectual fashion in the wake of the Holocaust (Miller, 1989). Aboriginal peoples themselves began to chafe at segregationist barriers. Many had fought alongside whites in the Second World War, and they were no longer content with the second-class treatment prescribed in an Indian Act that prevented them from going to a pub or entering a polling booth (Moran, 1988).

By the mid-1940s there was pressure for changes to official policy. Rejecting the principles of wardship and control, government sought to 'normalize' relations with aboriginal peoples by doing away with special and separate status (Boldt and Long, 1988). Select aspects of aboriginal culture and tradition (such as the potlatch) were increasingly accepted as part of a growing commitment to the principles of cultural pluralism (Gibbins and Ponting, 1986). Self-sufficiency was encouraged not only to curtail public expenditures, but also to facilitate aboriginal entry into the outside world. The former commitment to assimilation gave way to the principles of integration and formal equality as successive governments sought to redefine their responsibilities to aboriginal peoples.

In 1947 the government's decision to abolish separate status and administrative structures was formally announced before a Parliamentary Joint Committee (Boldt and Long, 1988). As long as aboriginal peoples were mired under the discriminatory and paternalistic provisions of the Indian Act, it was argued, they were destined to remain outside the mainstream as less than full and equal members of society. The spiralling cost of maintaining a separate structure and special programs was a contributing factor in the decision (Frideres, 1990). Strategies were discussed to abolish restrictive laws and paternal programs, to desegregate aboriginal peoples, and to integrate them into the mainstream (especially after passage of Canada's Bill of Rights in 1960).

By 1969 the Liberal government under Pierre Elliott Trudeau had proposed legislation for restructuring aboriginal–government relations (Weaver, 1981). Designed largely to shield Canada from external criticism rather than to meet the needs defined by aboriginal people themselves (Gibbins and Ponting, 1986), the White Paper ('The Statement of the Government of Canada on Indian Policy') recommended the eventual elimination of 'privileges' for aboriginal peoples. By 'normalizing' their entry into Canadian society as 'equals', the White Paper attempted to do away with special and separate status as set out in section 91(24) of the Constitution Act (Boldt and Long, 1988). It sought to abolish Indian status (by repealing the Indian Act), accelerate absorption into the mainstream, terminate federal obligations, allocate reserve resources to individual ownership, devolve services and support to the provinces, and phase out the Department of Indian Affairs, in the belief that separate and special aboriginal status was undemocratic and counterproductive (Miller, 1989).

Aftermath: From White Paper to Red Power

Federal policy-makers were caught off guard by the aboriginal reaction to the White Paper. Deeply committed to liberal values, and resentful of special status as discriminatory and regressive, many of those policy-makers were convinced that conferral of formal equality and protection of individual, civil, and human rights represented a step forward for aboriginal peoples, accelerating their movement into the twentieth century. To their surprise, aboriginal groups condemned the White Paper as racist in its intent and potentially genocidal in its consequences. Obviously Ottawa had miscalculated aboriginal grievances and aspirations (Comeau and Santin, 1990). Aboriginal peoples did not want Ottawa to get out of the aboriginal business. Rather, they wanted the right to conduct their political, social, and cultural affairs without excessive interference from Ottawa. Nor did attainment of formal equality amount to integration into the mainstream; after all, formal equality was not equivalent to real equality, for it overlooked the bias inherent in cultural differences and the unequal distribution of power and resources (see also Steinlien, 1989). The solutions, they argued, lay in differential treatment as befitting a 'distinct society' with unique political status, veto power, resource ownership, and collective entitlements (Kymlicka, 1991). Decades of enforced assimilation had already proven that inequality, racism, and discrimination would not be wiped out by decree.

Aboriginal groups were galvanized into action to protest the White Paper. In an unprecedented display of unity and singularity of purpose, they unanimously rejected any proposed diminution in formal status, preferring instead a distinctive arrangement that acknowledged their special status in society, along with corresponding entitlements. Foremost among their concerns was the attainment of justice and equality on aboriginal terms: terms imposed unilaterally by the central policy structures, even with the best of intentions, were rejected. Chastened by this collective show of strength, the government retracted the White Paper in March 1971, leaving both the political and public sectors in limbo over the status and powers of aboriginal peoples in Canada.

Limited Aboriginal Autonomy (1973-present)

With the demise of assimilation and integration as official guidelines for managing aboriginal–state relations, a policy vacuum appeared by the early 1970s. Repudiation of the White Paper marked the formal end of the colonialist policy era, although many of its underlying assumptions have continued to infiltrate aboriginal–government relations even into the present (Comeau and Santin, 1990). A period of confusion and indecision followed. Without any direction on a national aboriginal agenda, it was nearly impossible to develop mutually acceptable initiatives. To facilitate a new policy agenda, Ottawa established a Core Funding Program in 1971 to provide aboriginal groups with the resources necessary to promote their causes through research, legal channels, and publicity (Axworthy and Trudeau, 1990). Still, a common ground for hammering out policy compromises acceptable to both political and aboriginal sectors did not materialize until a critical 1973 Supreme Court decision in favour of aboriginal principles ushered in a policy commitment to limited autonomy. Although only three of seven judges ruled in favour of Nishga aboriginal title, the Calder case proved pivotal, for it showed that aboriginal rights and land claims could no longer be casually dismissed. According to Trudeau (Axworthy and Trudeau, 1990), the Calder case allowed him to reconsider the colonialist assumptions underlying government aboriginal policy, and to acknowledge the possibility of self-determination, aboriginal and treaty rights, and self-government as key organizing principles (Ponting, 1986).

As the whole issue of aboriginal problems and solutions, and the possibilities for development, was reopened for discussion and debate, government perception of the aboriginal agenda began to change. Acceptance that aboriginal title and rights existed prior to European settlement raised a host of questions regarding (a) the nature of aboriginal rights and (b) whether such rights can exist apart from aboriginal title to land. Debate centred on whether aboriginal rights continue into the present or if they were extinguished upon provincial entry into Confederation, the signing of treaties, or acceptance of treaty benefits and access to reserve land (Morrisseau, 1991). The answers provided by the courts have been double-edged, with positive decisions such as that in the Sparrow case offset by retrograde rulings for the Gitksan-Wet'suwet'en and Teme-Augama Anish Nabai.

The government's immediate response to the 1973 ruling was a policy of devolution for limited community control over administrative services (but not necessarily over design or funding of programs) (Comeau and Santin, 1990). Until 1964, for example, the government delivered programs directly to qualifying individuals on reserves. By the mid-1970s it had transferred many of its program delivery responsibilities to band councils. In 1979 it established a Band Support Funding program to assist local authorities in the administration of community programs as part of an overall commitment to devolution and aboriginal control over local government spending (DIAND, 1991e). This policy commitment to limited autonomy has paid dividends in improved bilateral negotiations and decision-making, comprehensive land-claims procedures, constitutional entrenchment of aboriginal and treaty rights in 1982, reaffirmation of federal trust obligations in 1985, endorsement of aboriginal self-government structures, and promotion of aboriginal collective rights. Particular attention has centred on aboriginal initiatives to transform the federal policy agenda along lines consistent with the distinct-society status implicit in the 'nations within' concept. In time this focus on self-determination through self-government has become more politicized, more assertive, and more directly aimed at the constitutional entrenchment of aboriginal self-governing rights.

That political receptivity to aboriginal assertions has also increased is not surprising, given the government's avowed commitment to a consultative, co-operative approach that stresses collaboration and consensus in pursuit of mutual goals (DIAND, 1989c). Federal authorities have continued to explore the potential of a limited-autonomy model.

There is a growing willingness to renegotiate federal contractual obligations with aboriginal peoples in light of the policy void created by the wholesale rejection of assimilation and integration as policy paradigms (Cross Cultural Consulting, 1989). The key word here is 'negotiation'. Since the final decision is not controlled by a 'disinterested' third party, namely the courts, the government is willing to underwrite the costs associated with the negotiation process (Frideres, 1991). This represents a significant reversal from the previous decade, when aboriginal and treaty rights were derogated as contrary to liberal-democratic values (Morse, 1985). In short, the Canadian government has formally acknowledged the legitimacy of aboriginal claims for self-determination over political, cultural, and economic affairs. As we shall see, however, subsequent efforts to specify the nature of these rights have lurched from one crisis to another.

Recent Policy Developments: Economic and Political

In recent years two major policy initiatives can be discerned as part of the government's strategy to renew its relationship with the aboriginal sectors. First is aboriginal economic development, with its focus on arresting the cycle of poverty, dependency, and abuse through provision of skills, tools, and resources. Evidence to date suggests that economic development programs have missed the target (Comeau and Santin, 1990). Billions have been squandered since the White Paper, but most aboriginal peoples (a total of 66 per cent in 1986) continue to receive some type of social assistance. In what is a cruel joke for long-suffering communities, some programs for local economic improvement have contributed towards the destruction of reserve life (Shkilnyk, 1985a) by increasing exposure to mainstream influences (e.g., alcohol) and sharpening social inequalities within the community. In other cases, federally-sponsored programs appear to be little more than public-relations gestures, rather than concerted or comprehensive efforts to build the groundwork for a viable local economy. Moreover, no one can minimize the difficulty of mounting a co-ordinated economic attack on remote reserves with small populations that have next to nothing as collateral for lending agencies in exchange for capital funds. To be sure, success stories exist, of which the creation of Creebec Airlines in Quebec is one. But the government has been singled out as a major culprit in detracting from aboriginal self-sufficiency through near-sightedness, mismanagement, and miscalculation. This overall lack of development may inhibit aboriginal political aspirations for an economically secure self-government system.

A National Strategy for Aboriginal Economic Development has been proposed and implemented (DIAND, 1989d; 1990b). Under this strategy for the economic empowerment of aboriginal businesses and entrepreneurs, funds (in the vicinity of $900-million) will be allocated to appropriate government departments such as Industry, Science, and Technology on a continuing basis (in contrast to the block funding, of limited duration, used in the past). The immediate goal is to provide aboriginal communities with long-term employ-ment and business opportunities by underwriting better-managed entrepreneurships, commercial establishments, and joint ventures, and by improving skills through job training and human-resource development. The long-range goals are enhanced economic self-reliance, decreased politi-cal and economic dependence on the government, and improved aboriginal participation in the national economy. To achieve these goals, the government plans to create three regional aboriginal economic development boards in con-sultation with aboriginal communities, on the grounds that community involvement is crucial to the success of these endeavours.

The second major development is at the political level, where a major restructuring is currently in progress. The overhaul of existing govern-ment structures in exchange for aboriginal self-government arrange-ments has been heralded as a positive step towards transcending the limitations of the Indian Act (DIAND, 1990h). In April 1986, federal authorities announced a two-track approach to enhance aboriginal self-government (DIAND, 1991c). One track seeks to reach a consensus on con-stitutional entrenchment of aboriginal self-government; the other seeks practical new arrangements to advance community self-government negotiations within the framework of the existing constitution (DIAND, 1990h). The latter, according to the government, is an interim step that provides an opportunity for aboriginal communities to exercise greater authority through legislative rather than constitutional change. Individ-ual bands are free to negotiate self-governing arrangements with Ottawa, setting out what powers they need, which services they plan to control, and how their community will fit into the larger picture (Goar, 1991).

For the state, the concept of community self-government entails a host of activities and initiatives that collectively aim at establishing a new relationship based on local control and self-reliance in collabora-tion with provincial authorities and in line with Canadian sovereignty and constitutional structures. These self-governing agreements are intended as non-constitutional initiatives directed primarily at design-ing practical arrangements through specific legislation for municipal-style governments, consistent with Cabinet-approved guidelines but outside any federally-imposed blueprint. The negotiation process is founded on the following principles (DIAND, 1990h):

1. to transcend the limitations of the Indian Act by enhancing local control and scope for community decision-making;

2. to ensure that the negotiation process is flexible enough to accommodate the social, cultural, political, and economic diversity of aboriginal communities across Canada;

3. to make community self-governments more accountable, politically and financially, to local groups rather than to federal structures;

4. to negotiate these agreements within the existing constitutional framework and federal/provincial laws, but without prejudice to treaty or aboriginal rights or to future land claims;

5. to conduct negotiations only with aboriginal communities who occupy reserves or lands obtained through comprehensive settlements.

Topics for negotiations are open, but include procedures of government, legal status, membership, land and resource management, financial arrangements, service delivery, and social assistance. In short, self-government is now touted as the cornerstone of the government's aboriginal policy (Canadian Government, 1990). But while central authorities are willing to tolerate a wider range of self-governing structures combining municipal, provincial, and federal jurisdictions, they cannot tolerate the notion of a sovereign aboriginal nation with the potential to transform Canada into a 'swiss cheese' perforated by independent aboriginal states. As put by Indian Affairs Minister Thomas Siddon, Ottawa is willing to 'move over' and make jurisdictional room for aboriginal self-government, 'but not if it means yielding the ultimate sovereigny of the Crown and of Canada' (in Platiel, 1991b). That aboriginal models for self-government (a 'distinct' tier) are not necessarily consistent with the government's limited ('negotiated' and 'community-based') proposals can only lead to additional strife.

A revised social-political contract based on the principle of aboriginal self-government has achieved moderate success. To date, two examples of community self-government are in operation, although both preceded the official government announcement. Self-governing arrangements have been implemented among the Cree-Naskapi of James Bay in 1984 and the Sechelt in British Columbia in 1986, with negotiations currently under way elsewhere. These include 8 projects (involving 30 bands) in the advanced stages, another 15 (involving 29 bands) at the substantive phase, and about 170 bands in the initial stages of negotiation (DIAND, 1991c). Other bands have reclaimed some degree of control over the design and delivery of service programs, in addition to a say in spending priorities through 'alternative funding agreements' and 'community-based negotiations' (Frideres, 1990; Weaver, 1990). Alternative funding arrangements have proven attractive since they allow aboriginal groups tc set priorities, design programs consistent with aboriginal sensitivities, take responsibility for the delivery and effectiveness of local programs, and assume accountability to band members for management of resources, services, and programs (DIAND, 1989b).

THE HIDDEN POLICY AGENDA:
THE POLITICS OF FISCAL CONSTRAINTS

The Tories are looking for ways to get out of the native business.
—Murray Angus, 1990

Aboriginal policy at present is shaped in a context dominated by fiscal restraint and reduction of federal expenditures (Angus, 1990). Downsizing of the public sector in general and of aboriginal services in particular has coincided with a political resolve to control escalating expenditures (Pratt, 1989). Since the Neilson Report of 1985, the government has embarked on paths to reduce 'unnecessary' spending. Of the approximately $4-billion now spent annually on aboriginal constituents, according to Department calculations, only about 25 per cent is necessary to meet legal obligations (Angus, 1990). The remainder is discretionary and (theoretically, at any rate) subject to negotiation.

Keeping aboriginal peoples off the reserve also represents a potential cost-cutting measure. According to the Department of Indian Affairs, the annual value of federal benefits to off-reserve aboriginals is $635 per person. By comparison, the figure stands at $12,108 per annum for Natives returning to the reserve in the first year, and $5,353 for each year thereafter (*Toronto Star*, 1991b). Expenses mount in other ways too. On-reserve Indians pay no property, income, or sales tax; receive subsidies for housing; and are eligible for free social services. Off-reserve Indians get assistance in health and education, but must pay income and property tax (*Globe and Mail*, 1990).

Outright curtailment of federal expenses represents another option. In recent years the government has been looking to dismantle the Department of Indian Affairs and transfer some programs and responsibilities to other departments (Angus, 1990). At the same time it has attempted to (a) cut back on federal programs for aboriginal peoples, (b) transfer responsibility for delivery of social services to local communities under the guise of self-determination, and (c) delegate authority to the provinces (or territories). While the cost factor looms large, this is not the only reason for such moves: from the federal perspective, there is much to be gained by displacing public displeasure and transferring aboriginal dissatisfaction from Ottawa to the provinces and local communities (Abele, 1990).

The politics of jurisdiction are played out at provincial as well as federal levels. Beginning with the 1969 White Paper proposals, federal authorities have cast about for ways to establish provincial responsibility for delivery of government programs (Clancy, 1990). Current debates focus on the nature and scope of provincial sharing in the special trust ('fiduciary') obligations incurred by federal authorities under section 91(24) of the 1867 Constitution Act (Boldt and Long, 1988; Morse, 1989). In light of the costs and difficulties involved in servicing aboriginal constituents, federal authorities are anxious to transfer both jurisdiction and responsibility to the provinces (Pratt, 1989). This move is consistent with efforts in other areas to restructure federal obligations in a manner that pares Ottawa's responsibility down to purely legal requirements. It is also consistent with the broader goals of assimilation and integration of aboriginal people into Canadian society. This suggests that the spirit of the White Paper continues to influence government aboriginal policy (Comeau and Santin, 1990).

The provinces, for their part, are reluctant to integrate aboriginal programs into their delivery systems despite federal promises of compensation for costs. While anxious to establish control over Indian lands and resources, most provinces show little enthusiasm for extending costly services to aboriginal people off the reserve. There is even less eagerness to assume responsibility for 'troublesome' and 'costly' constituents whose collective and special rights are likely to embroil the provinces in legal wrangles and electoral backlash. These caveats notwithstanding, by 1988 the provinces controlled 13 per cent of the federal government's $1.7-billion Indian Affairs budget (Comeau and Santin, 1990). Evidence suggests that provincial involvement will continue to increase as trilateral negotiations become the norm rather than the exception (Long and Boldt, 1988; Hawkes, 1989).

Aboriginal groups are equally ambivalent about the prospect of increased provincial involvement. In general they resist moves that may jeopardize the special relationship with federal authorities set out in the Royal Proclamation of 1763, the Constitution Act of 1867, and the Indian Acts of 1876 and 1951. Increased assimilationist pressures (not to mention loss of citizen-plus status) are an ever-present concern should the provinces take steps to control aboriginal resources in exchange for provincial delivery of social services (Pratt, 1989). Although several tripartite arrangements (federal, provincial, and first nations) have appeared, most aboriginal groups have shied away from any scheme that involves a jurisdictional shuffle with unknown ramifications.

Political Reactions: Smokescreen or Substance

Aboriginal affairs are rapidly becoming an arena in which competing groups—including federal/provincial authorities, aboriginal organizations, and resource-based industries—are each staking claims to protect and promote their own interests. Federal authorities appear to view aboriginal problems as a losing proposition: no amount of government largesse will match public expectations, administrative functions are bulky and costly at a time when down-sizing is in order, and aboriginal expenditures constitute anathema to a fiscally conservative government. Certainly moves towards fiscal restraint, curtailment of federal services, political rationality, and debureaucratization of the social policy agenda are evident in other areas (see Prince, 1987). Comparable initiatives for coping with the 'Indian problem' through cut-backs and termination of special status may appear callous; however, they do not represent a significant departure from the past, when government policy routinely swept it aside.

Both federal and provincial reactions to aboriginal demands are shaped by a fundamental dualism regarding the nature of the 'Indian problem', with predictable consequences for policy resolutions. As Ponting (1988) notes, policy-makers are confused by competing definitions of equality: one entailing equal treatment and no special privileges, and the other acknowledging the necessity of special treatment for certain sectors if true equity is to be attained. When applied to aboriginal policy and administration, this duality of meanings breeds ambiguity and confusion, since some favour federal spending cuts, abolition of the Department of Indian Affairs, and curtailment of federal services (*Globe and Mail*, 12-13 March 1986; 11 May 1988), while others endorse self-government and aboriginal rights as basic human rights (Penner, 1983; *Globe and Mail*, 20 May 1986). Failure to establish a coherent and enlightened policy framework has been detrimental to the development of an acceptable formula for aboriginal–government relations.

A New Aboriginal Agenda?

They have given us a longer leash and a bigger playpen, but they are determined to keep us under control
— Chief Bill Two Rivers, Kahnawake Mohawk Council, at the
Indigenous Peoples Conference, London, Ont.;
quoted in *London Free Press* (1991).

Federal authorities have continued to explore the logical consequences of a commitment to limited autonomy and power-sharing. Since the early 1970s, policy discourse has shifted towards a greater tolerance of aboriginal languages and culture, and has often included proposals for institutional control over health and education under self-governing arrangements. Geared to preserving the special place of Canada's first citizens within the constitutional framework of Canadian society, current government objectives rest on the four policy pillars of economy, land, political relations, and legal status, as announced by the Prime Minister in September 1990 (DIAND, 1990g). (See p. 97.)

To its credit, the government has accepted the idea that aboriginal peoples (a) are a separate people, (b) possess a threatened culture and society that require massive government intervention for survival, (c) need special measures to bring about renewal, and (d) depend on central authorities and legal obligations to ensure aboriginal progress as self-determining people (see also Steinlien, 1989). Towards the latter end, the government has shifted its policy in the direction of limited autonomy. Part of the shift consists in a restructuring of aboriginal–state relations along the lines of self-government, while another part concerns recognition of aboriginal land and treaty rights. Equally significant are moves to establish separate aboriginal structures or to modify existing institutions at the level of objectives, style, or personnel. The combined impact of these concessions suggests a new paradigm in the making, based on decolonization of the aboriginal agenda.

Appearances, however, are deceptive. Nearly two decades of tinkering have not fundamentally altered the national aboriginal agenda—at least not in any substantial sense. The basic principles of assimilation remain in place, suggesting that changes over the past 150 years have been largely illusory and rhetorical, with major developments restricted to strategies and symbols rather than objectives and content (Boldt and Long, 1988). Assimilation remains so deeply entrenched in practice that, despite its formal rejection as official policy, efforts to dislodge it still appear futile (Frideres, 1990).

Consider, for example, the government's current push for community self-government negotiations. While Ottawa is anxious for aboriginal peoples to assume control over land and institutions, its initiatives focus on creating 'more space' to accommodate aboriginal self-governing structures rather than on setting up sovereign entities (Siddon, 1991). While aboriginal groups advocate a distinct third level of self-government, equivalent in status to that of the provinces, Ottawa offers a limited degree of autonomy that may in part in respond to aboriginal demands, but remains consistent with federal goals for reducing both financial and statutory obligations (Comeau and Santin, 1990). Not only does the municipal style of self-government promoted by Ottawa put aboriginal aspirations under provincial domination, but federal initiatives also have the consequence (if not necessarily the intent) of setting up aboriginal leaders as lightning rods for criticism and second-guessing. By contrast, government officials are 'let off the hook' in what can be seen as a worthy attempt to cut costs while conferring the appearance of political and economic independence (Frideres, 1991). In the process of making local leaders accountable to the community for government programs, political and bureaucratic officials relieve themselves of the responsibility for procedural mistakes and program failures.

Not unexpectedly, as Sally Weaver (1990; 1991) has cogently argued, recent changes in aboriginal–government relations are more symbolic than real. With the exception of the Constitution Act of 1982 (which entrenched aboriginal and treaty rights), there has been little appreciable gain with respect to aboriginal empowerment. What we have instead are promises and proposals that, if they are acted on at all, are often followed by breakdowns in negotiations. The courts repeatedly uphold aboriginal and land rights, but Ottawa continues to maintain a 'trench warfare mentality' (Harold Cardinal, in Comeau and Santin, 1990: 20; Cassidy, 1991) and to demand additional court cases to test the legality of federal obligations. Too often, Ottawa has appeared willing to appropriate the rhetoric of change, distort it to suit political purposes, and put 'token' aboriginals in positions of 'power' to legitimate the reform process in the eyes of the public.

In short, evidence suggests that, despite moderate improvements, a gap remains between aboriginal aspirations and political concessions. Substantial changes will not come easily. It will take more time for the Canadian public to appreciate the logic underlying aboriginal aspirations, to understand the dynamics governing aboriginal–state relations, and to become aware of aboriginal peoples' needs and concerns as 'nations within'. Given the structural forces working to the contrary, it may take even longer to put these principles into practice.

SUMMING UP: PARADIGMS IN THE MAKING

> We're halfway through. From the old, paternalistic we-will-do-everything-and-tell-you-everything to an evolution where we discuss and implement self-government.
> —Bill McKnight, Indian Affairs Minister; quoted in Smith (1986a).

Aboriginal–state relations in Canada are undergoing a stage of rapid change and reassessment. Ottawa is anxious to forge a new working relationship based on mutual 'respect' and agreeable levels of power-sharing. Aboriginal sectors are equally anxious to establish a working relationship that would allow the 'healing' process to begin (Turpel, 1992). But the shift in aboriginal policy and administration is riddled with inconsistencies and plagued by turmoil as opposing parties with competing interests and ideologies debate the contours of a national aboriginal agenda. The long-standing commitment to assimilation and integration as the rationale for government policy and administration has proven inadequate and destructive to aboriginal interests. But a new paradigm based on decolonization of aboriginal–state relations has not yet taken hold. Inconsistencies in government policies and programs serve to reflect and reinforce the gap between the old and the new. While current policy and administrative initiatives for limited aboriginal autonomy are more promising than their predecessors, real change will require greater sharing of both power and resources, as well as a fundamental shift in the collective mind-set of central authorities. Not surprisingly, in light of the politics involved, the rethinking of aboriginal–state relations is blocked by political deception and bureaucratic obfuscation.

At the core of this breakdown is a fear of advancing aboriginal interests to the point where 'costs' (electoral or financial) become prohibitive. Problems arise from a failure to appreciate the nuances underlying the principles of citizen-plus, aboriginal, and treaty rights, land claims, and self-determination through self-government. No less detrimental to the aboriginal cause is the pervasive commitment to assimilate aboriginal peoples into Canada's institutional framework (Boldt and Long, 1988). The cultural-assimilationist ethos that prevailed prior to the 1970s is still evident; only its style has changed. It is reflected in efforts to (a) phase out separate institutional structures, (b) formally rationalize aboriginal–government relations through land corporations and municipal governing structures, (c) transfer federal responsibility to the provinces, and (d) incorporate aboriginal peoples into the legal, administrative, and political structures of Canadian society.

Will this gap between expectations and reality spawn a new round of Oka-like confrontations and violent outbursts? Predictions are difficult at this point. Even leaving aside the question of overt hostilities, however, the magnitude of the difficulties in reconstructing aboriginal–government relations cannot be overstated. Innovative policies cannot undo decades of inertia and commitment to the status quo. The restructuring process is fraught with ambiguity and stress, not to mention potential for confrontation, as new ways of thinking collide with old ones without displacing them. Nevertheless, it cannot be avoided. With or without open conflicts, aboriginal grievances over land, treaty and aboriginal rights, culture and identity, and empowerment will continue to prod central authorities into action.

The Politics of Self-Government

INTRODUCTION

Federal policy regarding aboriginal peoples has historically been defined by a commitment to protect, assimilate, and civilize those wards of the state under federal custody. A paternalistic element has permeated government perception and treatment of aboriginal peoples under the Indian Act, giving rise to a federal bureaucracy whose mandate extends to control and domination. Policy has also been shaped by ideologies that have upheld white supremacist views while denigrating racial and aboriginal minorities as inferior stock—doomed in the face of relentless evolutionary pressures unless properly socialized into the Western mould. The combination of these constraints and ideologies established a context in which the conquest and subjugation of aboriginal peoples were promulgated as necessary and normal. It also served to reinforce the irrelevance, dependency, and underdevelopment of aboriginal peoples within the Canadian nation.

Arguably, however, Canada's aboriginal peoples constitute 'domestic dependent nations' comparable in status and stature with aboriginal tribes in the United States. Both France and Britain dealt with aboriginal tribes on a nation-to-nation basis to secure their assistance as trading partners and military allies (Royal Commission, 1992). In recent years, the concept of aboriginal self-government has been linked with the general promotion of aboriginal and treaty rights as part of broader advances towards aboriginal self-determination.

Aboriginal leaders are resolute in rejecting any colonialist model at odds with an inherent right to self-rule. Self-governing structures are paramount, derived from first principles rather than legal authority, and preferably at a distinct level of polity alongside the provincial and federal governments.

What, then, is the nature of aboriginal self-government? On what grounds is it justified, by whose power and under what authority? Where are the boundaries and jurisdictions? Will collective rights clash with individual rights? Who will pay for self-government? What about Natives in cities? Will Canada dissolve into a quagmire of sovereign principalities? Will aboriginal inherent rights take precedence over Quebec's distinct-society aspirations? This chapter will examine these issues and focus on the impact of self-governing overtures for both aboriginal peoples and society at large. Aboriginal and government perspectives on self-government will be analysed and assessed, with particular reference to recent self-governing initiatives in Quebec and British Columbia. Finally, the politics of self-government will be discussed in more detail in relation to the constitutional debate over self-government between 1983 and 1987.

ABORIGINAL PERSPECTIVES

In Chapter 2 the concept of self-government was defined and defended as critical to aboriginal aspirations. In the next chapter we indicated that federal authorities prefer a negotiated, community-based style of self-government, in opposition to aboriginal demands for a more expansive arrangement. Crucial here is the notion that authority resides with aboriginal people, and is not delegated to them by central powers. Aboriginal peoples have defended self-governing rights as intrinsic and irrevocable. While provincial and federal authorities may possess sovereignty over their citizens, as Ovide Mercredi has argued, they have no moral right to divest aboriginal people of their sovereign powers, and the particular rights that flow from that sovereignty can be infringed only with aboriginal people's consent (Lenihan, 1991).

The right of self-government on unceded lands is derived from guarantees promulgated by the British Crown in the Royal Proclamation of 1763: '[T]he several Nations or Tribes of Indians . . . should not be molested or disturbed in the Possession of such Parts of Our Dominions and Territories as, not having been ceded to or purchased by Us, are reserved to them.' With this instruction, aboriginal peoples were to be protected from non-Native intrusion—whether commercial or legal—on unceded lands. The very act of signing treaties across much of Canada implied some recognition of aboriginal rights to land by virtue of original occupancy and use. Moreover, the right to aboriginal self-government has never been relinquished, although it was curtailed by the Indian Act (Royal Commission, 1992). It is interesting to note that Canada's highest courts have upheld this reading of aboriginal sovereignty in a series of cases. For example, in the Sparrow decision of 1990, the Supreme Court ruled that aboriginal rights (in this case pertaining to fishing) could be removed only with explicit legislation divesting aboriginal groups of land, resources, and self-government rights.

The implications of aboriginal self-rule as a distinct and unique level of government are as powerful as they are provocative. First, if aboriginal self-government is viewed as intrinsic and entrenched, three distinct civil jurisdictions exist in Canada: federal, provincial, and aboriginal (Raphals, 1991). Should this be the case, as Clark (1990) argues, federal and provincial authorities can no more encroach upon aboriginal jurisdictions than they can upon one another's. Nor can central authorities extinguish aboriginal self-governing rights, since existing federal fiduciary obligations refute any such extinguishment as part of a comprehensive land-claims settlement. Aboriginal jurisdiction would prevail over lands never explicitly ceded by treaty or in situations where treaties were shown to be invalid or fraudulent (McMillan, 1988). Boundaries between jurisdictions would still be open to negotiation, but aboriginal peoples would be guaranteed full and inherent rights to manage their political, social, economic, and cultural affairs. It is this meaning of sovereignty—that is, independent civil jurisdiction over internal matters—that takes priority over the concept of sovereignty in terms of independence, state-style (Clark, 1990).

This line of reasoning is not without problems. Difficulties arise in determining whether the Proclamation remains the law of the land or whether it has been rendered inoperable by federal and provincial legislation (Frideres, 1991; Raphals, 1991). Some argue that each major constitutional document—the BNA Act, 1867; the Statute of Westminster, 1931, and the Canada Constitution Act, 1982—superseded the provisions of the Royal Proclamation. Others such as Bruce Clark (1990) disagree, contending that each document built upon the last to guarantee aboriginal protections and intrinsic rights to self-government.

The elevation of self-government to a key negotiating principle has sent out a powerful message. Aboriginal leaders categorically reject the view of aboriginal peoples as a collection of 'ethnic' Canadian citizens who happen to live on reserves. They see themselves as sovereign and self-governing nations with a distinct political status within the Canadian confederation. Certain inalienable rights and claims follow upon that fundamental recognition. As 'nations within', they are anxious to deal with federal authorities on a government-to-government basis. Modified models of self-government such as the largely municipal arrangement negotiated by the Sechelt in British Columbia in 1986 may be seen in private as worthy of emulation, but in public they are denounced as inadequate and dangerous—inadequate because the jurisdiction is seen as limiting comprehensive social reform and economic development; dangerous because legally municipalities are entities under provincial authority (Miller, 1989). It remains to be seen if Ottawa is willing to negotiate a new social contract with aboriginal people based on an inherent right to self-government that has existed from time immemorial and has never been surrendered or extinguished by provincial statute or federal legislation (Lenihan, 1991).

FEDERAL RESPONSES

Policy Dilemmas

Political authorities appear receptive to aboriginal peoples' claims to be legitimate contenders for power and resources within society. In 1983 the Penner Report on Indian Self-Government recommended that self-governing channels be constitutionally entrenched as one way of severing the dependency cycle. The government rejected this proposal, although it does appear anxious to break that cycle and see aboriginal peoples assume greater responsibility in setting priorities and programs without unnecessary federal intrusion (Mulroney, 1985).

Yet federal authorities have been cautious in responding to aboriginal demands for self-government. Despite lofty promises and reassuring speeches, there remains a noticeable lack of political will for implementing much of this rhetoric (Weaver, 1990). Policy officials are understandably less than eager to dissolve once-habitual patterns of domination (Boldt and Long, 1985). Disagreement is particularly vocal with regard to the nature and scope of aboriginal self-government. Government officials prefer to view Indian self-government as a political concession, rather than as an inherent aboriginal right derived from first principles (Tennant, 1985). They see self-government as a 'contingent' right, delegated by federal authorities through negotiated agreements on a band-to-band basis (Cross Cultural Consulting, 1989). Self-governing structures must be limited to those that are consistent with Canada's constitutional make-up and subject to Canadian law. In the government's view, those who are delegated such devolutionary powers remain answerable to central authorities.

Government foot-dragging in this area appears to be attributable to self-interest and a perception of the general public as poorly disposed towards radical reform, preferring to see tribes as municipalities rather than self-determining nations. The administrative and operating costs of self-government also loom menacingly, however, as do the impending costs of reparation to aboriginal groups for federal dereliction of past duties and responsibilities (Frideres, 1991). Moves to put the principle of aboriginality into practice, as well as to clarify its meaning and nature, have thus proceeded slowly. Any effort to accommodate the principle of aboriginal self-government in the overall polity of a sovereign state faces formidable barriers (Asch, 1984).

SELF-GOVERNMENT IN ACTION

Ottawa is openly committed to the principle of self-government for aboriginal bands. In the context of its ongoing comprehensive land-claims policy, the government has acknowledged a need for continuing aboriginal involvement in managing land and resources under self-governing structures (DIAND, 1987). Since 1985 Ottawa has been negotiating practical self-governing arrangements with up to 200 bands within the existing constitutional framework but outside the restrictions of the Indian Act; the government has also stated its willingness to enter into tripartite self-governing agreements with the provinces and aboriginal peoples and Métis (Canada, 1991). Bands are now offered some degree of flexibility to meet the exigencies of particular circumstances, to take control over aboriginal community affairs, and to reflect greater accountability to the local community. Much of this shift can be attributed to the recommendations of the Coolican Report (1985), which called for flexible agreements recognizing the principle of intrinsic aboriginal sovereignty and self-determination for all aboriginal peoples who continue to occupy and use traditional lands (McMillan, 1988).

Federal authorities have rejected constitutional guarantees for still-to-be-defined inherent aboriginal self-government rights. Their preference is for municipal-style local governments created through an increase in delegated powers and negotiated on a community-to-community basis under either the Indian Act or alternative legislation. Although flexibility and aboriginal input are encouraged, federal authorities are resolute in imposing guidelines for community-based self-government negotiations. Self-government structures must respect existing constitutional principles and be consistent with current government policy (DIAND, 1987). In making self-governing structures subject to the Charter's equality provisions, they are likely to run afoul of aboriginal demands that inherent rights to self-government not be constrained by the Charter's liberal bias (Lenihan, 1991). In addition, terms for the implementation of self-governing structures and conferral of law-making authority need to be specified and negotiated before legislative approval is granted. No constitutional entrenchment of these structures is anticipated, apart from certain exceptional cases.

The following case studies examine two examples of negotiated self-government structures; others are in varying stages of completion.

Case Study: The Cree-Naskapi (of Quebec) Act, 1984
The Cree-Naskapi (of Quebec) Act originated in two agreements involving the governments of Canada and Quebec, three provincial Crown corporations, the James Bay Cree, the Inuit of Quebec, and the Naskapi of Schefferville. In 1984, the Act replaced band councils in northern Quebec with band corporations as part of a comprehensive land claim originating in the James Bay and Northern Quebec Hydro Agreement in 1975 (Peters, 1989; Feit, 1989). According to the terms of the Act, aboriginal title to vast tracts of land was surrendered in exchange for reserve land, financial compensation, hunting-fishing-trapping rights, and self-determination over local affairs. The agreement exempted one Naskapi and eight Cree bands from the provisions of the Indian Act except for individuals living off reserves. Band corporations were granted greater independence and power to make by-laws than had been the case under previous provisions. Among the new provisions were the rights to sell land under special circumstances, to borrow from private sources, and to take measures for securing a viable economic base. The administration and management of band affairs are the responsibility of an elected band council, which also has local governing powers over service delivery, taxation, and resource use (DIAND, 1989a). A collaborative arrangement involving federal, provincial, and local governments has been established to improve the delivery of health, welfare, and educational services.

While sound in theory, this historical experiment to make the Cree-Naskapi the first aboriginal group with a self-governing structure under federal legislation has not lived up to expectations (York, 1986). Delays in resource transfers, inadequate resources to support new self-governing powers, and unwarranted Treasury interference in financial affairs have largely undermined the spirit and intent of the Act. Furthermore, the Cree-Naskapi leaders have called for an injunction against further hydro development because of federal and provincial government failure to live up to treaty obligations.

The politics of development have become even more pronounced with proposed development of Phase II of the James Bay Hydro Project. In a series of incidents at the $12.6-billion Great Whale project, Cree groups have threatened to sabotage the mega-project unless their rights are acknowledged in an environmental assessment. In what is being hailed as a milestone decision, a Federal Court ruling is forcing Ottawa to intervene in the massive project until a full environmental impact assessment is conducted. Not only has Quebec decided on a one-year moratorium, but the court decision reinforces federal responsibility to intervene in all projects that have an impact on aboriginal peoples, according to James O'Reilly, a Montreal lawyer representing the Cree (*Toronto Star*, 1991i).

The broader question of aboriginal status *vis-à-vis* Quebec's aspirations as a 'distinct society' has also become pertinent: aboriginal groups feel that, should Quebec decide to separate from Canada, they have a right to separate from Quebec and take much of the province with them (*Kitchener-Waterloo Record*, 1991b). This argument comprises three intertwined strands. First, aboriginal peoples in Quebec have claimed virtually all of Quebec, thus making it illegal for the province to secede without explicit aboriginal consent. Second, it is argued that secession by Quebec may render the James Bay project of 1975 invalid. Since the original agreement involved a contract between Ottawa, Quebec, and aboriginal nations, loss of one signatory could put the entire tripartite arrangement in jeopardy. Third, constitutional experts argue that Quebec may be entitled only to the region it comprised in 1867—the St Lawrence River valley—and that Ottawa retains the rights to the lands transferred to Quebec in 1898 and 1912, as well as fiduciary responsibilities for aboriginal peoples in federal territories. The resulting conflict involving Ottawa, Quebec, and aboriginal peoples is likely to escalate in the near future as competing 'distinct societies' sort out their respective claims.

Case Study: The Sechelt Indian Band Self-Government Act, 1986
Current government policy is focused on non-constitutional initiatives in local self-reliance, better known as community-based self-government negotiations (DIAND, 1991a). Up to 70 community self-governing proposals are under federal review, but the conferral of self-government on the Sechelt band is unique in that the latter was the first band to negotiate self-government as a separate issue. Thus the legislation was tailored to fit local community needs rather than a broader scheme of development, as was the case in the James Bay agreements of the 1970s and the Cree-Naskapi (of Quebec) Act in 1984. With passage of the Sechelt Indian Band Self-Government Act in 1986, the 650 members of this BC band became the first in Canada to achieve self-governance without pressure from a development project.

The Sechelt model is a legislated and negotiated form of self-government that falls outside aboriginal demands for constitutional entrenchments of inherent self-governing rights and aboriginal title (Taylor and Paget, 1989). The Sechelt Act was negotiated to bypass restrictions within the Indian Act, but without prejudicing Sechelt aboriginal claims against the Canadian state (Cassidy and Dale, 1988). The delegation of powers under federal enabling legislation allowed the Sechelt community to assume more direct control over land, resources, health and social services, education, housing, and local taxation. Removal of the authority of the Indian Act and its replacement by a band constitution and legitimized tribal authority is perhaps the most significant innovation (Taylor and Paget, 1989). Unencumbered by the Indian Act provisions that prevented direct dealing with private or government sectors, the new Act established the Sechelt band as a legal entity with the powers and responsibilities of a natural person, granted it title to reserve lands (including the right to dispose of property without Departmental approval), defined the basis and powers of local government, conferred quasi-municipal authority over non-aboriginals, established an elected council with rights to draft laws and a constitution, and provided for an ongoing funding arrangement with the federal authorities (DIAND, 1986). In short, as Taylor and Paget (1989) point out, the Sechelt have achieved a relatively autonomous form of self-government with a wide range of delegated powers exercisable within the context of their constitution and under the control of the band itself.

The Sechelt arrangement has been subject to criticism. Some aboriginal leaders are concerned by the apparently modest, municipal-style level of self-government it provides, preferring to hold out for a distinct third order of government based on an inherent right. Others see the Sechelt as victims of a government plot to downscale involvement in the 'Indian' business—in effect, as nothing more than the 'lead buffalo' in what became known as Ottawa's 'buffalo jump' policy (leaked to the public in the mid-1980s). Still others are content to remain under the Indian Act, preferring only a form of self-government that would enhance their own control over internal affairs (McMillan, 1988). The Sechelt themselves recognize that a model developed for a highly urbanized, stategically located, and relatively prosperous band with vast development potential may not apply to other groups who are less favourably situated (Taylor and Paget, 1989). Despite ongoing criticism of Sechelt self-government, this precedent-making initiative is drawing both national and international interest as a workable compromise for self-determination through self-government.

Developments such as the Sechelt agreement are encouraging. They reveal a commitment on the part of Ottawa and the provinces to address aboriginal issues on a bilateral basis. They also suggest a willingness to renegotiate Canada's social contract with aboriginal people not as a colony but as a 'nation'. That recent talks have linked aboriginal demands with those of Quebec, given a mutual interest in collective rights and distinct-society status, is indicative of a shift in aboriginal strategy (*Globe and Mail*, 1991p). But failure to achieve satisfactory self-governing arrangements in other areas—despite constitutional guarantees to this effect—indicates that further struggles are in store.

CONSTITUTIONAL POLITICS AND ABORIGINAL RIGHTS

Decades of federal domination and bureaucratic control have done little to satisfy aboriginal aspirations towards self-government. Recognizing that political self-determination is central to renewal, aboriginal leaders have proposed to eliminate the paternalistic agenda underlying government–aboriginal relations in favour of one consistent with the principles of aboriginality. Proclaiming a right to self-determination through self-government, they have turned to the courts for definition of aboriginal and treaty rights, as well as resolution of outstanding land claims. In addition, aboriginal leaders have used the constitutional arena to define themselves and their place in society, on the assumption that guaranteed self-governing arrangements are critical for meeting political, social, and cultural needs (Platiel, 1991a).

First Ministers Conferences, 1983-1987

The politics of the Canadian Constitution became highly visible during the four First Ministers Conferences on Aboriginal Constitutional Matters convened between 1983 and 1987, which brought together federal authorities and provincial premiers in an effort to define precisely the content of constitutional provisions. That these conferences ultimately failed to achieve their objective is widely known. Yet they drew attention to the hard-nosed politics and diverse logics involved in sorting out the aboriginal agenda.

Participants
Status Indians were represented by the Assembly of First Nations (AFN), the largest and most powerful of all aboriginal lobby groups; among the groups that did not participate, however, were the 100,000-strong Prairie Treaty Nations Alliance, the Inuit Committee on National Issues, the Native Council of Canada representing non-status Indians, and the Métis National Council.

Claiming to speak on behalf of status Indians at federal levels, the AFN represents the latest in a series of attempts to establish aboriginal organizations dating back to the nineteenth century; earlier efforts were made despite prohibitions within the Indian Act that made it illegal to organize politically beyond the local level. It was not until the twentieth century that national, pan-tribal organizations such as the League of Indians in Canada and the North American Indian Brotherhood came into being. Both, however, failed as a result of lack of support, the pervasiveness of internal discord, and federal suppression (Frideres, 1988; Bressette, 1991).

In 1954 the precursor of the AFN, the National Indian Council—

comprising Métis, status, and non-status Indians—was formed, later splitting into two factions: the Native Council of Canada (composed of Métis and non-status Indians), and the National Indian Brotherhood (composed of status Indians). As the official voice of status Indians, the National Indian Brotherhood emerged as a powerful force during the 1970s, lobbying on behalf of status Indians and scrutinizing government policy. But criticism of its lack of representativeness, reliance on federal funding, and absence of accountability to diverse constituents led to its dissolution in 1980-82 and its replacement with the current structure.

The AFN carries on much of the work of its predecessor, although structural changes have been made. The original pyramid of hierarchically organized aboriginal associations was replaced by an organization of chiefs and 15 affiliated associations. In its role as an 'institutionalized' pressure group with a mandate to advise and monitor (Fleras, 1986), the Assembly has spearheaded the aspirations of status Indians through a decade of negotiation with federal and provincial authorities, especially in areas related to treaty issues and the constitutional entrenchment of inherent aboriginal self-governing rights.

An Overview

On the surface, the four constitutional conferences were concerned with the clarification of 'existing aboriginal and treaty rights'. At each of three conferences after 1983, constitutional recognition of aboriginal self-government as a 'freestanding' right, independent of any specific negotiated agreement, emerged as a pivotal issue (Canada, 1991). Beneath the surface, however, lay more fundamental concerns related to such issues as power-sharing, resource allocation, jurisdiction, and costs; equally significant was the question of whether the details of self-government were to be defined politically or by the courts, *ex post facto*. But in the end this emphasis on self-government, with its implied recognition of aboriginal peoples as 'nations within', was rebuffed, and Canada lost its chance to entrench aboriginal self-governing rights as part of the national Constitution. Federal and provincial leaders rejected what appeared to be a nebulous concept with potentially undesirable implications for the existing distribution of power and wealth. This rejection left current government–aboriginal relations in disarray and arguably, in conjunction with the exclusion of aboriginal peoples from the Meech Lake proceedings, contributed to Elijah Harper's filibuster in the Manitoba legislature, as well as to the 78-day standoff at Oka and Kahnawake in the summer of 1990.

Background

Many of the difficulties in these discussions could be traced to the wording of relevant passages within the Constitution. Section 35(1) of

the Constitution Act of 1982 recognized and affirmed the 'existing aboriginal and treaty rights' of Canada's first nations. Section 25 went on
to say that interpretation of the guarantees contained in the Charter of
Rights and Freedoms would not detract from aboriginal or treaty rights.
Section 37 made allowances for the convening of a conference among
First Ministers and aboriginal leaders to further explore aboriginal
rights, suggesting a distinction between existing aboriginal rights and
the possibility of additional rights acquired through negotiations
(DIAND, n.d.).

The intent may have been noble, but these clauses did not specify
what existing aboriginal rights were. Nor did it elaborate on how these
would be exercised; in particular, it remained silent on the concept of
self-governing rights. Each party operated on a different set of first principles. For the government, existing aboriginal rights consisted of
those that either existed in the present or would be acquired through
future land-claims settlements; rights lost prior to the Constitution Act
of 1982 could not be revived or restored by section 35. For aboriginal
peoples, however, existing aboriginal rights encompassed the full
range of rights that aboriginal peoples possessed in the past, which
they regarded as continuing into the present unless specifically extinguished (DIAND, n.d.). In effect, the government saw the section 37
process as an occasion for the *identification* and *protection* of new
rights acquired through negotiation. In contrast, the aboriginal view
treated the section 37 process as one of *restoration* and *clarification* of
aboriginal rights (Royal Commission, 1992).

The Issue
At the crux of this debate was the question of aboriginal self-governing 'rights' as interpreted through the prism of section 35. The dispute
focused on whether section 35(1) represented an 'empty box'—containing no specific rights until such were negotiated politically—or,
as aboriginal spokespersons asserted, a 'full box' of rights, requiring
only clarification by the First Ministers. Aboriginal representatives
argued that aboriginal groups possessed an *inherent* right to self-government by virtue of their status as the 'ancestral occupants' of the
land, whose right to political sovereignty and land entitlement had
never been extinguished either by treaty or by conquest. The inclusion
of section 35(1) merely reaffirmed what aboriginal peoples had perceived as existing from 'time immemorial': namely, their status as a
'distinct nation' whose self-governing rights existed in the past, persist
in the present, and will continue in the future. The distinction
between contingent and inherent rights is critical. According to
Michael Asch and Patrick Macklem (writing in the *Alberta Law
Review*), if aboriginal rights are contingent they depend upon formal

political or constitutional recognition, whereas if they are inherent they are independent of any Canadian law (Simpson, 1991a). Ultimately, then, inherent rights challenge the authority of Canada to unilaterally declare sovereignty over aboriginal nations.

For aboriginal groups, the entrenchment of an intrinsic, unconditional right to self-government was crucial to severing the bonds of dependency and underdevelopment engendered by the Indian Act. But verbal promises by the government to negotiate in good faith could not be accepted in light of the historical record. Only with virtually iron-clad guarantees of a constitutional amendment recognizing an inherent right to self-government, and access to the courts for protection, could aboriginal groups feel secure in the decolonization process. Towards that end, aboriginal groups refused to accept any self-governing concessions that were subject to a provincial veto.

Federal and provincial officials, on the other hand, proposed what might be termed a *contingent*-rights approach, under which aboriginal rights to self-government as implied in section 35(1) of the Act would be 'contingent' upon prior negotiations over details with the various levels of government (Platiel, 1987). No proposal for self-government would be enshrined in the Constitution unless it had been politically negotiated, specified in detail, and consented to beforehand by the provinces (Calder, 1988). Thus, in contrast to aboriginal groups who proposed to entrench the principle of self-government first and negotiate the specifics later, the provincial and federal governments insisted on negotiating the terms and powers of self-government first, and only then constitutionally protecting what had been specified (Opekokew, 1987). To the extent that the 'principles first' perspective of aboriginal representatives did not coincide with the government's 'specific agreement first' approach, a serious communication gap existed between the two competing sectors. Even a federal proposal to entrench self-governing rights, and to negotiate the specifics politically without infringing on provincial or federal powers, was unsuccessful.

The Process

The government's rejection of aboriginal self-government as an inherent aboriginal right was based on political and economic expediency. Financial and jurisdictional considerations proved to be major stumbling-blocks. Most provinces feared that an unrestricted right to self-government would mean excessive costs and substantial cost-sharing with the federal government in areas such as welfare. Also worrisome were the logistics of implementing self-governing provisions. British Columbia, a province not noted for its support of aboriginal issues, was particularly adamant about any prior entrenchment of aboriginal self-government. The province contained 197 bands (one-third of all those in Canada), and 1,628 reserves (72% of the Canadian total). If the constitutional rights of Native persons were guaranteed, Premier Vander Zalm argued, the province would find itself in the daunting position of having to negotiate self-government agreements with up to 350 tribal nations. This concern was compounded by the inability—or unwillingness—of aboriginal leaders to specify in detail the nature of self-government structures. The absence of consensus regarding either its form or its function left provincial officials perplexed and apprehensive over its ramifications and costs.

Nor would the provincial premiers agree to any amendment to transfer jurisdictional control over aboriginal government to the courts. Fearing judicial challenges to provincial monopoly over natural resources, they disputed the right of judges to define the meaning of vaguely worded constitutional agreements regarding aboriginal self-government—especially since court decisions in the past had been inclined towards a liberal interpretation of human rights in general and aboriginal rights in particular. Finally, at the core of the debate lay the problematics of power and its redistribution. According to Opekokew (1987: 45):

> The provinces are concerned with the possible transfer of powers to a third order of government. Once aboriginal self-government is clothed with powers similar to those in section 91 and 92 of the Constitution Act 1867, the provinces argue that there is a transfer of powers. . . . If there is a transfer of power to an aboriginal self-governing entity within a province, it can adversely affect other parts of the provincial powers. The provinces assert that aboriginal self-government must be practical, in that it must be compatible with municipal and provincial regimes that are adjacent to it. The provinces are also concerned about the resourcing of self-government, which they state is more than the fiscal aspect. It probably includes whether a land base must be provided for those who are now landless. The form or model of the institutional arrangement of aboriginal self-government is at issue. The form will have its basis on this authority. The decision for 1987 is whether it is created by delegation, such as the municipal status of the Inuit villages, or if it has a constitutional basis with a guaranteed jurisdiction, such as the section 91 and 92 powers of the federal government and the provinces.

Not surprisingly, despite aboriginal assurances that self-government represented only a progressive search for bilateral power-sharing—not a plot to undermine existing powers—provincial authorities steered clear of any proposal to open a Pandora's box of aboriginal self-governing rights.

The Outcome
It came as little surprise that no consensus was attained; given the politics of power at the core of the constitutional debate, nothing

short of a miracle could have produced a solution. The gap between aboriginal demands and what the provinces were willing to concede proved unbridgeable, despite several compromise proposals. For Ottawa, inherent self-government incurred the risk of creating a patchwork of independencies, each with the potential to seek international recognition as a sovereign nation. British Columbia and Alberta opposed any effort to entrench an unfettered guarantee of self-government within the Constitution; Saskatchewan and Newfoundland were troubled by the concept of entrenching an unqualified right, and decided eventually to reject the compromise. In addition, for these and other provinces, the difficulty of entrenching the principle of self-government for landless Métis and non-status Indians in urban areas appeared insurmountable. Also problematic was the whole notion of collective rights in relation to deeply entrenched individual and equality rights (Platiel, 1987). Ontario and the remaining Atlantic provinces appeared willing to make a compromise, but Manitoba was the only province unreservedly prepared to accept an intrinsic right to aboriginal self-government. The talks collapsed, leaving aboriginal peoples in constitutional limbo over the entrenchment of 'distinct' self-governing rights.

Why did the constitutional conferences fail to resolve the self-governing issue? The lack of political will was a contributing factor (Brock, 1991). Native groups were neither powerful enough politically nor sufficiently concentrated in territorial terms to constitute an electoral force worth deferring to. Equally significant was the absence of any potential for 'issue-linkage': whereas the Meech Lake accord offered the provinces resources and power in exchange for renewing Canadian federalism, the aboriginal issue never really presented any material incentive to reach a compromise. If anything, entrenchment of aboriginal self-government implied a redistribution of power and funds that would infringe on provincial autonomy and resources. Without a tangible payoff in return for their support, the notion of an aboriginal 'distinct society' did not appear to warrant serious consideration among the premiers.

In the end, the fact that aboriginal rights were entrenched in the Constitution at all can be attributed largely to the vigorous lobbying by aboriginal groups in England, not to any fundamental commitment among the First Ministers. The evidence suggests that political leaders were uncomfortable dealing with aboriginal peoples on a government-to-government basis (Brock, 1991). Many were perplexed by aboriginal demands for recognition of inherent self-governing rights whose collective character puts them beyond the provisions of the Charter or the Constitution. Nor did the First Ministers appear capable of making fundamental changes to the cultural assumptions and colonial mentality underlying the relationship between aboriginal peoples and the state.

The Aftermath

The distinct society perpetuates a myth. Canada was not born when the English and French cultures joined. It was born when the treaties were signed with the First Nations. We allowed people from Europe to come here and settle peacefully.
—Georges Erasmus, Assembly of First Nations; quoted in *Maclean's* (1990b).

Aboriginal leaders reacted with dismay to the constitutional logjam. To some, the politics of constitutional reform was yet another manifestation of 'institutionalized' racism. To others, the constitutional debacle reflected the pervasiveness of Canada's internal colonialism. Still others were simply daunted by the challenge of swaying Canadian decision-makers to accept the concept of aboriginal self-government as an inherent constitutional right.

This dismay, however, turned to outrage when a month after the final conference, in April 1987, the same First Ministers met at Meech Lake and hammered out an arrangement to preserve and protect Quebec's 'distinct society' aspirations. For aboriginal peoples the double standard was unconscionable. How could the First Ministers reject aboriginal self-government as poorly defined, yet accept an equally ill-defined, yet-to-be-worked-out concept as a basis for constitutional reform? Aboriginal peoples, no less than the Québécois, see themselves as a 'distinct society' whose rights to preferential self-governing treatment are entrenched in law (the Royal Proclamation) and the 1982 Constitution. Like their Québécois counterparts, they constitute a founding ('charter') element in Canadian society, with special rights relinquished by neither treaty nor conquest. As the co-chair of the Inuit Committee on National Issues, Zebedee Nungak, put it, 'If there is any distinct society in this country, it's us' (reported in the *Kitchener Waterloo Record*, 7 Aug. 1987). Their failure to recognize aboriginal peoples as a distinct yet integral component of Canadian society would come back to haunt the First Ministers during the constitutional crisis that followed the demise of the Meech Lake agreement.

The Post-Meech Era

Recent developments support the notion of aboriginal peoples as distinct societies. In a somewhat interesting turn-around, public support for the concept of aboriginal people as a distinct society is growing, while English-speaking Canadians continue to repudiate a similar status in the case of Quebec. Supreme Court rulings such as the

Sparrow decision in 1990 have supported the distinct-society position, in the process exempting aboriginal peoples from certain laws of
the land. Nova Scotia's Micmacs have received constitutional rights to
fishing, and limited immunity from government regulations (*Globe
and Mail*, 8 March 1990). Similarly, Ontario's 160,000 status Indians
are unofficially exempt from regulations related to hunting and
fishing. Expanded hunting and fishing rights, it was announced by
Ontario's Native Affairs Minister, Bud Wildman, meant that aboriginal
people would not be charged under game laws since aboriginal rights
to game (for personal or community consumption) take precedence
over all but essential matters of conservation. This exemption stems in
part from an earlier Supreme Court ruling that upheld aboriginal
access to wildlife resources, and in part from the NDP government's
endorsement of inherent aboriginal rights to self-government, with
promises of authority, jurisdiction, and finances to put the principle
into practice (*Toronto Star*, 1991c). In rejecting the legitimacy of state
laws on aboriginal peoples, the courts have taken steps towards
restructuring the status of aboriginal peoples as distinct societies and
nations within.

Equally impressive changes are evident in the political agenda. There
is growing federal willingness for bilateral consultations in decision-
making, particularly with the collapse of the Meech Lake accord and the
ensuing national-unity crisis. With the possibility of revising the constitutional agenda to deal with Quebec's proposed sovereign status,
aboriginal leaders are pinning their hopes on meaningful involvement
in the next round of constitutional talks. Their demands are fundamental: constitutional recognition of aboriginal distinctiveness; the
right to self-government; limited political interference in aboriginal
jurisdictions; and full participation in all constitutional talks (*Globe
and Mail*, 1991o). In an effort to strike a new constitutional deal and
to capitalize on this historic opportunity to redefine aboriginal status
in society, aboriginal people have been promised an 'appropriate
place' at the upcoming constitutional talks, thus ensuring aboriginal
issues a higher national profile than in the 1987 Meech Lake negotiations, and a role at First Ministers Conferences not aimed specifically
at aboriginal concerns. As well, a Royal Commission on Aboriginal
Issues has been formed with majority Native representation to look
into sweeping changes in Canada's treatment of aboriginal peoples.
The mandate and composition of this Commission confirm that, in
contrast to the situation in the past, when Canada would address aboriginal concerns only in terms of isolated issues and crises, at last it is
prepared to take a co-ordinated approach to aboriginal affairs. Clearly,
aboriginal issues have moved to the forefront of the national agenda
(Simpson, 1991b; Deputies Council, 1991), and recent federal moves

Table 5.1 Models of Self-Government

Aboriginal Position	Federal/Provincial Position
1. Distinct order of government with provincial-like powers	Municipal-type government under provincial control
2. Powers defined by Constitution, specifics to worked out later	Powers specifically defined by legislation, to be constitutionally entrenched following negotiations
3. Charter individual rights plus collective aboriginal rights	Strict application of Charter rights
4. Total ownership of resources plus institutional autonomy	Limited ownership and decision-making input
5. Content and style of self-government accountable to Native communities	Self-governing structures accountable to parliament or constitutional law
6. Powers inherent in aboriginal status and conferred by the Creator from 'time immemorial'	Powers to be delegated from central authorities as a 'privilege' that must conform to Canadian laws

to include aboriginal peoples in drafting constitutional reforms on a government-to-government basis suggest the dawning of a new era.

SELF-GOVERNMENT: COMPETING VISIONS

The politics of aboriginal self-government reflect competing visions of the status of aboriginal people in society, and of their relationship with central authorities. The government claims to be anxious to establish a new working relationship with the aboriginal people 'that reflects modern Canadian realities and legitimate aboriginal expectations' (Prime Minister Mulroney, DIAND, 1991h). Yet there is a failure to communicate. Government initiatives centre on the concept of community control and self-reliance under the jurisdiction of the appropriate federal or provincial authority (Canadian Government, 1990). But aboriginal peoples claim an inherent right to self-government and demand a distinct third order of government alongside federal and provincial authorities. Conversely, the state proposes to restrict self-governing powers to municipal-style control over the design and delivery of community programs (DIAND, 1989c). Figure 5.1 compares the federal and aboriginal positions. Recently the federal government has proposed a 'stand-alone' right—neither inherent nor negotiable—emanating from the Constitution which would be 'justiciable' (enforceable by the courts) after a ten-year delay. This compromise proposal appears to be unacceptable to most aboriginal groups (Morse, 1991), but is consistent with federal efforts to ensure Canadian sovereignty and the primacy of the Constitution (Royal Commission, 1992).

In short, aboriginal and federal perspectives on self-government are diametrically opposed. For aboriginal peoples, the basic premise underlying self-government is relatively straightforward. By linking their collective rights to those of Quebec as part of an overall strategy, proponents of aboriginal self-government underline their right to govern themselves, within the framework of Canadian society and as equals with Ottawa and the provinces (Comeau and Santin, 1990). Aboriginal rights to authority over land and institutions are not delegated but intrinsic and natural, reflecting inherent rights that remain intact (Royal Commission, 1992). Central authorities, by contrast, envision self-government as a municipal-administrative arrangement in which aboriginal functionaries would carry out federal responsibilities transferred to them under provincial supervision. This clash of visions has been both reflected in and intensified by the constitutional frenzy that has attended the politics of 'distinct societies' in the aftermath of Meech Lake. It also suggests that constitutional renewal of aboriginal–state relations on a mutually respectful footing and in a spirit of co-existence and reciprocity will not come easily, despite growing public support for a lasting reconciliation with aboriginal peoples as equal partners in Confederation (Royal Commission, 1992).

The Department of Indian Affairs: From Bureaucracy towards Empowerment?

A precondition of internal colonial systems is the establishment of state bureaucracies to administer government policy (Blauner, 1972). Ostensibly directed at the protection and assistance of client groups, these administrative agencies have in fact been more concerned with the indirect control and domination of aboriginal peoples. At present, in response to societal change and social protest, aboriginal departments are undergoing modifications in structure, function, and process. Of particular note is the proposed dismantling of bureaucratic mentalities and structures as part of a broader shift of focus from 'administration' to 'development'. Nevertheless, ambiguities persist as new ways of thinking jostle with the old. Competing agendas and mutually exclusive priorities are not conducive to the unity of purpose required for addressing aboriginal concerns and aspirations. What we are left with are aboriginal, political, and bureaucratic sectors at odds with each other over a workable national agenda.

Such is the case in Canada, where a federal department has long controlled and exploited the direction of aboriginal policy and administration. From 1867 onwards, comprehensive legislation has been instituted to govern every aspect of aboriginal life, even to the point of curbing constitutional and citizenship rights. Aboriginal languages, cultures, and identity were suppressed, while band communities were locked into patterns of dependency from which there was little escape (McMillan, 1988). The Indian Affairs Department's complicity in the control and exploitation of aboriginal peoples under the Indian Act has been well documented (Ponting and Gibbins, 1980; Ponting, 1986; Shkilynk, 1985a), and little can be gained by rehashing the negative consequences of even well-intentioned actions by officials often more interested in careerism and empire-building than in assisting aboriginal communities. In keeping with government policies for self-reliance and limited aboriginal autonomy, the Department has tried to put some distance between itself and the stifling provisions of the Indian Act. Calls for outright abolition of the Department and transfer of its functions to government agencies and aboriginal bands are balanced by claims that the Department has served as a buffer, shielding aboriginal peoples from predatory private interests. Condemnation of the Act as antiquated and paternalistic is equally widespread, yet aboriginal leaders are reluctant to do away with it for fear of undermining the government's legal obligations to them. Difficulties will persist until serious steps are taken to overhaul the Indian Act in consultation with aboriginal leaders as recommended in the government's current four-part aboriginal policy agenda.

This chapter examines the largely ambivalent role, past and present, of the Department of Indian Affairs and Northern Development (DIAND) in shaping the contours of aboriginal–state relations and demonstrates how the mandate of the Department is constrained by organizational imperatives at odds with aboriginal ambitions. The Department's obligation to carry out the objectives of the Indian Act has also weakened its capacity to address contemporary issues. Thus recent efforts by the Department to engage in more meaningful interaction with its clients have been riddled with inconsistencies and breakdowns. While some criticism of DIAND is misplaced and unjustified, there remains good reason to believe that the presence of a still formidable bureaucracy may prove an insurmountable barrier to true empowerment of aboriginal communities.

The Mandate: Indian Acts, 1876, 1951

Aboriginal relations with the government and the state as a whole are reflected, reinforced, and mediated by the Indian Acts of 1876 and 1951 and their implementation by the Indian Affairs Department. The original Victorian-era Act gave sweeping power for the Department to invade, control, and regulate every aspect of aboriginal life, from consumption of alcohol to loitering at pool halls (Moran, 1988). It defined who, legally, was an Indian, what aboriginal peoples were entitled to under the government's fiduciary obligations, who could qualify for enfranchisement, what could be done with Indian lands and resources, and how they were to be ruled (by Indian agents and band councils with quasi-municipal powers). Any change to aboriginal life on the reserve, from the personal to the community level, had to be approved by the federal representative (the Indian agent).

It was not until 1985, when passage of Bill C-31 reinstated enfranchised aboriginal persons (especially women who had lost status by marrying non-Indians), that major changes were made to the Indian Act. The 1951 Indian Act had softened the most blatantly discriminatory provisions of the 1876 Act. It legalized certain aboriginal customs such as the potlatch, lifted the prohibition on raising money for political purposes, and permitted drinking at hotels—though not on reserves for another five years. Yet despite the appearance of local control through band councils (Gibbins and Ponting, 1986), the powers of the Minister remained largely intact. The 1951 Act permitted a limited degree of local input into program administration, but departmental approval was required for a broad variety of services, programs, and obligations, for which DIAND was accountable to the Auditor-General (*Toronto Star*, 2 Nov. 1986). Little was done to foster band control over the design, delivery, and monitoring of federal services such as housing.

Attempts at social renewal or economic development have continued to suffer because of confusion over jurisdiction and channels of authority. Bureaucratic encumbrances still thwart even moderate aboriginal ambitions. While certain provisions are beneficial in protecting special status, the Indian Act places aboriginal peoples under the authority of the federal government, with a corresponding diminution of local initiatives for reform and development. Under the Indian Act, aboriginal people cannot hold title to land or private property (land title is held in trust by the Crown, and band members cannot dispose of land and resources without initially surrendering them to the Crown). Bands thus have difficulty financing commercial endeavours on reserves, since neither land nor property is subject to mortgage, collateral, or legal seizure (McMillan, 1988).

That the Indian Act remains on the books is perplexing, in view of recent shifts in policy and administration. It has been denounced by aboriginal men and women as inflexible and restrictive, at odds with even limited aboriginal aspirations. Aboriginal leaders are vehement in condemning the Act as racist and regressive, although they acknowledge its usefulness in affording legal protection. Federal authorities from the Prime Minister down have decried the Indian Act in its present form as a recipe to foster dependency, to frustrate aboriginal self-sufficiency, and to deny aboriginal self-respect (DIAND, 1990g; Harry Swain, Deputy Minister of Indian Affairs, quoted in *Toronto Star*, 1990a). This outcry suggests that the days of the Indian Act are numbered.

In what can only be ironic twist for many Canadians, the Indian Act and its administration by the Indian Affairs Department have been likened to South Africa's system of apartheid, with its convoluted efforts to exclude and exploit the indigenous Black populations on the basis of racial characteristics (Hall, 1990). Some of the parallels are deceptively compelling. In the past, an outdated and paternalistic perception of aboriginals as wards of the state meant that aboriginal peoples were denied equal rights and full participation in Canadian society on racial grounds. For example, until 1960 they did not have the right to vote in federal elections; in principle they required a pass from the Indian agent to leave the reserve; until 1956 they were not permitted to consume alcohol on the reserve; and they were barred from political office off the reserve. The reserve system itself bore a striking resemblance to the system of bantustans ('homelands') for Blacks in the outlying areas.

But these comparisons can be taken too far. Aboriginal peoples in Canada today possess a whole range of rights and options that are still routinely denied to Blacks in South Africa. They possess equal rights as set out in the Canadian Charter, as well as special aboriginal rights to enhance collective and individual interests. Mobility rights are no longer curtailed in any way, nor are aboriginal individuals forced to carry 'identification' cards with them and to live in designated areas. Hence, while parallels to apartheid are useful in drawing media attention to legitimate grievances, they ignore the fundamental difference in management of aboriginal–government relations.

History and Status of DIAND

> Its continuing presence is an affront to the concept of Indian self-determination.
> —Kevin Christmas, Executive Director, 1991 Union of Nova Scotia Indians; quoted in Halifax *Chronicle-Herald* (1991).

The 1876 Indian Act created the legal framework for the paternalistic administration of aboriginal affairs by a federal agency. The Act consolidated existing Indian legislation in the provinces and territories, and delineated the responsibilities of the federal government towards aboriginal peoples as stipulated in the BNA Act of 1867. It also established the principle of government control over and responsibility for managing aboriginal assets (land, funds, and properties). Perception of aboriginal peoples as wards of the state, in need of superior guidance and protection, gave rise to the colonialist/paternalistic character of the Department. Aboriginal people were seen as inferior legal minors who had to be pacified, controlled, managed, and educated in hopes of achieving the ultimate goal of enfranchisement (loss of Indian status) and absorption into society.

In 1867 the federal government assumed jurisdiction over aboriginal affairs with the establishment of the Indian Affairs branch under the Secretary of State (Ponting and Gibbins, 1980). Later, responsibility for aboriginal affairs was transferred to the Department of Interior, then to the Department of Health and Welfare in 1945 and the Department of Citizenship and Immigration in 1949. It was not until 1966 that the Department of Indian Affairs and Northern Development was created by an Act of Parliament, with a Minister responsible for the Indian and Inuit Affairs Program (DIAND, 1990d).

The Department's early policy and administration were consistent with the provisions of the Indian Act. Foremost among its objectives were the protection (guardianship), settlement, and assimilation (through exposure to Christianity and the arts of civilization) of aboriginal peoples, and, through agricultural self-sufficiency, their transformation into productive citizens of the country. The success of the Department's policy was to be measured by the numbers of enfranchised Natives—that is, those who formally renounced Indian status and assumed all the rights, duties, and obligations of citizenship in Canada (Ponting and Gibbins, 1980).

At present the Department retains a comprehensive range of responsibilities towards aboriginal peoples as stipulated in the Indian Act. The diversity of programs directly or indirectly under its management is unique in that it corresponds to the full range of services provided to other Canadians by provincial and municipal governments (DIAND, 1990d). Federal programs for reserve communities include services in education, social assistance, housing, community infrastructure, justice, culture, and economic growth. National Health and Welfare Canada is responsible for aboriginal health services, although the governments of the Northwest Territories and Newfoundland have assumed responsibility for delivery of certain services under a cost-sharing agreement with federal authorities.

Administering aboriginal affairs has been expensive. Since the mid-1960s, the Department has spent more than $30-billion on the administration of reserve programs and services. DIAND's budget for 1990-91 stood at $2.5-billion (another $1.5-billion was to be spent by other government departments and agencies), of which nearly 70 per cent would be administered by band councils or Indian agencies (DIAND, 1990d). In real dollars, this expenditure had increased by 76 per cent since 1975-76. The areas receiving the bulk of funds are education, social assistance, welfare services, and housing. In addition, a good deal of money has recently been directed to various programs to enhance economic self-sufficiency and development on reserves through the Department's Economic Development Sector in partnership with other government departments; an increasingly large proportion of these expenditures takes the form of 'alternative funding arrangements', with nearly $200 million in lump-sum payments destined for certain bands to spend at their discretion for 1990-91. Finally, the number of people employed by DIAND has continued to decline, dropping from 6245 'person years' in 1984 to 4102 in 1990-91. The number of aboriginal personnel within DIAND has increased by 19 per cent in the same period.

Manifest Functions/Latent Consequences

> Indian Affairs is holding you with a noose around your neck—they've got
> you with just your toes on the ground—dangling that money over you.
> —Juanita Perley, Tobique Women's Political Action Group, New
> Brunswick; cited in Silman (1987: 223).

Firmly rooted in the antiquated 1951 Indian Act, the Department remains a largely custodial agency devoted to regulation and control rather than development (Weaver, 1990; Frideres, 1990). Ponting (1986) has referred to DIAND as a 'money-moving' agency whose primary role is to allocate funds on the basis of compliance with organizational directives (also Penner, 1983; Franks, 1987). For example, all reserves are governed by an elected band council and band chief whose essential function is to administer funds from Ottawa and deliver basic services pertaining to health, housing, sanitation, and education (Comeau and Santin, 1990). For the most part it is Ottawa that decides how much money each band can spend and where, with the result that band governments are more accountable to federal authorities than to the local community. Overspending by the band in any fiscal year is treated as irresponsible behaviour, and an equivalent amount may be withheld from the next budget. In response to aboriginal demands for more autonomy in this area, Ottawa has loosened its purse-strings somewhat in recent years, and certain bands are now allowed to administer global budgets (a lump sum over five years) with some degree of discretion in spending ('alternative funding arrangements'). Nonetheless, the budget is still set in Ottawa, which remains the only source of revenue for many band governments.

Other observers have described DIAND as a system of containment whose bureaucratic imperatives collide with aboriginal realities (see Fleras, 1989a). Too often, administrative decisions are made by people whose values differ from their clients', and who are not always answerable to the latter for their actions (Deputies Council, 1991). This remoteness creates problems of credibility (Miller, 1989). Rather than promoting change from within, the Department attempts to ensure control and predictability—primarily by (a) reinforcing rules, (b) proper communication ('going through proper channels'), (c) conformity ('going by the book'), and (d) pervasive hierarchy (see Weber, 1947). To no one's surprise, the potential for meaningful interaction is diminished when aboriginal–government relations are conducted on the basis of impersonal and hierarchical authority, formal rationality, a complex division of labour, and rigid observation of procedures and rules.

The Department has cast around for ways to improve its image. Some efforts have focused on creating a culturally sensitive working climate; others have been directed at a broader restructuring of the organization in terms of power (devolution), responsibility (delegation), and structures (decentralization). The introduction of people-oriented management styles and the proposed removal of systemic discriminatory barriers are promising innovations, but they have yet to take hold (Deputies Council, 1991). Most notable have been the commitment to 'community self-government negotiations' and the promotion of 'alternative funding arrangements'. The paternalism of the past is being phased out with the transfer of some responsibilities to aboriginal bands and increasing decision-making powers for band councils (McMillan, 1988). A growing number of bands now exert limited control over finances, and, as we have seen, several have negotiated self-governing arrangements.

Yet the Department's 'hidden' agenda has remained remarkably steadfast (Ponting and Gibbins, 1980; Weaver, 1981). Reflecting the commitment to assimilate and 'civilize', Departmental policy has historically labelled aboriginal peoples as a 'problem' whose cultural and social idiosyncracies preclude smooth absorption into society. Strategies to purge aboriginal peoples of their so-called backwardness have evolved over time. After the Second World War, the political emphasis shifted from cultural assimilation to the eradication of poverty at several levels—physical, social, cultural, and psychological (Shkilnyk, 1985a). Obstacles to economic development in Native communities had to be removed through encouragement of off-reserve migration. Provision of social services and upgrading of reserve infrastructure, coupled with increased local responsibility for community-based initiatives, were also seen as critical in accelerating the transition from backwardness to modernity and progress. For the 'war on poverty' to be won, moreover, it was considered necessary to attack certain attitudes and values related to work and lifestyle that were seen as detrimental.

Modest improvements in socio-economic status notwithstanding, the continued impoverishment and alienation of aboriginal communities points to a fundamental misreading of the causes underlying the 'Indian problem' (Shkilnyk, 1985a). From the government's point of view, the problem lay in the communal (read 'communistic') aspects of tribal life, and it was the community that needed to be upgraded by increasing government expenditures on the reserve in the form of programs relating to job creation, infrastructure, and economic self-sufficiency. But throwing money at the problem has not solved it. The inadequacy of economic solutions to essentially political problems is reflected in the fact that, although Canada spends more on its aboriginal peoples (about $8,000 per capita, or $13,000 if we include only on-reserve Indians) than any other country in the world, conditions in many aboriginal communities have scarcely been raised above Third World standards. Thus complex questions need to be asked. Are we talking about inadequate implemention of solutions to clearly articulated problems? Or are various well-intentioned solutions doomed to failure because the problems themselves have been inappropriately defined? The challenge, in other words, is not more modernization and accelerated development. At the heart of the matter for aboriginal peoples is the lack of the power and resources they need to take control of their lives—a condition aggravated at times by an insensitive bureaucracy.

Debureaucratizing Indian Affairs: Self-Administration or Self-Determination?

The assimilationist objective of various Indian Affairs departments has not wavered over the years (Ponting and Gibbins, 1980). Since 1966 and possibly earlier, however, the formal mandate of the Indian and Inuit program within DIAND has shifted towards support of aboriginal efforts to achieve self-government, to secure economic self-sufficiency through community-based development, to settle accepted land claims, and to ensure that Canada's statutory and constitutional obligations to aboriginal peoples are fulfilled (Canadian Government, 1990). Devolution has become the catchword in recent years. Here too the emphasis is on community participation in the design and delivery of local services in hopes of enhancing local self-sufficiency by way of programs developed for 'people development', not 'people administration' (Ponting and Gibbins, 1980; Rawson, 1988). The establishment of a 'community negotiation process' and modified block funding arrangements ('alternative funding') that allow some discretion in spending and leeway in priority-setting, and enhance local accountability, has revised the explicit role of the Department. Instead of focusing on control and administration, as was once the case, DIAND claims it is moving into local development and community assistance in conjunction with federal and provincial bodies (Frideres, 1990). The oft-repeated statement that bands currently administer nearly 70 per cent of DIAND's $2.5-billion budget lends an air of credibility to these assertions.

But Indian Act restrictions continue to apply, hampering local and regional endeavours. Some question whether aboriginal peoples have merely won the right to administer the Department's definition of the problem, rather than to control the design and delivery of programs according to aboriginal needs and definitions (*Toronto Star*, 2 Nov. 1986). Other ambiguities are present as well. For instance, the federal allocation for aboriginal affairs continues to escalate yearly; yet per capita spending has declined because of inflation and population increases (Angus, 1990; *Toronto Star*, 18 Nov. 1990). Finally, studies continue to suggest that management is not always sensitive to aboriginal culture, and that aboriginal employees may be denied opportunities for advancement because they do not fit the traditional bureaucratic model (Deputies Council, 1991).

In light of the current fiscal crisis, suggestions that the government intends to dismantle the Department and redistribute its functions to existing line departments in both the federal and provincial sectors come as no surprise. Rumours to that effect have been circulating since the mid-1980s, fuelled in large measure by the leaked 'buffalo jump' document of the 1980s. The objective is the devolution of DIAND to an 'intergovernmental' affairs department that, apart from certain trust responsibilities, would divest itself of remaining program delivery responsibilities (Deputy Minister Harry Swain, in MacIntyre, 1991). There is also talk of scrapping the Indian Act and converting the Department into a developmental agency for transferring funds from the government to self-government structures in the same way that provinces receive block funding from federal coffers for programs and services. A similar plan has recently been implemented in New Zealand with, as we shall see, some success (Fleras, 1991). Although few at this point can predict what the future has in store, a restructuring of aboriginal policy and administration will clearly entail a massive shift in our perceptions of and approaches to aboriginal concerns.

DIAND: MULTIPLE MANDATES/COMPETING AGENDAS

That the Department of Indian Affairs remains a convenient target for criticism is understandable, given its reputation as an instrument of colonial domination, control, and assimilation (Ponting, 1986). As well, the Department has an impossibly sweeping mandate to administer the provisions of the Indian Act, to provide a broad range of services and programs to status Indians, and to advance the cause of aboriginal self-sufficiency and community self-government within the parameters of the Indian Act. Yet this outdated legislation not only fails to address aboriginal concerns and aspirations, but also diminishes the possibility of real change and aboriginal control of local affairs (Thomas Siddon, in DIAND, 1990c).

Since the mid-1960s the Department has undergone a series of internal reorganizations that have left the bureaucracy in a state of flux if not turmoil. Among these changes was a shift in focus towards community development, increased openness, and aboriginal input as part of a decentralization/devolution process in the mid-1970s. By the late 1970s, however, growing rationalization and an increasingly technocratic orientation had undermined much of that earlier progress and again put DIAND at cross purposes (Ponting and Gibbins, 1980). This lack of organizational continuity detracts from the Department's credibility as a positive force for change, and weakens morale and motivation among its staff. The wider environment in which the Department must operate is turbulent and complex, at best sceptical of and often hostile to any concession it makes as concealing a hidden agenda. Difficulties also arise from DIAND's efforts to balance the competing demands of some 600 bands, not to mention those of numerous government departments and agencies. At the same time, the Department's relatively low status within the government has cramped its effectiveness as a forum for aboriginal grievances.

Relations between aboriginal peoples and the Department can be described as ambiguous. Lobby groups such as the Assembly of First Nations play a useful role in terms of 'demand aggregation' and artic- ulation of various interests, but differences in operating principles and organizational priorities make clashes inevitable (see Ponting and Gibbins, 1980, for a detailed discussion). If DIAND has been taken to task for doing 'too much' for aboriginal peoples—robbing them of initiative while deterring self-reliance though excessive red tape, top-heavy administration, and welfare-dependency—it has also been criticized for doing 'too little' to advance aboriginal interests and aspirations. Often accused of failing to meet its trust (fiduciary) obligations, the Department has also been criticized for excessive spending, financial mismanagement, and careless accounting procedures. Other charges stem from DIAND's central function as a regulatory agency responsible for allocating funds to aboriginal groups and organizations—a situation conducive to allegations of abuse, favouritism, and paternalism.

How justified are these attacks? We believe that much of the criti- cism fails to acknowledge the difficult circumstances in which the bureaucracy finds itself. On the one hand, the Department is required by an Act of Parliament to implement and observe the Indian Act, an outdated mandate that is likely to bring bureaucrats and aboriginals into direct collision. On the other hand, many of the Department's fail- ures reflect its status as a bureaucracy, and the high degree of rigidity and inefficiency intrinsic to any large organization (Handelman and Leyton, 1978). That this bureaucracy is embedded within the state creates other problems. The Department is an agency of the state, and its functions cannot be separated from those of any state in a capitalist society; thus they include the function of legitimizing the distribution of wealth and power in society, as well as that of preserving the social order through the state's monopoly on the use of force (Panitch, 1977). Hence we agree with Ponting (1986) that the primary (if latent) function of the Department is to contain and control aboriginal peoples, in large part by channelling aboriginal aspirations into avenues that are acceptable to outside interests.

The Department therefore finds itself in the unusual position of intermediary between the state and the aboriginal nations. This middle ground means that it must fulfil its obligations to the government and state, yet at the same time be responsive and answerable to its aboriginal clients—without much support from either sector. Confusion arising from this dual mandate has made DIAND a convenient target, and a lightning rod for aboriginal anger and frustration. The transition that the Department is currently undergoing has compounded the difficulties. The old paradigm of administration and control under the Indian Act is drawing to a close, but remains entrenched despite efforts at de-bureaucratization. A new paradigm emphasizing consultation and development, devolution and decentralization, has gained a foothold, but in implementation it remains unclear and inconsistent. Until the new paradigm replaces the old, competing agendas and expectations will continue to frustrate the decolonizing of aboriginal–state relations (see Weaver, 1990).

SEVEN

Aboriginal Protest, Symbolic Politics, and Political Reform

Examination of the white-dominated world of policy and administration makes it tempting to see aboriginal peoples as passive victims, with minimal control over their destiny. But such a label risks perpetuating a number of undesirable stereotypes. The view of aboriginal peoples as unwitting victims of decisions by remote and powerful authorities reflects the long-standing stereotype of the 'noble savage', admirable but ultimately doomed in the face of evolutionary progress. Certainly this image is more benign than its counterpart: some see aboriginal peoples as 'ignoble savages', hell-bent on impeding societal progress and undermining national prosperity; others see them as 'dirty savages'—worthless, lazy alcoholics and welfare bums, oblivious to material pursuits and modern values. That these stereotypes are false is beyond dispute. Nevertheless, the victim image has served to reinforce both the subjugation of aboriginal peoples and the assimilationist thrust of aboriginal policy and administration (Allen, 1986).

As pointed out by Sylvia Van Kirk (1980), albeit in a different context, the concept of victimization is inadequate as an explanatory variable in any case, since it oversimplifies the dynamics of aboriginal–government relations. While at times their leeway for action was constrained by the circumstances in which they found themselves, aboriginal peoples have always taken the initiative as 'active agents' to make the most of the opportunities available to them. Nor would the process of decolonizing aboriginal–state relations and the restructuring of the political agenda to meet aboriginal demands have even begun without their activism and protest, as well as negotiation and compromise. Activism—from the use of civil-disobedience tactics by the Innu of Labrador to the violence at Oka—has been effective in drawing public and political attention to aboriginal grievances when conventional channels of redress are ineffective or unavailable. Political compromise and constitutional negotiations (documented in Chapter 5) are equally important. Lobby and pressure groups including the Assembly of First Nations and the three other national aboriginal associations provide a powerful national forum for aboriginal concerns and aspirations (Ponting and Gibbins, 1980).

This chapter will consider the relationship between aboriginal protest and political reform at the level of symbolic politics. The first section examines how symbols are manipulated by aboriginal leaders as part of the negotiating process with federal authorities. The second section looks at the potential for collaborative efforts by political and aboriginal sectors to improve aboriginal involvement in national politics; here the concept of New Zealand-style guaranteed aboriginal representation in Parliament is examined in terms of its rationale, structure, and potential impact for Canada. The third section will examine the incidents leading up to Oka, and discuss the impact of this event as a possible watershed in aboriginal renewal.

SYMBOLIC POLITICS

> Whites liked the Indians when they were being passive.
>> —Juanita Perley; cited in Silman (1987: 51).

It is commonly accepted that marginalized groups do not enjoy a 'level playing-field'. In order to overcome disadvantages and remove discriminatory barriers and labels, these groups must redefine their socio-economic and political status in society (see Breton, 1984).

Such has been the case with aboriginal peoples in general and Canada's first nations in particular as they seek to redefine the symbolic order in which they are situated. But aboriginal peoples' demands and aspirations outstrip the formal political power at their disposal for initiating fundamental social change (Jhappan, 1990). Neither their relatively small population nor their restricted access to the corridors of political or economic power provides an adequate base from which to negotiate. To overcome these disadvantages, aboriginal peoples have had little choice but to resort to alternative tactics, and one of these is the use of symbols. In fact, terms such as 'self-government' and 'treaty rights' have come to constitute something more than devices to draw political or public attention to aboriginal grievances. To the extent that they evoke emotional responses and value judgements, and are sufficiently imprecise to allow numerous interpretations, making it possible to create an illusion of consensus that masks factions and divisions, these terms constitute symbols (Jhappan, 1990). These symbols are manipulated to shape public opinion, to shame the government into action through public pressure, and to influence the underlying terms of aboriginal–government discourse (see Dyck, 1985).

In recent years aboriginal groups have shown a flair for dramatic actions in photogenic settings that are deliberately used to attract maximum media exposure and inflict embarrassment on the government. Key among these are demonstrations of civil disobedience, particularly with relation to land or resource conflicts; more general policy protests with respect to sovereignty issues; appeals to international agencies and opinion; and, occasionally, violent confrontations. The protest activities of the Haida, the Lubicon, the Teme Augama tribes, and, most recently, the Mohawks at Oka come to mind as symbolically astute gestures designed to publicize aboriginal concerns and aspirations. While these actions always incur the risk of backlash, they have been highly effective in moving aboriginal issues to the centre of the national agenda.

Political responses to these symbolic initiatives are mixed at best. Central authorities are naturally inclined to resist them because of the potentially immense costs, both political and economic, associated with the entrenchment of aboriginal claims to title, rights, and self-government (Jhappan, 1990). They cannot be seen as moving too quickly, for that might risk electoral rebuke and grave social consequences. By contrast, moving too slowly incurs the risk of stoking the fires of another Oka in one of numerous hot spots across Canada (*Toronto Star*, 1991e). By the same token they cannot afford to be seen as weak and vacillating, passively accepting all aboriginal demands. Finding the proper political response, in other words, is critical if diverse publics are to be placated.

THE POLITICS OF SYMBOLS:
SEPARATE ABORIGINAL SEATS IN PARLIAMENT

Federal efforts to improve aboriginal relations with the state reflect Ottawa's unease over the general lack of aboriginal participation in the institutional and symbolic life of Canada. The lack of participation in the political process, at least south of the 60th parallel, is worrisome, as is the fact that, since 1867, only 12 MPs out of 11,000 elected have been aboriginal people (*Toronto Star*, 1991k). The costs of this alienation, coupled with growing resentment and threats of violence, cannot be ignored, especially in light of Oka. This section examines one effort to incorporate aboriginal peoples into the political mainstream.

Central authorities throughout the liberal-democratic world have struggled to find an acceptable formula for re-integrating minorities into the political mainstream. This search has been particularly urgent in countries, such as Canada, where the aboriginal peoples appear reluctant to take part in the electoral process. Meaningful involvement in the federal electoral process continues to elude most aboriginal groups outside of the Northwest Territories and Yukon. Different strategies have been explored to improve electoral participation and aboriginal representation, but few have attracted as much attention as a proposed system of aboriginal electoral districts integrated into the national framework and modelled after a comparable arrangement in New Zealand.

Aboriginal demands for political self-determination have also taken on a sharper focus. Canada's aboriginal leaders agree on the need for self-governing powers, but remain divided over how to attain them. Of the many avenues proposed for bringing aboriginal peoples into the political mainstream, few are as controversial—or as enticing—as the concept of constitutionally-guaranteed aboriginal seats in Parliament. This concept is attractive for two reasons in particular. First, aboriginal voters are largely excluded from the electoral process south of the 60th parallel (Marchand, 1990); even where the aboriginal population is uncommonly high, their presence is diluted by higher concentrations of non-aboriginals (*Globe and Mail*, 18 Jan. 1991). Second, representation based on geography (that is, a system of territorially-defined electoral districts) or focused around political parties fails to take into account the specific needs and identity of a community of interests. What is required to enhance aboriginal participation and representation in the electoral process is some way of overcoming the problem of geographical dispersal.

Various recommendations have been put forward to secure equitable aboriginal participation in Canada's electoral democracy. Proposals for aboriginal-based self-government in the Northwest Territories have included discussions about guaranteed aboriginal representation in the legislative assembly (with jurisdiction over matters of aboriginal importance such as land and culture) in tandem with a majority-rule principle for decision-making (Watt, 1990b). New Brunswick has recently seen a different proposal to set aside at least one non-voting seat in the legislative assembly, although a lack of consultation with key aboriginal leaders in the province, coupled with disagreements over specifics (*Globe and Mail*, 19 March 1991), has dampened enthusiasm for this plan. Of particular note, however, is the proposed designation of seats in the federal Parliament for representatives of distinct aboriginal constituencies as one way of dealing with the marginalization of aboriginal people in the political process (Hall, 1991b).

Numerous obstacles stand in the path of implementing a system of aboriginal electoral districts. Legal, geographical, historical, and cultural factors serve to separate aboriginal peoples, making consensus an elusive ideal. Nor is there any guarantee that increasing their presence within the federal electoral process will enhance aboriginal peoples' influence on policy. Indeed, a key government report (Penner, 1983) concluded that the advantages of such a plan would be offset by its potential to distract central authorities from more fundamental social, economic, political, or cultural concerns. Others have repudiated the concept of aboriginal electoral districts as (a) irrelevant in advancing aboriginal interests; (b) a logistic nightmare, given the diversity and breadth of the aboriginal constituency; and (c) inconsistent with the values and principles of Canada's political culture.

How, then, do we establish an electoral system that addresses aboriginal claims for self-governing status, yet ensures aboriginal involvement in the political mainstream? Are the demands for aboriginal political self-determination and aboriginal representation mutually exclusive? Do we proceed by more 'fine tuning' of the present system? Or is it time to introduce bold initiatives that reflect, reinforce, and advance the unique status of aboriginal peoples? Perhaps the lessons learned in New Zealand can serve as a guide towards implementing a comparable system of aboriginal electoral districts in Canada.

SEPARATE MAORI REPRESENTATION IN NEW ZEALAND

Provision of separate Maori seats constitutes one of the more contentious aspects of New Zealand's pioneering efforts at managing race relations. For nearly 125 years, the system of separate electoral districts has worked both for and against Maori aspirations. On the one hand, Maori seats have over time become widely regarded as integral to Maori status as the *tangata whenua o aotearoa* ('indigenous occupants of New Zealand'). On the other hand, the racial element in this separate representation has been criticized as sabotaging Maori aspirations for power-sharing; Maori concerns have been compromised, compartmentalized, diminished, or derailed by a system that serves an instrument for containment and control. Thus questions have arisen as to whether this system should be retained as is, reformed by enlarging the numbers of Maori seats in line with the population, or abolished and replaced by either a separate Maori parliament or voting on a common roll (Fleras, 1985b).

The Maori Representation Act of 1867 introduced a dual system of representation by superimposing four Maori seats upon the existing arrangement in the House of Representatives. A temporary expedient of largely assimilationist intent, this system was expected to last for five years, or until such time as the Maori qualified for inclusion on the European roll (pending conversion of communal land tenure into individual freehold). Dividing New Zealand into four electoral districts, the Act entitled Maori males to elect one representative from each of the Northern, Southern (South Island), Western, and Eastern electoral districts. All adult Maori men not previously convicted of treason or any 'infamous offence' received the right to vote irrespective of any property means test—twelve years before universal male suffrage was extended to Europeans. 'Half-castes' were permitted to vote on either the Maori or the common roll—or, if they met the appropriate property qualification, on both (Love, 1977). When the double vote was abolished in 1893, the concept of separate Maori representation became formally entrenched.

The distinction between Maori and general ridings does not reflect differences in content or style. Each of the 97 general and 4 Maori seats elects one candidate every three years in a first-past-the-post ('plurality') electoral system. Maori representatives do not sit in a separate chamber, but possess full voting rights on all issues dealt with by their Parliamentary colleagues. All major political parties nominate Maori candidates for the Maori seats and contest them every three years as part of the general election. Maori voters are likewise indistinguishable from their counterparts in the general electorate. Those who choose to exercise the 'Maori option' (see below) follow the same procedures and are subject to the same restrictions as voters on the general roll.

Where differences do exist is in the regulations governing the eligibility of voters and candidates. First, while eligibility for the general electorate is determined by territory ('where you live') and the principle of universal suffrage (McRobie, 1981), Maori representation is based on racial criteria ('who you are'), since only Maoris can vote in these electorates. Second, only a New Zealand Maori—defined as a person of the Maori race of New Zealand, including any descendant of such a person as set out in Electoral Amendment Act of 1980—has the option ('Maori option') of voting for a candidate to one of the four reserved seats. Registration on a Maori roll is a precondition for exercising the Maori option. Having once registered on the Maori roll, however, a voter may not transfer to the general roll until the following quinquennial census. Third, nominations for election to Maori seats are generally (though not exclusively) restricted to Maori candidates. At one time, only 'full-blooded' or 'half-blooded' Maoris could stand as candidates in Maori electoral districts; this discriminatory provision was abolished in 1967, when the government opened candidacy to both races in either the Maori or general ridings. As pointed out elsewhere (Fleras 1992), the system does not necessarily work according to plan. Rather, it is riddled with inconsistencies that leave it open to criticism and demands for reform or abolition.

Lessons From 'Down Under'

The system of separate Maori representation provides a useful departure point for designing a viable system of aboriginal electoral districts in Canada. Current proposals by the Royal Commission on Electoral Reform and Party Financing suggest establishing aboriginal electoral districts across Canada in proportion to the aboriginal population (approximately 3.6 per cent); this would yield 8 to 10 aboriginal seats out of the existing 295 general seats. Each aboriginal voter would have the option of voting either for a candidate in the general riding or for the aboriginal candidate in one of the aboriginal districts. Candidates in the aboriginal districts could run either as independents or as party representatives (*Globe and Mail*, 1991c). Ideally, such an arrangement would assist aboriginal peoples in formulating input at the highest level of decision-making. It would provide a forum for (a) debating and discussing aboriginal issues at the national level, (b) sorting out and organizing aboriginal concerns, needs, and aspirations, (c) articulating aboriginal viewpoints in a coherent fashion, and (d) protecting aboriginal interests at the highest levels of decision-making. Guaranteed aboriginal involvement in the national electoral process could not only legitimize aboriginal political and social concerns, but also avert the further alienation of an already marginalized people. It could also enhance aboriginal participation in the electoral system at a time when the very existence of Canada as a unified society is in question.

Perhaps the most important lesson to be learned from New Zealand is that aboriginal electoral districts constitute only one component in the overall drive to entrench aboriginal rights through self-determination on many fronts: political, social, economic, and cultural. Any electoral reform must be complementary to aboriginal self-governing demands, and must not detract from aboriginal initiatives in this area or infringe upon related areas of self-determination (Len Marchand, *Globe and Mail*, 1991c). Aboriginal electoral districts, in other words, are not meant to prejudice aboriginal title and demands, but to complement and strengthen the process of constitutional renewal and aboriginal self-government (Committee for Aboriginal Electoral Reform, 1991). An equally important lesson is the necessity of involving aboriginal peoples at all levels of decision-making in the design and implementation of a new electoral process; anything less can only give rise to charges of appropriating aboriginal rights to self-determination. Finally, aboriginal electoral districts must be established in the true spirit of power-sharing, not as a conflict-management device with public-relations overtones.

What would constitute an equitable system of aboriginal electoral districts? Numerous possibilities exist, from proportional representation to a first-past-the-post arrangement, and these have been discussed elsewhere (Fleras, 1992). Problems related to numbers (should these be based on proportion of voters, total population, some fixed number?), boundaries (tribal or administrative?), registration procedures (who votes? who can stand as a candidate?), and implementation would not be easy to resolve. But the potential benefits are significant: not only would a guaranteed aboriginal voice in Parliament reinforce the unique status of Canada's first nations, but the major parties would be forced to compete for aboriginal votes. In the end, by making the electoral system more accountable to aboriginal voters, separate representation would finally legitimize aboriginal involvement in the electoral process.

The general concept and framework of aboriginal electoral districts, together with proposed rules and procedures for implementation, were set out in a consultation paper entitled 'Aboriginal Electoral Districts: The Path to Electoral Equality', produced by the Committee for Aboriginal Electoral Reform under the broader mandate of the Royal Commission on Electoral Reform and Party Financing (1991). Among its key points were these:

1. Aboriginal electoral districts would be designed to increase aboriginal participation and representation in the democratic process. Under this arrangement based on the principle of community of identity and interest (rather than territory), properly registered aboriginal voters would have the option of electing members of Parliament who would represent them and be directly accountably to aboriginal constituents through the electoral process.

2. The number of aboriginal electoral districts would reflect the proportion of aboriginal people in the total population of Canada. (This paper differed from the more recent proposal in suggesting that existing ridings be maintained for non-aboriginal voters, while a second tier of one or two aboriginal ridings per province, depending on population, would be added [*Toronto Star*, 1991k].)

3. Aboriginal electoral districts would correspond to federal electoral district boundaries within the province. The boundaries themselves would be decided by electoral boundaries commissions in consultation with aboriginal people. In some cases (e.g., provinces entitled to only two seats), aboriginal electoral districts need not cover separate geographic areas but merely provide

separate lists for 'separate' aboriginal peoples (for example, Métis and status Indians).

4. Aboriginal voters would retain the option of voting in aboriginal electoral districts or in the ridings where they live.

5. Candidates in aboriginal electoral districts would meet the same eligibility criteria as candidates in general. They would also have the option of affiliation with a major political party, forming an aboriginal party, or standing as independents.

6. Aboriginal members of Parliament would be full members of the House, with equal rights and voting privileges.

7. A constitutional provision would be required to create a single aboriginal electoral district for the Atlantic region, where the aboriginal population is too small and dispersed to warrant separate provincial districts.

A proposal for aboriginal electoral districts is likely to be greeted with dismay—even derision—by many Canadians. In a society based on a geographically defined one-person/one-vote system, where some reject even existing legal obligations to aboriginal peoples, the idea of introducing a racially-based system of representation will undoubtedly prove contentious. Moreover, while the benefits of such an arrangement (practical, symbolic, and strategic) are significant, the potential drawbacks—including the danger that aboriginal issues will be wrapped up in a single package and relegated to the periphery —are undeniable. The New Zealand system has demonstrated all too clearly the dangers of electoral neglect, party considerations, and political indifference (Fleras, 1985b). Nor do all aboriginal groups agree with even the most basic premise of the proposal: the Mohawks, for example, do not recognize the legitimacy of Parliament (Len Marchand, *Globe and Mail*, 1991c). Extreme caution must be exercised to ensure that any system of aboriginal electoral districts is receptive to Native concerns over aboriginal and treaty rights, land settlements, and self-government. Yet if the events at Oka and Akwesasne have taught us anything, it is that aboriginal commitment to Canadian society is brittle and easily ruptured. Fine-tuning the existing system through electoral add-ons may no longer be enough. Imaginative and bold proposals are required if we are to ensure equitable and productive aboriginal involvement in Canada's electoral system.

OKA: A WATERSHED IN ABORIGINAL RENEWAL

It annoys our minds to imagine golfers tramping on the grave of Mohawk grandmothers. It annoys our minds to think, to feel, that we are less than

sovereign peoples in our homelands. And it annoys a good many Canadians now too.

—Lee Maracle (1990: 9)

Memories of the 1990 Oka standoff remain etched in our collective
consciousness as Canadians. Scenes reminiscent by turns of Beirut and
the Hollywood Wild West only compounded the bewilderment as the
struggle dragged on. Among the more prominent images were masked
warriors in battle fatigues armed with automatic weapons, defiant in
defence of their territory; up to 3,700 army personnel in full battle
regalia awaiting orders to tear down the barricades 'in the pines'; a
young soldier and a Mohawk standing each other down for a seeming
eternity; angry demonstrators at the Mercier bridge clashing with the
police and burning Native effigies; white protesters hurling rocks and
construction debris at the cars of fleeing Mohawk elders, women, and
children while police and soldiers looked on with apparent disinterest.
Reports of violence and abuse of human rights were juxtaposed with
moving accounts of acts of courage and self-restraint.

Few events in aboriginal–government history have so clearly called
into question how we see ourselves and our relationship with the
first peoples. Not even the firebombings and killings at Akwesasne
(in a dispute over casinos and self-determination) received as much
publicity. The impact of Oka is such that it constitutes a watershed in
aboriginal–state relations. The following section will take a closer
look at the issues and rationale underlying that conflict.

Towards Conflict: Property and Politics

The issues leading up to the confrontation at Oka are familiar
enough. The village of Oka (40 kilometres west of Montreal, along
the Ottawa River) wanted to extend its municipal golf course onto
land claimed by the Kanesatake Mohawks, and when the lengthy
negotiations had broken down, violence erupted. On 11 July the
Sûreté du Québec launched an unsuccessful raid on a four-month
blockade of a road leading to the disputed land at the Oka municipal
golf course. In sympathy, the Kahnawake Mohawks blockaded a
main arterial bridge into Montreal later that day, sparking protests
and racial confrontations by enraged commuters. Police failure to
dismantle a barricade erected by warriors and Mohawk sympathiz-
ers at Oka resulted in a 78-day armed standoff in which Corporal
Marcel Lemay lost his life, and that ended as it had begun, in confusion and bitterness. For their part, federal and provincial authorities had agreed to negotiate, but not with a gun to their heads, and
certainly not without an unconditional Mohawk surrender. A public
inquiry failed to fix the blame on any particular group (Hughes,

1991), although all the participants—the government, the municipality, the police and armed forces, and the aboriginal protesters—
were held partly responsible for the fiasco.

The conflict at Oka had no more to do with a golf course than Elijah
Harper's filibuster had to do with the specific details of the Meech
Lake Accord. While the precipitating cause lay in some questionable
moves by the Oka Village Council, the root causes extend back two centuries. In many ways these underlying causes are typical of aboriginal
grievances in general as they relate to land, self-determination, and
authority. Yet the situation at Oka was also unique (DIAND, 1990f; Hughes,
1991). There is no reserve at Oka, but a series of blocks of federally-
owned land set aside for the benefit and use of the Kanesatake Mohawks.
Non-aboriginal properties interspersed among the Kanesatake lands
made it doubly difficult to avoid friction and open confrontation. These
blocks are remnants of land granted in 1717 by the King of France to the
Sulpician religious order, which brought aboriginal peoples from Montreal to reside at the Mission in 1721. The suggestion that the ancestors
of the present Mohawks arrived in the Oka region only after Europeans
were established there is critical, since federal recognition of aboriginal
title depends on pre-European ownership.

Disputes over ownership rights flared up between the religious order
and the Mohawks now and then during the nineteenth century. A parliamentary statute in 1841 and a 1912 ruling by Judicial Committee of
the Privy Council in favour of full Sulpician propriety did not resolve
the issue, as the Mohawks did not accept them. In 1945, the Department
of Indian Affairs assumed ownership of all unsold Sulpician land, in
addition to all non-spiritual obligations to the Mohawks. This transaction was disputed by the Oka Mohawks, who argued that all Sulpician
lands had been bequeathed to them over time, and that the disposal of
land and obligations without Mohawk consent was therefore invalid.

In January 1975, the Mohawks at Oka together with the bands at
Kahnawake and Akwesasne presented a joint claim of aboriginal title
to this land to the federal and Quebec governments. The Department
of Indian Affairs rejected this claim later that year on the grounds that
(a) the Mohawks could not assert aboriginal title because they were
not the original occupants of the land 'since time immemorial'; and
(b) any aboriginal title that may have existed was extinguished by the
King of France in 1717, and later by the British Crown when it opened
the lands for settlement; the Mohawk presence at Oka did not pre-date
European settlement, but occurred after establishment of the mission in
1721. The Kanesatake claim, in short, did not fit the established criteria for comprehensive land claims or aboriginal title. A specific claim
submitted in 1977 was also rejected by the Department of Justice on the
grounds that the federal government did not have a lawful obligation to

the Mohawks at Oka. The Mohawks, for their part, continued to claim ownership over the land prior to the land grants by the King of France. In any case, they argued, no legal international principle existed that would allow a European power to assert sovereignty over any territory in the absence of conquest or cessation (Hughes, 1991).

Still, the government has recognized some historical validity in the Mohawks' claims, and has sought ways to deal with the problem. In 1986 Bill McKnight, the Minister of Indian Affairs, proposed redress for Mohawk grievances through a federal land-reunification package of the disputed land. Assembling land under federal jurisdiction for a united and contiguous reserve at Oka, however, meant co-ordinating land-use policies among the municipality, the Mohawks, and private interests, and this made conflict even more likely.

Factional disputes were no less a contributing factor (Hughes, 1991). Like aboriginal groups in general, the resident Kanesatake Mohawk community of 838 was split between those wishing to govern themselves according to traditional values and hereditary styles of leadership and those supporting the system of governance prescribed in the Indian Act of 1876. The latter Act had recognized certain 'band customs' pertaining to local government, but only as temporary measures until elected councils were put in place. Such was the case among the Kanesatake Mohawks, who in 1899 were brought under the Indian Act through the establishment of a Band Council. But when ambiguities were found in the wording of the revisions to the 1951 Indian Act, certain customary aspects of governance were allowed back in.

Hence several competing factions were in place: namely, supporters of an Indian Act Band Council based on elected officials either in accordance with band custom or under the Indian Act system of governance (Hughes, 1991), and supporters of the traditional Longhouse system of government, based on traditional chieftainship, who resolutely opposed any Indian Act initiatives as contrary to Mohawk law and inimical to Mohawk sovereign ambitions. Compounding this factional arrangement was the uneasy juxtaposition of private, municipal, and Mohawk land which, given the lack of any official status for Kanesatake land under the Indian Act, made it doubly difficult to demarcate lines of authority for local control and administration.

Thus the reasons for Oka are complex. Rejection of the Mohawks' comprehensive and specific land claims created a situation in which their faith in the judicial and political system was shaky at best, leaving them little recourse except to circumvent normal negotiation channels. By 1987 the Kanesatake community was again in turmoil over the preferred style of governance. Federal refusal to accept Mohawk claims for implicit sovereignty was viewed as an insult to aboriginal peoples and indicative of the government's hidden agenda. Hopes for settlement were further dashed when the First Ministers Conference failed to specify the nature of aboriginal and treaty rights. Failure to resolve the issue through further discussion set into motion the chain of events that culminated in the 'Indian summer' of 1990.

Fallout From Oka

The small town of Oka has taken on something of the mythical symbolism that surrounds an equally small and once obscure town in the South Dakota badlands. The similarities between Oka and Wounded Knee are striking (York, 1991). In both cases we saw a violent encounter with police following an armed seige; young warriors defending property and lives; the moderating influence of the army; and factional divisions between supporters of traditional chiefs and elected tribal leaders. Even the durations of the two standoffs—71 days at Wounded Knee and 78 at Oka—were similar, as were the underlying issues.

Oka represents a textbook study of symbolic politics (see Edelman, 1964; Jhappan, 1990). It served as a forum for protest against government policy, for criticism of the sluggishness of government land-claims negotiations, and for assertion of aboriginal sovereignty in matters of internal jurisdiction. Mohawk leaders and Warriors manipulated a dramatic political setting for maximum national and international publicity. Given the vast resources at the disposal of the Canadian state, Oka certainly posed no military threat to Canada. Nor was victory the point for the Mohawks. In a society where democratic traditions and pluralistic philosophies prevail, their goals at Oka were to publicize aboriginal grievances, heighten public awareness, foster public sympathy, and increase public pressure for reshaping the discourse over aboriginal–government relations (Jhappan, 1990).

The strategy has paid off. In the wake of Oka, political authorities have indicated a willingness to avert another such incident, and aboriginal concerns have been propelled to the forefront. As the Acting Chair of Trent University's Native Studies Department, Peter Kulchyski, put it:

> Non-Natives gained an appreciation of the seriousness of the issues as well as the level of frustration and anger in aboriginal communities, and aboriginal peoples have been empowered by being taken seriously (*Globe and Mail*, 1991f).

Among the consequences of Oka are initiatives by Ottawa and two provinces (New Brunswick and Quebec) to establish aboriginal seats in their legislatures. In addition, BC, Saskatchewan and Ontario have taken land-claims issues more seriously, and each has gone on record as endorsing the principle of inherent aboriginal rights to self-government.

Political changes are in evidence as well. On 25 September 1990,

Prime Minister Brian Mulroney formally announced a new federal aboriginal agenda. To nurture a new working relationship that may preserve 'the special place of our first citizens in this country, based on their aboriginal and treaty rights recognized in the Constitution' (DIAND, 1991c), he announced four central commitments: (a) to accelerate land-claims settlements (both specific and comprehensive) through increased funding, the appointment of a land-claims commissioner, fast-tracking for smaller claims, and greater discretion on the part of the Indian Affairs Department to approve claims without Treasury approval; (b) to improve aboriginal social and economic conditions, particularly housing and sanitation; (c) to revitalize aboriginal relations with the government through reforms in aboriginal justice; and (d) to address aboriginal concerns, including the concept of self-government within a Canadian framework. Built into these commitments were promises of further consultation with aboriginal peoples on constitutional affairs, a Royal Commission on aboriginal affairs, a streamlining of the land-claims process, a revamping of the antiquated provisions of the Indian Act, and continued maintenance of the Crown's fiduciary responsibilities (*Globe and Mail*, 10 July 1991).

For the government, the massive publicity over Oka drew attention to growing public awareness and support for aboriginal concerns. It was important for government officials to move, and to be seen as moving, in response to public-opinion polls that registered considerable public sympathy for the plight of aboriginal peoples in Canada. An Angus Reid telephone poll that surveyed 1,735 adult Canadians between 19 and 27 September 1990 (considered accurate within 2.5 percentage points 19 times in 20) indicated that Canadians were critical of both provincial and federal politicians and of Ottawa's handling of aboriginal issues (*Kitchener-Waterloo Record*, 13 Nov. 1990). More than 67 per cent believed the government had broken its obligations to aboriginal peoples. Another 70 per cent believed the government had failed to honour its treaty obligations, and 62 per cent supported land-claims settlements. Prime Minister Mulroney received the lowest credibility rating among various leaders for dealing with aboriginal issues, garnering only 21 per cent support. Recent surveys continue to reflect a high level of support for aboriginal issues—at times beyond what federal authorities are willing to concede in areas such as constitutional recognition of oboriginal peoples as a founding nation with rights to provincial-like self-governing powers (*Toronto Star*, 1991m).

These conclusions are consistent with previous findings. As noted earlier (Ponting, 1990; also Wohlfeld and Nevitte, 1990), Canadians generally display positive (if regionally varied) attitudes towards aboriginal peoples and their concerns. Many endorse aboriginal issues when they pertain to the principles of land claims, resource development, cultural retention, and limited self-governing structures. This is not to suggest that Canadians are free of stereotypes or misconceptions of aboriginal concerns and aspirations as representing a no-win situation of ever-escalating demands. Evidence also indicates that Canadians are uncomfortable with the concept of aboriginal peoples as sovereign, with territorial claims as independent nations, or as 'distinct societies'—with all that term implies in the way of special privileges or threats to individual rights (*Globe and Mail*, 5 June 1991). Nevertheless, in light of the consciousness-raising at Oka, Canadians as a whole appear favourably disposed to aboriginal demands, even if the support may be a 'mile wide and an inch thick' (Simpson, 1991c).

Oka: A Watershed?

There is little doubt of Oka's contribution to the aboriginal profile in Canada. Government support for aboriginal issues is now viewed as desirable—at least in principle, if not always in specifics or practice. Politicians are now swinging around to the concept of aboriginal self-governing structures as a negotiable right. In some cases, this endorsement is born of expediency; in others, of misunderstanding and fear. But the potential for change is now present, and Oka can be seen as the symbolic blow that softened Canada's collective indifference.

What can we conclude from Oka and the long Indian summer of 1990? First, public concern and political attention have been drawn to inadequacies in the government's aboriginal policy and administration. By late 1991, the government appeared ready to recognize the right to aboriginal self-government explicitly in the Constitution, without prior negotiation (Royal Commission, 1992). Second, while images of violence and confrontation abound, one cannot help being struck by the high levels of restraint and order shown by all parties after the initial salvoes. Such willingness to negotiate and to seek compromise as a basis for conflict resolution bodes well for the future of restructuring aboriginal–government relations. Third, although Oka provoked physical retaliation from law-enforcement agencies, there is little evidence of the attitudinal backlash from Canadian citizens that might have been expected in response to such a challenge to the legal system and the authority of the Canadian state (Jhappan, 1990). Rather, urged on by groups in Europe and the UN, public sympathy for aboriginal issues appears to be growing, as does public awareness of aboriginal grievances regarding land and treaty rights (*Maclean's*, 1991). Release of the Spicer Commission Report on the Citizens Forum for Canada's Future in late June 1991 confirmed overwhelming public support for equitable resolution of aboriginal land claims and establishment of appropriate self-governing structures where warranted. There is additional support for proactive government involvement in addressing aboriginal concerns related to land, resources, culture, and identity. The Royal Commission on Aboriginal Affairs, announced in April 1991 (*Globe and Mail*, 1991a), has come out in support of inherent aboriginal self-governing rights as a basis for a productive partnership (Royal Commission, 1992).

Political good will and public support are one thing. But restructuring the attitudes, institutions, and values of Canadian society may be quite different. More often than not, the rhetoric on aboriginal self-determination is long on principle but short on specifics. In the spate of articles marking the first anniversary of Oka, most conceded that the situation at Oka remained unresolved, and that factionalism and strained relations between Mohawks and community members would prolong the crisis that had already cost taxpayers $235-million and weakened Canada's international credibility (Picard, 1991). Nor are proposed government solutions to the problem seen as always consistent with aboriginal values, priorities, or aspirations.

Not surprisingly, aboriginal leaders are sceptical about fundamental changes to the agenda in light of Oka, a point made clear at the Indigenous Peoples Conference at London, Ontario, in the spring of 1991 (*London Free Press*, 13 May 1991), where ratification of an Indigenous Peoples Support Group (made up of aboriginal and non-aboriginal organizations) all but conceded the likelihood of further confrontations. High-profile leaders such as Saul Terry, President of the Union of BC Chiefs (*London Free Press*, 13 May 1991), have suggested that any apparent gains are illusory; aboriginal grievances and social injustice may be more widely publicized, but the government has responded with publicity-seeking tactics that do little to address the real issues of poverty, land claims, and self-government. In the words of Terry:

> Our expectations are more publicly exposed but governments are just paying lip service . . . Oka exposed the injustice that we have been experiencing for generations but the government responded with nothing more than public relations announcement. It's despicable manipulation, not progress (in Picard, 1991).

Towards a Restructuring

Much of the ambiguity in the restructuring process has been highlighted by events in Ontario, where the NDP government and many of the province's aboriginal chiefs have entered into an unprecedented agreement to recognize 'inherent aboriginal right to self-government within the Canadian constitutional framework' (*Toronto Star*, 1991c), Hailed by many as a milestone, this 'statement of political relationship' was described by Chief Gord Peters as a 'major, major breakthrough' (*Kitchener-Waterloo Record*, 1991c), and by Grand Chief Joe Miskokomon as 'just shy of a constitutional agreement' (*Toronto Star*,

11 Aug. 1991). It makes five major points in defence of aboriginal self-governing rights:

1. The relationship between Ontario and aboriginal peoples must be based on inherent aboriginal rights to self-government, and conducted on a government-to-government basis.

2. Inherent self-governing rights are rooted in the principle of original occupation of the land.

3. Implementation of self-governing rights reflects both aboriginal and political commitment.

4. Political commitment, however, neither increases provincial responsibilities over aboriginal peoples nor detracts from federal responsibility.

5. Political commitment is not equivalent to a treaty. Nor does it create, redefine, or prejudice the rights of aboriginal and non-aboriginal peoples.

This admittedly historic declaration can be read in two ways. On the one hand it is an essentially symbolic agreement (not a treaty) that fails to define the parameters of self-government or to specify the nature of aboriginal sovereignty. According to Premier Bob Rae, the document represents a statement of political intent—not a transfer of power, establishment of local government, or redefinition of legal relationships, but merely a framework for further negotiation (*Toronto Star*, 1991f). It remains vague about specifics, provides no timetable, allocates few resources, and ignores the problems of implementing this right to self-government within the constitutional framework. It remains to be seen how willing the province will be to transfer the resources and share the powers that would allow aboriginal communities to take control over land, resources, services, and programs.

On the other hand, this announcement heralds the demise of colonialist attitudes and asserts the possibility of new interaction with Ontario's aboriginal peoples as a basis for future negotiations. It acknowledges the existence of aboriginal self-governing rights prior to European contact, and concedes the principle that aboriginal rights to self-government have not been extinguished by provincial statutes; these rights serve as a point of departure for practical concessions and transfer of jurisdiction over education, health, social services, and resource management. It also establishes the principle of aboriginal peoples in Ontario as a distinct society—a 'nation within'—with the sovereign capacity to negotiate with the government over transfers and resources on a government-to-government basis. In becoming the first government anywhere to recognize the principle of intrinsic aboriginal rights to self-government, Ontario made a significant start towards establishing a basis from which to negotiate a new political relationship. Again, to what extent the Ontario government is willing to follow through on these principles, and to ensure their visibility at the next round of constitutional talks, is open to speculation at this point. But the province's precedent-setting agreement to transfer (without federal compensation) $60.5 million and 610 square kilometres of land to six bands in northern Ontario is a promising sign, especially since Ontario has waived the 50-per-cent claim to resource rights that it and other provinces enjoy on most reserves across Canada (*Kitchener-Waterloo Record*, 1991f).

Conclusion

Nearly fifteen months after Mulroney's widely touted 'four pillars' speech in September 1990, aboriginal leaders are profoundly disappointed by the apparent lack of progress in redefining aboriginal–government relations (Henton, 1991). The consensus is that the new policy initiatives amount to little more than exercises in federal public relations, are essentially a regurgitation of the past with some minor embellishments, and were destined to appear regardless of the new proposals. While federal authorities point to achievements and progress on various fronts, many of the improvements proposed by the government are now enmeshed in bureaucratic red tape or jurisdictional wrangling. Even the headway made in land claims involving the Tungavik Federation of Nunavut, the Council of Yukon Indians, and the Gwich'in in the Mackenzie delta has come under criticism for trampling on intrinsic aboriginal rights as a condition for settlement at a time when the courts continue to define and expand those rights. The lack of constitutional guarantees for inherent aboriginal self-government, coupled with little visible progress in the fight against poverty, has taken much of the lustre from Mulroney's promise to restructure government relations with Canada's first nations.

The restructuring process is likely to proceed slowly, at least until both politicians and the general public begin to understand the meaning and implications of a collective aboriginal right to self-government within the structure of the Canadian state (Pangowish, 1992). Moreover, any fundamental restructuring will continue to languish as long as aboriginal–government relations reflect the centuries-old Eurocentric assumption of a right to exercise sovereignty over Canada's original inhabitants by virtue of a unilaterally-declared 'right of discovery' (Platiel, 1991c). But public awareness of and political receptivity to aboriginal issues are at unprecedented levels. With the quincentennial celebration of Columbus's 'discovery' of the 'new world' now upon us (Gray, 1991) there is even greater incentive for Canada's 'nations within' to define who they are in relation to society at large.

Métis and Inuit Nationalism

The preceding chapters have focused mainly on status Indians. The aims of the Métis and Inuit are broadly similar to theirs, but for various reasons their respective situations are quite different. This chapter will examine the historical background and nationalist aspirations of these two distinct groups.

THE MÉTIS NATION

In August 1991, the federal government announced a Royal Commission on Aboriginal Peoples, to be headed by Georges Erasmus, the former national chief of the Assembly of First Nations, and Mr Justice René Dussault of the Quebec Court of Appeal. Included within the Commission's far-reaching terms of reference is the mandate to examine 'the position of Métis and off-reserve Indians'. In essence, the Commission is being called upon to assist in the formulation of a new, more equitable paradigm for métis people's relations both with other aboriginal peoples and with the Canadian government and society as a whole. It is the objective of this section to examine the need for a new paradigm in métis-government relations specifically, beginning with a brief outline of the historical background to Métis nationalism. (Following the accepted convention [Foster, 1986: 375], the lower-case 'm' refers to those Canadians who might identify themselves as métis because of a mixed aboriginal and European ancestry, while the upper-case 'M' is reserved for those who identify with a particular community or with the Métis nation.)

Métis Nationalism: The New Nation

In response to the 'ethnicity' question in the 1986 census, 128,640 Canadians (18 per cent of the aboriginal population) replied 'métis' (Norris, 1990: 35-9); of these, two-thirds live in the Prairie provinces. While the first métis, in a genetic sense, could have appeared nine months after the arrival of the first Europeans, the Métis nation had a much longer gestation period. Indeed, the emergence of the 'New Nation' may be traced to the settlement that flourished in the early nineteenth century at the confluence of the Assiniboine and Red rivers in the area of Manitoba that is today Winnipeg.

From 1670 to 1870, the Canadian Prairies and northwest essentially constituted a fur-trade empire managed by rival trading companies— the Hudson's Bay Company (HBC) and the North West Company (NWC). The Métis played vital roles in the fur-trade economy, and their sense of self gradually coalesced around these roles. The Métis nation was born in conflict, caught in the middle of the struggle for monopoly control by the HBC and NWC (Morton, 1978: 27) before the merger of the two rivals in 1821.

Nationalism gradually emerged as the English- and French-speaking Métis united in common opposition to policies such as the Scottish immigration to the western plains sponsored by Lord Selkirk and the HBC. Their written protests to the HBC were repeatedly ignored, and their frustration rose following the establishment of the Red River Selkirk colony in 1812. The situation reached a climax in 1816 when the Métis, under the elected leadership of Cuthbert Grant, successfully engaged the settlers in an armed conflict, known as the Battle of Seven Oaks, that was to be the first of many continuing attempts—both diplomatic and military—on the part of the Métis to secure public recognition and title to their land. From that point on, 'the Métis knew they were a distinct people with a way of life that was worth defending' (Dickason, 1985: 31). Peterson (1985: 64) describes the 'new people' of the Red River after 1815 as 'not merely biracial, multilingual, and bicultural, but the proud owners of a new language; a syncretic cosmology . . . distinctive modes of dress, cuisine and architecture, vehicles of transport, music and dance; [with] a quasi-military political organization, a flag, a bardic tradition; a rich folklore and a national history'. The Métis people's sense of themselves as a nation—or what Barth (1969) would term their 'ethnic boundaries'—intensified in the following decades under the pressure of threats from outside, as more and more homesteaders arrived on the Prairies, the fur trade waned, the buffalo were depleted, and Métis river lots were resurveyed by Ottawa without regard for Métis claims and occupancy.

The New Nation faced its first major crisis in 1869-70, when ownership of Rupert's Land—the vast territory that included all of what is today Manitoba, as well as most of Saskatchewan and portions of Alberta and the Northwest Territories—was transferred to Canada from the HBC. After the acquisition of Rupert's Land, Ottawa sought to extend its control over the Métis nation. It did not, however, consult with the Métis either before or after the transfer. In response to this affront, the Métis rallied around their leader, Louis Riel. Acting for the first time in a formal, foreign-affairs diplomatic capacity, they sought to negotiate with Ottawa the terms under which they would agree to enter Canada, having previously rebuffed overtures from the United States. As a result of these negotiations, the Manitoba Act of 1870 promised Métis heads of families more than 1.4 million acres for their children. In practice, however, only about 15 per cent of this land ever found its way into Métis hands (Berger, 1987). The issuing of land scrip consti- tuted tacit recognition by Ottawa of prior Métis land rights, and in 1985 Thomas Berger, a former Chief Justice of British Columbia, launched two land claims on behalf of the Manitoba Métis Federation (MMF). It is Berger's opinion that the Manitoba Act—which the Métis continue to regard as a treaty—has the same legal weight as the Charter of Rights; that is, it is part of the Constitution (Berger, 1987: 196), and Canada has no choice but to honour it. The Métis are not seeking to have the land that Winnipeg currently occupies returned to them, but they wish to have just compensation for their river lots and the 1.4 million acres of land granted them in the Manitoba Act. The Royal Commission will no doubt have to examine the provisions of the Manitoba Act and their implementation as one of many issues that have bearing on the larger question of the position of the métis in Canadian society.

Métis–Government Relations

The Manitoba Act is not the only piece of federal legislation that has had a profound impact on the position of the métis in Canada. In 1876 the Indian Act, which consolidated various statutes relevant to the abo- riginal peoples, deliberately *excluded* métis from all federal trust responsibility, focusing exclusively upon Indians (and later Inuit) with respect to federal entitlements.

Over a century later, the Constitution Act of 1982 reversed the exclu- sionary provision of the Indian Act, explicitly *including* métis along with Inuit and Indians as aboriginal people. (The Act is unclear on the subject of non-status Indians). But while the existing aboriginal rights of the métis, Indians, and Inuit are affirmed in section 35(1), they are yet to be fully defined. Soon after the patriation of the Constitution, in the 1985 Musqueam case, the Supreme Court of Canada recognized the legal Indian ownership of reserve land, establishing that the ownership of Musqueam reserve land was based on an Indian legal order existing in the pre-European contact period, and not on British or Canadian actions (Sanders, 1989). While there has been no equivalent Supreme Court ruling concerning métis land claims, the critical point in the Musqueam decision—that aboriginal land rights pre-date and are independent of any government legislation or treaty—will likely be highly significant for métis land claims.

Since there is no parallel to the Indian Act spelling out the position of the métis *vis-à-vis* the federal government, and the Constitution does not define the nature of aboriginal rights—seemingly leaving the latter up to legislative bodies and the courts to define as in the Musqueam case—the 1991 Royal Commission has the potential to break new ground. In the course of investigating the legal, political, and socio-cultural status of the métis, it must also address the questions of whether a federal (as opposed to provincial) métis policy is needed and, if so, what the extent of such a policy should be. Métis leaders have repeatedly called for a 'new and mutually beneficial relationship between Native people and the federal government' (Native Council, 1978). It is clear that the federal aboriginal paradigm consisting of treaties, reserves, band council governments, and a federal Indian department concerned with the on-reserve population does not apply to the métis. Herein lies the potential significance of the Royal Commission.

Like the 1982 Constitution Act, the Royal Commission has reinforced the conceptualization of métis, Inuit and Indian as distinct peoples. Before and even after 1982, there was an increasing tendency on the part of the federal government to subsume, on an *ad hoc* basis, all aboriginal peoples under the 'Native' heading for the purposes of policy and program planning (Weaver, 1985a). Thus when Métis were included in federal programs such as the Native Economic Development Program (DRIE, 1983), even though they were not a federal responsibility, they were defined as a 'special needs group not as a special rights group . . . [to be viewed] clinically, not ideologically' (Weaver, 1985a: 86). Métis leaders such as Harry Daniels (1978) have argued that the inclusion of métis as 'Native' has a debilitating effect on the Métis people's sense of themselves as a national minority, regardless of any practical benefits it might have in making them eligible to receive federal largesse. Furthermore, as Dyck and others (e.g., Watson, 1981) have argued, 'the difficulty with using the term "Native" to refer to all peoples of aboriginal ancestry . . . is that this practice tends to homogenize and eviscerate historical and contemporary realities' (Dyck, 1980: 42).

Their sense of themselves as a national minority notwithstanding, before 1982 the Métis had allied themselves with the non-status Indians in an effort to assert maximum pressure on Ottawa; the main lobby group for this alliance was the Native Council of Canada. The similarities between the métis and the non-status Indians, both in their exclusion from the Indian Act and in their social and political concerns, were perceived to outweigh their historical and cultural differences. The rationale for such a political union largely dissolved, however, when the Constitution Act recognized métis as distinct from Indians (status and non-status). In 1983, the more nationalistic Métis left the Native Council to form the Métis National Council. Members of the latter acknowledge their roots in a western plains homeland, trace their ancestry to 'those who were dispossessed by Canadian government actions from 1870 on' (Peterson and Brown, 1985: 6), and base their claims against the state on their status as a nation. The métis who remain within the original council use the term 'métis' more inclusively and base their claims on aboriginal rights, not national status. Thus the Constitution Act served as a catalyst for a redefinition of métis identity that reflects the diversity in métis historical experience. With the formation of the Métis National Council, Métis nationalism asserted itself once again as an undiluted and potent political force.

Conclusion: From Denial to Recognition

The affirmation of aboriginal rights in the Constitution had a wider significance for the métis than for other aboriginal peoples. Before 1982, there was a dichotomy in aboriginal organization that set status Indians with clear entitlements, firmly defined by the Indian Act, on one side, and métis together with non-status Indians on the other. Traditionally, the métis had organized with non-status Indians in the belief that they shared common interests and would be stronger with a united front. The patriated Constitution, however, acknowledged the métis as a distinct aboriginal people for the first time, and in so doing placed all Native peoples on the same constitutional footing.

In addition to those métis who identify themselves as an aboriginal people in the general sense of having mixed Indian and non-Indian ancestry, there are some, such as the members of the Métis National Council, who clearly identify with the New Nation as it existed in the Canadian west before its entry into Canada. These Métis have a definite list of grievances and a specific political agenda. In short, they wish to hold Canada accountable for the provisions of the Manitoba Act. They also share many of the goals of other aboriginal peoples: namely, control over their own land and resources, self-government, and the preservation and promotion of their culture. What is needed is an avenue other than the judicial system through which the Métis can form new relationships with the federal and provincial governments, relationships attuned to their aboriginal rights and distinct history. This was the goal of Louis Riel and his provisional government when they presented Ottawa with the conditions under which the Métis would agree to enter Canada. The Manitoba Act met most of these demands. If its provisions had been adhered to and judiciously implemented, the terms of reference of the 1991 Royal Commission on Aboriginal Peoples would have been considerably different.

A contemporary Métis leader, Louis Bruyère, has commented on the general lack of historical knowledge and understanding for his people's position: 'What Canadians do not understand is that Louis Riel is a Father of Confederation. . . . He intuitively sensed the future for Canada and wanted to guarantee a place for Métis people in that future . . .' (in Kilgour, 1988: 148). The Constitution was the first step necessary to guarantee such a place. Perhaps the House of Commons resolution, in March 1992, recognizing Riel as a 'founder of Manitoba' will be the second. The role that the métis have played in Canadian nation-building will be adequately recognized, however, only when Louis Riel joins John A. Macdonald and George-Étienne Cartier in the history books as the third 'Father of Confederation'.

NUNAVUT: TOWARDS AN INUIT NATION WITHIN CANADA

The Inuit have experienced considerable socio-cultural change in response to political and economic pressures. As residents of Canada's last, vast frontier land, they were removed from the influences of the larger society, isolated and without a common awareness for collective action, until well into the middle of this century. Nevertheless, in the last three decades they have taken measures to redefine themselves in relation both to each other and to the Canadian state.

Most Inuit in Canada reside in the Northwest Territories, with smaller clusters of population, numbering from two to four thousand, in Labrador and northern Quebec. We have chosen to focus on the Inuit in the eastern Arctic within the jurisdiction of the NWT. Not only do these people account for the majority of Inuit in Canada, but since 1977 they have been engaged in political activity to establish a new territory and government known as Nunavut in the eastern sector of the NWT. An Inuktitut word meaning 'our land', 'Nunavut' has the same emotional connotation for Inuit as *mon pays* has for Québécois. The process of defining and promoting the vision of Nunavut provides a glimpse of the dynamics of nation-building as it affects not only the Inuit but other aboriginal peoples in the NWT as well.

Unlike status Indians in the south, the Inuit always have been the undisputed landlords of the north, never having signed treaties with the federal or provincial governments. Ottawa has had the legal responsibility for the welfare of the Inuit in the provinces as well as the territories since the Supreme Court ruling in 1939 that deemed Inuit to be the equivalent of Indians for purposes of program administration

(Diubaldo, 1981). The Inuit share some similarities in outlook with other aboriginal peoples in Canada concerning such fundamental issues as aboriginal rights, self-government, and land claims. Yet their aspirations and strategies for achieving their objectives are unique, reflecting their own historical and cultural background.

This section will examine government–Inuit relations and the implications of current policy initiatives for the future of Nunavut. The larger context of aboriginal politics in the NWT will be introduced first; then we will focus on the more specific matter of Inuit self-determination.

Ethnic Regionalism in the Northwest Territories

While contact with outsiders has posed a continuous threat to the survival of Inuit culture, not all threats have emanated from the south. The existence of self-determining movements among the Dene, métis, and Inuvialuit (Mackenzie Delta Inuit) in the western NWT has placed the Inuit in the eastern NWT in conflict and competition with other aboriginal peoples over such issues as the structure of government and the control of non-renewable resources, including mineral rights and off-shore oil exploration and development. Thus it is not possible to appreciate Inuit–government relations without considering the larger context of ethno-regional politics in the Northwest Territories.

Currently both the eastern and western Arctic are governed by the same territorial government, with its capital in the western NWT city of Yellowknife. The Yellowknife government enjoys fewer powers than a provincial government, and is thus controlled to a greater degree by Ottawa, although there has been a trend towards devolution of powers in recent years. Contrary to what one might imagine, the territorial government in the past decade has not been white-dominated. The election of the Ninth Assembly in 1979 was the turning point in aboriginal–white relations. Four Dene and Métis members were elected. 'They, the Inuit members, and a number of sympathetic non-native members transformed the consciousness of the assembly. For the first time, issues of concern to native people were given pre-eminence' (Dacks, 1988: 225). In the 1980s the government of the NWT was led by Richard Nerysoo, a Dene, and Nick Sibbeston, a Métis; in 1991 Inuvialuit Nellie Cournoyea was elected government leader.

The Dene and Métis support the process of devolution on the understanding that it will not undermine their aboriginal claims or prejudge the future constitutional structure of the western NWT (Dacks, 1988: 228). The Inuit's main priority, however, is the establishment of Nunavut. Consequently, they may not stand to benefit as much from devolution as the Dene and Métis. Since a main threat to Inuit aspirations for

Nunavut stems from the inter-ethnic competition in the western Arctic, a comparison of the different social and cultural systems found there will provide greater understanding of areas of potential conflict.

The NWT is composed of three distinct aboriginal societies—the Dene, the métis, and the Inuit—each of which comprises various sub-groupings. Taken as a whole, the Native population makes up approximately 62 per cent of the inhabitants of the NWT. The Inuit are about 34 per cent; the Dene, including such people as the Chipewyan, Slavey, Dogrib, Hare, and Kutchin (Loucheux), about 18 per cent; Métis about 10 per cent; and non-Natives about 38 per cent. Non-Natives form the majority in such Mackenzie District communities as Hay River, Fort Smith, Inuvik, and Yellowknife (*Canada's North*, 1983: 3-4).

In sum, while the population of the eastern NWT is 80 per cent Inuit, the western NWT can be viewed as a series of ethno-regional communities containing Dene, métis, and Inuvialiut. From the western NWT point of view, the Inuit in the eastern Arctic may pose a threat inasmuch as they have spearheaded the drive to partition the NWT in order to create a Nunavut homeland for themselves distinct from the western Arctic and its peoples. The sense of threat stems from the fact that partition would reduce the overall aboriginal majority in the Legislative Assembly, and the Dene and Métis rely on the Inuit members to bolster the Native ranks against those of non-Natives.

While philosophically the aboriginal peoples of the NWT support self-determination for themselves and others, the positions taken in the course of the partition debate serve to clarify the differences in goals and aspirations between the eastern and western Arctic peoples. Further analysis of the evolving aspirations and self-definitions of the aboriginal peoples in the eastern and western NWT is aided by Petrella's (1980) systemic approach to the study of regional and national movements, which distinguishes between those variables that are internal and external to a region.

With respect to external factors, the Inuit, the Dene and the Métis have the same constitutional status under section 35(1)(2). Yet they differ significantly in their treaty status. Aboriginal peoples in the western region of the NWT in the past signed two treaties, but the Inuit in the eastern Arctic have never signed any. Thus the Dene nation tends to take as its political reference group the aboriginal associations of the south such as the Assembly of First Nations, whereas the Inuit, not bound by past treaties, tend to look to the politics of the circumpolar indigenous peoples for inspiration and leadership. (The first Inuit Circumpolar conference, held in Barrow, Alaska, in 1977, was attended by Greenland, Canadian, and Alaskan Inuit; since the thaw in East–West relations, Russian Inuit have also been attending.)

It is when selected internal factors are examined, however, that the differences between the eastern and western Arctic social and cultural systems emerge in bold relief. The western Arctic is relatively more developed economically and the population is more diverse. Given that the eastern Arctic lacks the economic development seen in the western sector, it is thought that Nunavut would be almost entirely dependent upon the federal government for support—a rough estimate by a DIAND official ran as high as 95 per cent (Baker, 1990: 18, 22). Moreover, some development and resource extraction projects may be more appealing to one sector of the Arctic than the other, depending on the environmental risk involved. (For example, except for Baker Lake, all the Inuit communities are in coastal locations; hence Nunavut would be more threatened by coastal tanker spillage than would communities in the western NWT, which are more vulnerable to a land-based pipeline crisis.)

Finally, with respect to the ethnic mix of the population, the eastern Arctic is almost exclusively Inuit, whereas the west is populated by Dene, métis, white northerners, and Inuvialuit (who may have cultural ties to Alaskan Inuit). Unlike the relatively homogeneous eastern Arctic, therefore, the western sector finds it difficult to speak with one voice. The Inuit depend upon the western sector to co-operate in the partition of the NWT, as their dream of Nunavut cannot become a reality without the western sector's agreement on such matters as the new boundary. As a Senior Assistant Deputy Minister with DIAND recently reminded the Inuit, 'From the perspective of the Government of Canada, the creation of Nunavut is not the creation of one territory —it is the creation of two' (Van Loon, 1990: 8). The federal government has consistently held that there are four conditions for partition: (a) continuing support for division by majority of northerners; (b) agreement on a boundary; (c) settlement of aboriginal land claims; and (d) agreement on the division of powers among various levels of government (Van Loon, 1990: 9).

The aboriginal peoples in the western Arctic have the potential to thwart—wittingly or unwittingly—the legitimate aspirations of the eastern Arctic Inuit. Moreover, it is in the immediate interest of the western sector to keep the Inuit in the Legislative Assembly, since a shift in the aboriginal/non-aboriginal ratio could have negative repercussions for the aspirations of Dene, métis, and Inuvialuit.

With the dynamics of aboriginal politics in the NWT as a whole in mind, let us examine more closely the status of Nunavut.

Nunavut: Vision vs. Reality

While early contact with the Eskimos—as they were called by European explorers—took place as early as 1576 with the voyage of Martin

Frobisher in the Baffin Island area and continued with the establishment of the Hudson's Bay Company in 1670, it was not until the nineteenth century that contact was made with the Central Inuit. Until the
1950s, the missionaries, the Royal Canadian Mounted Police, and the
federal and territorial governments were the chief institutional influences on life north of the 60th parallel. The traditional economy began
to break up in the mid-1950s with the proletarianization of labour
(Vallee, 1971). A wage labour economy was introduced on a minor
scale, with some Inuit finding sporadic employment in guiding, trans-
lating, and the construction and maintenance of radar defence instal-
lations. Commercial Inuit art—soapstone sculpture and print-making
—was also developed at this time in the Cape Dorset area with southern Canadian encouragement. Inuit-run co-operatives established in
the 1960s were successful in the merchandising of 'Eskimo art' and
other northern handicrafts (McMillan, 1988: 269).

The most complex unit in traditional Inuit society was the family.
Several families might live together in a band, but these groups seldom
comprised more than 50 people with the exception of Inuvialuit settlements, which numbered in the hundreds (McMillan, 1988: 258).
Given that knowledge of southern Canadian culture and life styles are
relatively new to the Inuit, the fact that in the space of a few decades
they have developed the sophisticated political organization and skills
necessary for the Nunavut campaign is a remarkable achievement.

The transformation from a family-based social group to a 'nation'
involves a change in social consciousness as well as in social structure. The formation of an ethnic group and the development of ethnic
consciousness are necessary precursors to the development of nationalistic feelings. Classic nationalism, in the sense of nineteenth-century
European political movements, challenges the legitimacy of the state.
Since the movement to establish Nunavut has not challenged Canadian authority, it is more correctly seen by outside observers as an
ethno-regional movement rather than a nationalistic one (Elliott,
1984). Nevertheless, the question remains: how did the Inuit make the
transition from family-based nomadic bands to the complex social
organization and political activity of the current era?

The Mathiassons (1978) answer this question by referring to the
'ethnicization' of the Inuit. In developing an awareness of themselves
as an ethnic group, a people look beyond their kin to recognize others
who are related to them by common ancestry—albeit distant—or by
language or culture. A feeling of 'we-ness' develops and intensifies
when confronted with its opposite: people with different ancestry,
language, or culture. Through heterogeneous interaction we/they feelings emerge, and ethnic consciousness becomes one component of the
individual's overall identity.

For the Inuit, ethnic consciousness emerged gradually through inter-action with outsiders: first whalers and explorers, then missionaries and traders, and finally government administrators, teachers, shop-keepers, and health professionals. Because famine and starvation had been all too commonplace among such groups as the Caribou Inuit in the Central Arctic (McMillan, 1988: 262), and for administrative con-venience in the delivery of services, the federal government from the 1950s on encouraged the consolidation of Inuit groups and the forma-tion of permanent settlements. The administrative centres of Inuvik in the west and Iqaluit (formerly Frobisher Bay) in the east developed as the result of federal policy and presence. As these centres contained significant numbers of non-Native bureaucratic personnel, a two-tiered life style quickly became evident in the Arctic, with non-indigenous northerners living more comfortably than aboriginal people.

Not all of the federal government's policies, however, were benign. In 1953, in an attempt to establish a Canadian presence in the High Arctic, the government used false pretences to persuade seven Inuit families from Port Harrison (now Inukjuak) in northern Quebec and three from Pond Inlet on Baffin Island to relocate to Cornwallis Island and Ellesmere Island. The Inuit were told that game would be more abundant there, and that their overall quality of life would be higher. Such was not the case, and the 'volunteer' migrants were forced to cope with isolation and harsh conditions including months of total winter darkness. Today the most northerly community in Canada, the Inuit community of Grise Fjord on Ellesmere Island achieved the purpose of establishing Canadian sovereignty over the Arctic archipelago.

The relocation experience was a bitter one for the Inuit; not only did it expose them to severe hardship, but it revealed the duplicity of the government in its dealings with them. In 1982, in an effort to achieve some compensation, the Inuit, through the Inuit Tapirisat of Canada (ITC), requested government assistance for those families who wished to return to Inukjuak. Finally, in 1990 a Parliamentary Standing Com-mittee on Aboriginal Affairs recommended that the government offi-cially recognize the role the Inuit played in establishing sovereignty, compensate them for their services, and make a formal apology for 'the wrongdoing inflicted upon them' (cited in Grant, 1991: 4). Although agreeing to assist the return to Inukjuak, the Mulroney government rejected the other recommendations of the Parliamentary Committee, and has done nothing to erase the Inuit's sense of having been treated like second-class citizens.

The psychological or ethnic boundaries of the Inuit were further sharpened and defined through their participation over the years in the Legislative Assembly of the NWT. The culmination of this process, marking the achievement of the Inuit's ethnic identity—their collective sense of themselves as a people—as well as their political maturity, can be seen in their negotiations with the federal government over two independent but related issues: the Nunavut proposal and a land claim in the eastern Arctic.

The earliest proposal to partition the NWT dates to 1960, when the Diefenbaker government suggested dividing the territories into Nunatsiaq in the east and Mackenzie in the west. The first Inuit proposal was put forward in 1977 by the ITC, with Nunavut having slightly different boundaries than Nunatsiaq. The Inuit have been the main thrust behind the proposed division ever since.

The initial Inuit land claim, submitted by the ITC in 1973, concentrated primarily on hunting rights. In 1975, however, the first comprehensive land claim in Canada was achieved with the James Bay and Northern Quebec Agreement. Learning from the experience of their Inuit neighbours in Arctic Quebec, who had signed that Agreement along with the Cree, the ITC filed a comprehensive claim (involving an area twice the size of Alaska) for the Inuit of the NWT, including the Inuvialuit. The Nunavut government proposal was not part of this claim.

The Inuit gained an active ally in their partition efforts in 1981 when the Dene Nation supported the idea, proposing that their land be established as a new territory to be called Denendeh. In the following year, a plebiscite concerning partition to create Nunavut in the east was held by the NWT with Ottawa's backing. When the plebiscite passed with a vote of 56.7 per cent in favour, Constitutional Forums were immediately established in the east and the west in order to examine in detail the implications of division and the structure of the new governments that would be formed.

Two years later, before the Constitutional Forums could report, the Inuvialuit in the west signed a separate land claim with Ottawa, without reference to the Inuit in the Eastern Arctic. It is not clear whether the Inuvialuit will eventually be part of Nunavut or Denendeh. This unilateral action shattered any monolithic view of the Inuit as an indivisible ethnic group; however, the legitimacy of the Nunavut proposal has not been undermined by the Inuvialuit's departure.

An agreement in principle to start negotiations was signed by the Inuit and the federal government in April 1990, and in December 1991 Ottawa announced that it intends to introduce legislation to create Nunavut in the fall of 1992, pending ratification by eligible voters in the area (estimated numbers range between 14,000 and 18,000) and 'a political accord with Northwest Territories . . . to settle the issue of government in Nunavut' (Delacourt, 1991). Under the terms of the proposed accord the federal government and Inuit people will have settled a massive land claim stretching from the tree line (the 60th parallel) in the eastern Arctic to the North Pole (ownership of nearly 350,000 sq. km and control over 2 million sq. km) in exchange for surrender of any future Inuit aboriginal-rights claims to land. Ottawa will also transfer $1.5-billion (with interest) over the next four-teen years to assist Nunavut in establishing an ethnically-based home-land and a democratic territorial government similar to that currently operating in the NWT (Henton and Walker, 1991).

The boundary line between Nunavut and the western territory remains an outstanding and contentious issue. Historically the Caribou Inuit and the Chipewyan people have hunted in overlapping territory (McMillan, 1988: 257), and in 1987 Dene-Métis demands for lands used by métis trappers in southern Keewatin led to collapse of the boundary negotiations. Each side believes that it has made concessions and the other is intransigent.

Matters are likely to be complicated by aboriginal groups in the south who are disenchanted by Inuit's apparent willingness to trade off any future aboriginal rights such as an inherent right to self-government (Sheppard, 1991). This ideological gap may pose difficulties; still, while no one is wagering a guess as to the precise birth date of Nunavut, most outside observers agree that it will take place before the end of this century.

If Nunavut is formed, it will have the status of a territory—eventually, perhaps, of a province. The Inuit government would be fundamentally different from any other Canadian government, aboriginal or non-abo-riginal, in that the aboriginal people would form the only government in Nunavut, and would have authority over Inuit and non-Inuit alike. Nowhere else in Canada does one district aboriginal group constitute a clear majority with the capacity to form a public government.

Nunavut would have English and Inuktitut as its official languages. To further preserve their culture, the Inuit would establish a three-year residency requirement before migrants would be permitted to vote (Nunavut Constitutional Forum, 1983). This would prevent newcom-ers from voting *en bloc* if a flood of short term in-migration should occur in conjunction with an economic development project, for example. However, since over 80 per cent of the population of Nunavut would be Inuit, there is little likelihood that they would be swamped by outsiders in the foreseeable future.

For the Inuit, the issue of aboriginal 'self-government' has neither the same political context nor quite the same significance that it does for other aboriginal peoples. The métis and Indians are attempting to secure their 'inherent' right to self-government by entrenching it in the Consti-tution, but except for Ontario (which recognized the inherent right to self-government in 1991), Saskatchewan, and BC, the provinces and the federal government have tended to view self-government as a contingent right, often preferring the municipal-government model. (For further discussion of the politics of self-government as it affects aboriginal peoples residing in the provinces, see Chapter 5.)

Even though the government of Nunavut would be fundamentally different from other aboriginal governments, the Inuit support the other aboriginal peoples in their quest for self-government. As Rosemarie Kuptana, the current head of the ITC, has emphasized, the Inuit demand that a revised Canadian Constitution guarantee a right to self-government for all aboriginal peoples that is 'not dependent for existence upon grants of power from the federal or provincial governments' (cited in Cox, 1991: A9).

Concurrent with the struggle for Nunavut are independent negotiations with the federal government regarding the Inuit comprehensive land claim (Jull, 1987, 1991). While it is federal policy to deal with the claim and the political structures separately, the two issues are closely intertwined at the level of strategy. To date the Inuit have not agreed to the terms of the claim because the federal government wishes them to sign an agreement that would extinguish their aboriginal rights to the land. The Inuit position is that if Nunavut is established as a territorial government, they might be willing to sign away their aboriginal rights because they could rely upon the government of Nunavut to protect their interests. Without the safeguards associated with such a government, however, the Inuit would feel vulnerable if they were to extinguish their aboriginal rights in order to settle the land claim. Nunavut is thus clearly the priority, since with its establishment a successful resolution of the land claim would be less critical to the preservation of their culture (Ittinuar, 1985).

Conclusion

The establishment of Nunavut would set a precedent inasmuch as to date no aboriginal government has been a public government. However, regional governments in parts of the Arctic other than the NWT have been in place for over a decade in areas where the population is almost exclusively aboriginal. The Kativik regional government in Arctic Quebec was formed in conjunction with the James Bay and Northern Quebec Agreement in 1975. Similarly, the Alaska Native Settlement Act in 1972 created an aboriginal regional government on the North Slope in Alaska in the region adjacent to the Inuvialuit on the Beaufort Sea. In Greenland the Inuit have enjoyed 'home rule', independent from Denmark, since the early 1970s (Sanders, 1989: 723). Hence the creation of Nunavut, although a precedent-setting move, would not be out of line with respect to other Inuit governments outside the NWT.

No matter how compelling the argument for Nunavut may be in terms of 'natural justice' or aboriginal rights, it should be stressed that the proposal is not a panacea for all the many deeply rooted social and economic ills that plague the eastern Arctic. The Inuit are the youngest and fastest-growing population in Canada (Norris, 1990: 58), with a high unemployment rate that, given their demographic and economic structure, is predicted to worsen (Irwin, 1989). Teenage suicide in epidemic proportions is indicative of the alienation and despondency currently suffered by the young. The social problems facing the Inuit are multi-faceted and will not disappear with the creation of Nunavut.

Nevertheless, the forces undermining efforts at cultural and language preservation are increasingly difficult to control under the present territorial system. Recognition as the 'nation' of Nunavut would allow the Inuit a greater measure of self-determination within the Canadian federalist system. As long as discourse about Nunavut remains within the framework of NWT devolution without partition, the potential of Inuit culture is blocked and its survival threatened. Transforming the vision of Nunavut into reality would go a long way towards making an Inuit renaissance possible and starting the healing process that is so sorely needed by young Inuit. More simply, the creation of Nunavut would acknowledge what has always been theirs.

The Canadian confederation will not be complete until the Yukon and NWT become provinces. In essence, the Nunavut proposal is an offer on the part of the Inuit to join confederation. Canada was confronted with a similar offer in 1870, when the Métis presented Ottawa with the terms under which they would have been willing to join the confederation. Ottawa did not honour the terms that it agreed to in the Manitoba Act of 1870, with consequences that have been tragic for our mutual history. Once again, Canada has the opportunity to welcome and legitimate an indigenous society on its frontier. How we respond this time around will be a measure of our maturity.

N I N E

Conclusion: From Periphery to Centre

Consensus among the forum's non-aboriginal participants is astonishing, verging on unanimity . . . they tell us that this has besmirched our international reputation and that it offends our collective principles of caring and fairness.

> — Keith Spicer, Chairman, Citizens Forum on Canada's Future, 1991.

Our fight in terms of constitutional issues . . . is to restructure Canada. We have to alter the fundamental thinking, of the legal and political systems. If we fail to accomplish that task, we will have to do what Quebec is doing and that is to seek a path that is independent of the dominant society.

> — Ovide Mercredi; quoted in *Kitchener-Waterloo Record* (1991a).

[The] vast majority of Canadian natives—and I mean ordinary native people, not just their political leaders—are deeply frustrated and profoundly disappointed with the way they perceive that they have been, and are today, treated by Canadian governments (of all levels) and with their current economic social and cultural position in the Canadian polity. They feel that their historical position in Canada, their traditions and values, and their aspirations, are not well understood by most non-native Canadians, and that they are not respected and supported by Canadian governments. . . . [Yet] the frustration and disappointment felt by many natives have not, perhaps surprisingly, given way to cynicism. . . . The reason for the absence of cynicism is, I believe, that most Canadian natives are remarkably decent, fair, tolerant and compassionate people. There was a palpable integrity about virtually all the native people I met. . . .

> — from a report by former chief justice Brian Dickson of the Supreme Court on the Royal Commission on Aboriginal Peoples ('A Real, Rare Opportunity', *Globe and Mail*, 29 Aug. 1991).

In 1969, aboriginal peoples in Canada were about to become an 'endangered species'. The White Paper had proposed to abolish separate status (by repealing the Indian Act), to terminate their unique relationship with the state (as set out in treaties and the reserve system), and to eliminate their special privileges (through conferral of formal equality). This decision to rescind the distinctive components of aboriginal existence (such as the Department of Indian Affairs) and to transfer residual responsibility to the provinces was not motivated entirely by political calculation or economic expediency. Fallout from the American civil-rights movement, as well as broader movements for human and individual rights, was equally important in revising the policy agenda. For the architect of the paper, Pierre Elliott Trudeau, replacing special status with equality was part of a grander vision of a just society in which all citizens regardless of race were similar under the law (Axworthy and Trudeau, 1990). Regardless of the motives, however, the net effect of these proposals would have been to eliminate the 'Indian problem' by abolishing aboriginal peoples as a recognizable entity in Canada.

Just over two decades later, aboriginal peoples are solidly entrenched as Canada's first citizens. Their situation has evolved to the point where they are recognized as distinct peoples with corresponding rights to sit with Canada's First Ministers and debate constitutional reform. On 5 July 1991 Ottawa officially endorsed a parallel aboriginal constitutional process in which aboriginal groups would provide a unified set of proposals to the House of Commons. On 12 March 1992 aboriginal leaders were offered full participation as distinct governments for the next round of constitutional talks; according to Joe Clark, Minister for Constitutional Affairs, aboriginal peoples will never again be excluded from the constitutional table, as was the case with the Meech Lake accord (*Toronto Star*, 1991d). On the strength of this constitutional inclusion, and threatening to form a secessionist movement similar to that in Quebec should current constitutional proposals reach an impasse, aboriginal peoples are poised to assert their case as 'nations within'—a distinct society and a founding people of Canada with the right to self-government, land, and treaty concessions. Finally, a Royal Commission with a broad mandate and sweeping terms of reference is now reviewing Canada's relationship with aboriginal people, and the impact of its findings could be as powerful as that of the Bilingualism and Biculturalism (Laurendeau and Dunton) Report, which culminated in the passage of the Official Languages Act in 1969 (Fraser, 1991).

In short, since 1969 aboriginal peoples have become actively engaged in defining self-government structures, negotiating land-claims settlements, and conferring with heads of government over constitutional matters (Comeau and Santin, 1990). How do we account for this profound shift in the status of aboriginal peoples, from a position of irrelevance to that of a 'distinct society' in Canada with aspirations comparable to those of Quebec? In 1969, in response to a suggested reopening of the issue of 'aboriginal rights', Prime Minister Trudeau responded with a resounding 'No' (Asch, 1989: 119). He defended this stance by asserting: 'We can't recognize aboriginal rights because no society can be built on historical "might-have-beens"' (see Weaver, 1981: 179). By 1984, Trudeau's opening remarks to the First Ministers Conference on Aboriginal Constitutional Matters revealed a reversal: 'We are not here to consider whether there should be institutions of self-government, but how these institutions should be brought into being; what should be their jurisdictions; their powers; how they should fit into the interlocking system of jurisdiction by which Canada is governed' (in Ponting, 1986: 400). Why did the issues surrounding the aboriginal agenda move from insignificance to an equal footing with other provincial and national concerns? Is the concept of 'nations within' about to become a reality in aboriginal–state relations?

The preceding chapters have attempted to answer these questions. They have outlined how the aboriginal agenda (with its focus on citizen-plus status, self-government, land claims, and treaty rights) has moved to the forefront of public and political consciousness, in large part through organized aboriginal efforts to combat the assimilationist intent of the 1969 White Paper. Aboriginal assertiveness and willingness to embarrass Ottawa into action have been equally critical in forging an environment receptive to change. That central authorities in Ottawa and the provinces have also been pivotal in engineering these changes is evident in the spate of legislation, policies, and programs seeking new ways of advancing both aboriginal and political interests. Nor can the role of the courts be discounted, for many of these political decisions have taken their cue from judicial decisions. From the Nishga (Calder) case in 1973 to the Sparrow decision in 1990, the courts have opened doors for aboriginal peoples by reinforcing the legal grounds for redefining aboriginal relations with the state.

The Canadian public has likewise been instrumental in exerting pressure for changes to the aboriginal agenda. As noted in the 1991 Spicer Commission report, the general public appears to be overwhelmingly in favour of aboriginal self-government and resolution of land claims. Admittedly, there is no assurance that the public's definitions of the problem and the solutions coincide with those of aboriginal peoples. Moreover, there is a groundswell of anger over certain 'special rights' accorded to aboriginal people, such as the announcements in Ontario and BC that aboriginal people will be permitted to hunt and fish without complying with provincial or federal laws except when essential for conservation purposes. Nevertheless, the growing receptivity among Canadian citizens has made it easier for both politicians and aboriginal leaders to take risks without fear of immediate backlash.

Finally, the ideological climate in Canada has changed dramatically in the last two decades. With the entrenchment of two official languages in conjunction with federal multiculturalism as a legal fact, a commitment to the principles of diversity and equality has become a fundamental characteristic of Canadian society, creating a climate conducive to managing diversity in a positive and productive manner. Under the sway of this and other social forces, aboriginal concerns have moved from the margins of political and public awareness to occupy a central place in Canadian nation-building.

Approaching the twenty-first century, Canada may well be on the threshold of a paradigm shift in aboriginal policy and administration. Aboriginal issues have become firmly locked into our public consciousness, as media reportage continues to dwell on aboriginal land claims, the plight of aboriginal peoples in the cities and on reserves, the politics of self-government, and concerns over racism and discrimination in the criminal justice system. In 1985, when Georges Erasmus was elected Grand Chief of the Assembly of First Nations, the results were buried deep inside the *Globe and Mail*; in 1991, the leadership convention that elected Ovide Mercredi received front-page headlines and extensive electronic coverage. This increase in media attention is only one indication of the prominence now accorded to aboriginal issues.

How this paradigm shift will manifest itself in practice is another question. Are the proposed charges in formal policy and administration rooted in substance, with a fundamental commitment to redefining the status and role of the 'nations within'? Or are they a matter of symbols and cosmetics only (Weaver, 1991)? Will aboriginal grievances be addressed in a spirit of co-operation and bilateral decision-making (Ponting, 1991)? Or will new aboriginal–government relations simply rearrange the furniture without much regard for the floor plan? To what extent is the government willing to concede to aboriginal demands for a new kind of nationhood, with fundamentally separate structures? In the end, will it endeavour to accommodate aboriginal peoples simply through greater institutional flexibility? The following case study illustrates the challenges and conflicts involved in any attempt at reform.

Case Study: Renewal in Aboriginal Criminal Justice

The justice system has failed Manitoba's Aboriginal people on a massive scale. It has been insensitive and inaccessible, and has arrested and imprisoned Aboriginal people in grossly disproportionate numbers. Aboriginal people who are arrested are more likely than non-Aboriginal people to be denied bail, spend more time in pre-trial detention and spend less time with their lawyers, and, if convicted, are more likely to be incarcerated.

It is not merely that the justice system has failed Aboriginal people; justice also has been denied to them. For more than a century the rights of Aboriginal people have been ignored and eroded. The result of this denial has been injustice of the most profound kind. Poverty and power-lessness have been the Canadian legacy to a people who once governed their own affairs in full self-sufficiency.

— Aboriginal Justice Inquiry of Manitoba (1991).

Many of the challenges and paradoxes that pervade the proposed restructuring of aboriginal–state relations are reflected in specific initiatives for reform. The recent release of the report of the Manitoba Aboriginal Justice Inquiry is a case in point. Repeating the familiar refrain that Canada's conduct toward aboriginal people is 'disgraceful', the authors accused the legal system of both explicit racism and systemic discrimination at the level of legislation, courts, law enforcement, and prisons (Roberts and York, 1991). Proof of mistreatment was abundant and scathing. Nearly 40 per cent of those in Manitoba jails are Native, although aboriginal people comprise only 12 per cent of the total population. Police actions have at times bordered on the overtly racist, especially during their investigations of the 1971 sex slaying of the Cree teenager Helen Betty Osborne, and of the shooting death of aboriginal leader J.J. Harper by a Winnipeg officer in 1988. The cumulative impact of these daily injustices, the report concluded, was unconscionable. The criminal justice system has penalized aboriginal peoples and ensured their exclusion from meaningful participation in Canadian society.

To redress this injustice and avert the further blackening of Canada's reputation, the report advocated the establishment of a parallel aboriginal justice system within the context of self-government. Aboriginal jurisdiction would be paramount across the country's 600-odd bands, thus ensuring aboriginal control over the design and delivery of criminal/civil/family laws. In the words of the report:

Aboriginal and non-aboriginal accused, arrested, and charged by aboriginal police officers, should appear in front of aboriginal judges, in an aboriginal court system controlled by aboriginal people . . . and the authority of aboriginal courts within aboriginal lands must be clear and paramount.

Other recommendations were aimed at improving existing criminal justice institutions and procedures, in part through affirmative-action hiring of aboriginal personnel, and in part by making the entire process more sensitive to aboriginal needs and culture.

Responses to the report of the Inquiry have been mixed, reflecting varied opinions about the nature and scope of the problem as well as the prospects for solution. The present system, rooted in English common law, was seen as isolating aboriginal people by excluding their cultural values from input into the social control process (Dafoe,

1991; Nagle, 1991). However, despite both federal and provincial efforts to devolve the delivery of service to aboriginal communities (Doherty and Currie, 1991), not all parties concurred with the concept of parallel criminal justice institutions as a viable solution. Some aboriginal leaders wanted a legal system entirely separate from the federal and provincial courts, while others endorsed a Native-run system consistent with Canada's Constitution and legal system. Still others were content with modifications to the existing system (*Globe and Mail*, 1991k). In a study conducted among the Nishnawbe-Aski Nation in northern Ontario (reported in the *Toronto Star*, 1991i), the vast majority of those who responded were content with the present arrangement and disagreed with the principle of parallel aboriginal justice as a solution to problems, especially when serious crimes were involved, although less grievous offences (such as drunkenness) could be better handled outside the Euro-Canadian system.

Federal and provincial authorities agreed that a problem existed, but, by contrast, repudiated the solutions recommended by the Inquiry. The federal Justice Minister, Kim Campbell, argued against a parallel system, preferring instead selective improvements through the addition of 'customary' practices to the existing arrangement (*Toronto Star*, 1991h; Doherty and Currie, 1991). For some, the very principle of a parallel system was anathema, a violation of cherished individual guarantees. To others, the logistics of implementation proved to be a stumbling block. How would a separate system carve out a niche in existing provincial and federal structures? Where do jurisdictions begin? Where do they end? Would individual freedoms and guarantees as set out in the Charter of Rights be respected in tribal courts? Would a parallel system apply to serious crimes both on and off reserves? What will happen with offences involving aboriginal and non-aboriginal persons?

How valid are these concerns about the philosophy and practice of aboriginal justice? Evidence suggests that tribal justice systems are workable, and do not necessarily entail conflicting standards and inconsistent levels of redress. In New Zealand, for example, the Maatua Whangai system was established in the early 1980s as an alternative to conventional court procedures for Maori youth (Fleras, n.d.). Unacceptably high rates of offending, coupled with the high costs of recidivism, made it clear that Maori youths were victimized by a *de facto* separation already inherent in the criminal justice system. Under Maatua Whangai, youthful offenders are given an option of settling accounts for minor criminal activities. They can be adopted into an urban Maori family for resocialization through gainful employment and exposure to Maori cultural values. Another option allows Maori offenders to return to their rural tribal homelands to rediscover their identities and local roots. In either case, rehabilitation and restitution are central components, and a high degree of community involvement is essential for success.

Many other examples confirm that 'the native system of justice is very different from the non-native' (Mary Ellen Turpel, Dalhousie Law School Professor, quoted in *Globe and Mail*, 1991n). In British Columbia, a pilot project at Mill Bay allows cases to be referred from the provincial court to a council of aboriginal elders who decide on appropriate levels of punishment (*Globe and Mail*, 1991k). Nowhere, however, is the concept of parallel aboriginal justice more evident than in the United States, where well over 100 tribal arrangements flourish (*Globe and Mail*, 1991m). Many date back to the early part of the twentieth century, when US policy encouraged limited sovereignty (under the 'domestic dependent nations' principle), in tandem with the introduction of conventional policing and court systems as tools of civilization. One of the more successful examples can be seen in the southwest, where the 200,000-strong Navaho nation has since 1959 operated a tribal court system that grafts traditional customs onto essentially American courtroom procedures. With a $5-million budget that handles up to 46,000 cases annually, the Navaho courts have unlimited jurisdiction over civil matters, a limited authority over non-serious criminal cases, and punishment powers extending up to one year in jail and $5,000 fines (although concurrent sentences are permissible). Problems are ever-present, to be sure, many of them arising from conflicts of jurisdiction with overlapping states. Nevertheless, the Navaho system can be termed a success in balancing American (the basic law that protects due process and individual liberties) and tribal styles, and in the process softening the adversarial process in favour of one geared towards a pursuit of justice that is community-based and culturally sensitive (*Globe and Mail*, 1991m).

• *Restructuring: modifications or upheaval?*   Proposed changes to the criminal justice system strike at the core of aboriginal–state restructuring as a whole. In both cases, the goal is to accommodate aboriginal demands within a coherent national framework. The accommodation process can take one or more of several forms. First, the system of criminal justice can be left intact for the most part, with only the operational reins turned over to aboriginal people. Increasing the numbers of aboriginal officers and judges may make a difference in individual cases, since the people behind the uniforms or sitting on the benches would be more culturally attuned. It is debatable, however, whether an infusion of aboriginal personnel can sensitize the system as a whole.

Second, the system may be modified to reflect aboriginal concerns and sensibilities. In this scenario, reform is achieved through modifications that attempt to integrate aboriginal realities into the existing system of sentencing, punishment, and restitution. One example might involve the elimination of circuit courts, in which judges and prosecution arrive inter-mittently at remote settlements, and its replacement by a system of an elder-based courts committed to the principle of restitution and rehabili-tation through the community (*Globe and Mail*, 1991l). The jury is out over the effectiveness of a proposal that bridges the criminal-justice gap, but the danger of co-optation into the mainstream cannot be dismissed.

The third option is to create a parallel system of criminal justice within the framework of aboriginal self-determination and self-govern-ment. According to proponents of this approach, the systemic limita-tions inherent in the existing criminal justice system would be left untouched by the preceding proposals. As put by Pearl Keenan, an elder of the Teslin Tlingit band of the Yukon (reported in the *Globe and Mail*, 1991l), the Canadian Constitution is poorly equipped to accept either aboriginal justice or self-government since the constitutional rights of the individual take precedence over those of group. 'In our group', Ms Keenan notes, 'the rights of the group must come ahead of the indi-vidual.' What is required instead is a model more cognizant of aborig-inal cultural values and geared towards collective aboriginal rights—even if these violate Charter rights and freedoms and fall outside the criminal code. The US evidence noted above suggests that aboriginal court systems are workable, despite numerous procedural difficulties. The extent to which central authorities are willing to relinquish both power and resources to implement such a system is open to question at this point. Given the stakes at hand, however, the likelihood of paral-lel structures without further political struggles is remote.

The broader picture

Debates about the criminal justice system cut to the core of the politics involved in restructuring aboriginal–state relations in general. Two alternative scenarios predominate. Should the empowerment of abo-riginal peoples rely on efforts to revamp existing arrangements in a manner consistent with aboriginal values and priorities? That is, can the present system be retained with only appropriate modifications at the level of program design, delivery of services, and personnel changes? The alternative is for aboriginal peoples to exercise full jurisdictional control by designing programs and procedures consistent with their self-governing status as 'nations within'. In this case the community itself would create parallel structures in criminal justice as well as in health and education, in effect giving practical expression to the principle of aboriginal self-government. In short, the choice is between, on the one hand, modification of existing structures, and, on the other, fundamen-tal change and creation of parallel structures.

Just as reasons for optimism exist, so too there are grounds for pessimism (Cassidy, 1991). In the aftermath of Oka both political and aboriginal sectors continue to distrust each other. As far as aboriginal peoples are concerned, the government is best described as 'oppressive', 'untrustworthy', 'interfering', 'aggressive', and 'uncivilized'; they themselves are 'sovereign', 'spiritual', and 'peace-loving' (Ponting, 1991). This dichotomization may be empowering for aboriginal identity. But the polarization of social reality into good and evil is hardly conducive to dialogue and compromise. The government for its part continues to act regressively. Too often it still appears anxious to marginalize aboriginal leaders, delegitimize aboriginal concerns, and destabilize movements perceived as threats to the prevailing social order. Even the recent federal proposals for court-entrenched aboriginal self-government in the Constitution within ten years if the provinces cannot negotiate a definition has brought angry denunciations from some aboriginal leaders. Mocking Mulroney's claim that self-government is a matter of 'fairness', 'justice', and 'equality', Ovide Mercredi termed the constitutional reform package a 'betrayal' for denying to aboriginal people the 'inherent right to self-government' (Toronto Star, 1991l).

Even positive moves are suspected of concealing 'hidden agendas'. The government's receptivity to aboriginal demands is not necessarily based on compassion or outrage but on politics and power. Compromises and negotiations that prove to be costly in political or economic terms may be abandoned when excessive media exposure leads public interest to wane. Frustration in dealing with seemingly intractable problems may also instil a mood of indifference and apathy. However, as Cassidy (1991) points out, no permanent solution can be anticipated without recognition of the first nations as the founding people of Canada; constitutional affirmation of their inherent powers as 'distinct societies'; reaffirmation in practice of aboriginal and treaty rights; establishment of a modern treaty process on a nation-to-nation basis and in a spirit of equity, justice, and fairness; continuation of Ottawa's special trust obligations; repeal of the Indian Act; and achievement of economic self-sufficiency.

In effect, then, no one can predict where recent developments in aboriginal–government relations will lead. Predictions of yet another hot 'Indian' summer for 1991 proved to be groundless as military confrontation gave way to inclusion in premiers' conferences, guarantees for a voice in future constitutional talks, and establishment of the Royal Commission on Aboriginal Affairs. But whether these concessions will solve aboriginal peoples' 'problems' or simply ratchet their expectations to yet higher levels is impossible to tell. What is predictable is that aboriginal issues will play a pivotal role in the ongoing reconstruction of Canadian society. Thus Canadians owe it to themselves and to their country to become more acquainted with these issues if we are to ensure our collective survival as a progressive society.

PART II

ABORIGINAL NATIONS WITHIN THE UNITED STATES OF AMERICA

T E N

America: One Nation . . .
With Liberty and Justice For All?

INTRODUCTION

Aboriginal issues in the United States in recent years have not occupied centre stage to the same dramatic degree they have in Canada and New Zealand. The aboriginal people are relatively few in number, representing less than 1 per cent of the total population, and are significantly overshadowed by those of African, Hispanic, and Asian descent, who together represent more than one in five of all Americans. The more numerous racial and ethnic minorities—especially Afro-Americans, who comprise approximately 12 per cent of the population—have tended to set the civil-rights agenda in the United States. Important as the civil-rights battle is for all Americans, however, it does not adequately encompass the pressing needs and aspirations of the aboriginal peoples.

For more than a century the United States has been engaged in a protracted and painful transition from an era in which institutionalized slavery flourished—formally ending in the latter half of the nineteenth century—to one in which universal constitutional guarantees and protections prevail. Although this transition is central to the health and vitality of a liberal democracy, the key concerns of aboriginal peoples have been focused elsewhere. First and foremost, aboriginal peoples seek to have their treaty rights respected and their collectivity, or nation, recognized. It is in this quest for collective rights that the goals of aboriginal peoples go beyond those of racial minorities who are seeking individual rights and freedoms.

This chapter examines how the aboriginal peoples of the United States have sought to keep the integrity of their political agenda intact and separate from the dominant and often competing concerns of other racial and ethnic minorities. The unique claims and entitlements of the aboriginal peoples *vis-à-vis* the state flow from their historic relations with the latter. We begin by examining how the 'nation' concept with respect to aboriginal peoples has evolved over time in the United States, and review the judicial rulings in the nineteenth century that—for better or worse—set the precedents that have determined aboriginal legal status today. Next we consider the ways in which aboriginal peoples have acted as nations prior to the twentieth century, primarily in their efforts to resist foreign encroachment. The analysis proceeds in the third section by focusing upon assimilationist policies and their impact on tribal social organization. It was predicted that by the mid-twentieth century the aboriginal peoples—both collectively and individually—were doomed. How they were able not only to step back from the precipice but to move towards revitalization is the subject of the fourth section. Finally, the concluding section speculates upon the future status of the 'nations within'.

ABORIGINAL NATIONS: SOCIAL CONSTRUCTION

It is generally thought that, prior to European contact, the predominant mode of social organization in North America was the band or tribe, a unit smaller in size and less complex in organization than the 'nation' (Cornell, 1988). If this is the case, why are aboriginal peoples in North America today referred to as nations? By what processes was aboriginal life, and the way we speak about it, transformed? How accurate is the 'nation' designation, and what are its implications?

Aboriginal 'nations' emerged through the interaction of three major players—(a) the settler societies, (b) the imperial powers of Europe, and (c) the aboriginal peoples themselves—all with their own agendas. Furthermore, none of these players was a homogeneous, one-dimensional entity: quite the opposite. Indeed, the cultural diversity of aboriginal peoples far exceeded that of the Old World invaders—Dutch, Spanish, French, and British. Given the range of cultures represented among the inhabitants of the Old World and the New, it is not surprising that different viewpoints have produced contradictory accounts of historical events.

To describe the historical development of aboriginal nations and New World culture in any exhaustive or comprehensive sense is beyond the scope of this book. Rather, we will attempt to recount the highlights, acknowledging that the telling of any history suffers from biases of selection and interpretation. However, in order to understand fully the contemporary dynamics of issues such as Native sovereignty in relation to the larger society, it is essential to review the unfolding of our mutual history from the perspective of the Old World and New, bearing in mind that the view presented here is only one among many.

The term 'nation' will be used here in a metaphorical as well as a sociological or geopolitical sense. Also, in keeping with the accepted usage in social-science literature and historical record, 'tribe' and 'nation' will sometimes be employed interchangeably; as Sturtevant (1983: 9) observes, from '1797 through 1803 the treaties use only "nation" without reference to "tribes". Thereafter, until at least the 1830s, "tribe" and "nation" are used interchangeably, often in the same treaty.'

Over time consolidations did occur: some bands increased in size and complexity to become tribes; some tribes expanded their sociopolitical organization to become nations; and some nations united to form confederacies. One notable example of the latter was the Iroquois League based in northern New York State; originally comprising the Seneca, Oneida, Mohawk, Onondaga, and Cayuga nations, it was joined by the Tuscarora from the south in 1712. The overall trend, however, seems to have been towards proliferation of distinct tribal units rather than consolidation. For example, the Algonquian-speaking tribes—Ottawa, Potawatomi, and Chippewa (Oneida)—'once formed a single nation living north of the Great Lakes' (Josephy, 1976: 101). According to Witt (1965: 94), the 'proclivity to separate off into autonomous tribes was the distinctive feature of Indian political development'.

Figure 10.1 presents the two basic types of aboriginal organization prevailing prior to contact with Europeans; each of these types is broken down into three levels of complexity. The less complex Type I groups ranged from family-based units of fewer than 50 people to band-based villages. While they shared language, culture, and to some extent territory with neighbouring groups, and might join together for hunting or ceremonies, these were autonomous units, lacking integration at a higher or tribal level; they had no shared political identity until contact or later.

Type II social organizations, by contrast, were characterized not only by linguistic, cultural, territorial, and kinship ties, but also by the common identity and political organization that we associate with tribes and nations. Confederations at the highest level of organization included, in addition to the Iroquois League, the Natchez and Pueblos. The first supra-village organization among the latter is thought to have come into existence in 1680, with the objective of driving the Spanish from the southwest. Once that objective was achieved, however, 'the unity of the Pueblos quickly disappeared. No confederacy was formed with a central council. . . . In short the organization of the Pueblos had been for a single, quickly accomplished purpose. Once done the various villages returned to the old form of life' (Spicer, 1962: 163).

Figure 10.1 Aboriginal Social Organization Prior to Contact

Level of Social Organization (from less to more inclusive)	Aboriginal Groups (example)
TYPE I	
Family (less than 50)	Paiute
Clan-based villages	Potawatomi
Band	Comanche
TYPE II	
Tribe	Cheyenne
Nation	Cherokee
League (multi-tribe confederation)	Iroquois

SOURCE: Adapted from S. Cornell, *Return of the Native* (1988: 74–5).

Archaeological evidence indicates that Type I societies were the most common, Type II societies being the exception (Cornell, 1988). Kroeber (1955: 313) sums it up this way: 'our usual conventional concept of tribe . . . appears to be a White man's creation of convenience for talking about Indians, negotiating with them, administering them.' It was only as interaction continued between aboriginal peoples and European interlopers that the Type II organization became dominant. Thus tribes are largely the result of the colonization process and relations with politically organized states (Fried, 1975).

The 'Nation' Concept: Pre-Twentieth-Century Conceptions

Legal thinking dating from before the twentieth century has determined the contemporary status of the aboriginal nation in the United States. The following are central to our understanding of this body of knowledge: the 'doctrine of discovery'; the Royal Proclamation of 1763; the Northwest Territory Ordinance, 1789; and the 'domestic dependent nations' ruling. We will consider each one in turn.

The 'Doctrine of Discovery'
The very act of treaty-making is an acknowledgement of mutual nationhood; only sovereign bodies can make treaties with each other. For this reason historians tend to stress the significance of treaties as a solid indicator of nation status, and the study of aboriginal–European relations often dates from the signing of the first treaty. However, the main

treaty-signing era did not begin in earnest until the 1780s, after the formation of the American Republic. Before that time, as Price (1972: 11) points out, 'the British governments ignored any Indian rights to sovereignty or land. By right of discovery they claimed complete supremacy against both their European rivals and the aborigines.'

Vine Deloria, Jr, a prominent legal scholar of Sioux origin, and Clifford Lytle (1984: 2) explain this 'right of discovery' as follows: 'Christian princes discovering new lands had a recognized title to them, subject only to the willingness of the original inhabitants to sell their lands to the discoverer.' In other words, territory that had not been settled was seen as fair game for the first invading power with the intention of permanently settling or colonizing the land. The British did not recognize the aboriginal settlements as sufficient proof of occupation. From the outset, therefore, differing conceptions of land use, ownership of property, and sovereignty placed the aboriginal peoples and the European powers on a collision course that would continue fundamentally unaltered through the centuries. Aboriginal scholars stress the contemporary relevance of the 'discovery doctrine': 'Every legal doctrine today that separates . . . American Indians from other Americans traces its conceptual roots back to the Doctrine of Discovery and the subsequent moral and legal rights and responsibilities of the United States with respect to the Indians' (Deloria Jr, and Lytle, 1984: 2; see also Williams, 1990).

The 'discovery doctrine' received the equivalent of judicial ratification in 1823 with the first of three Supreme Court decisions by Chief Justice Marshall (see also p. 134 below) that were to have profound implications for the legal status of aboriginal people. In his Johnson v. McIntosh ruling, Marshall established that aboriginal people did not hold title to their land and thus could not sell it directly to settlers or land speculators. The implications of this ruling will be discussed in more detail in the final section of this chapter.

The Royal Proclamation of 1763

The British Royal Proclamation of 1763 has been called the Indian Magna Carta. It set boundaries to the power of the Crown and established Native sovereignty and land rights. The wording of the Proclamation was in keeping with the philosophy of the 'doctrine of discovery':

> Whereas it is just and reasonable . . . that the several Nations or Tribes of Indians with whom We are connected . . . should not be molested or disturbed in the Possession of such Parts of Our Dominions and Territories as . . . are reserved to them . . . as their Hunting Grounds. . . . We do hereby strictly forbid . . . all our loving Subjects from making any Purchases or Settlements whatever, or taking Possession of any of the Lands above reserved (cited in Miller, 1989: 71-2).

Figure 10.2 Eastern North America after the Royal Proclamation of 1763

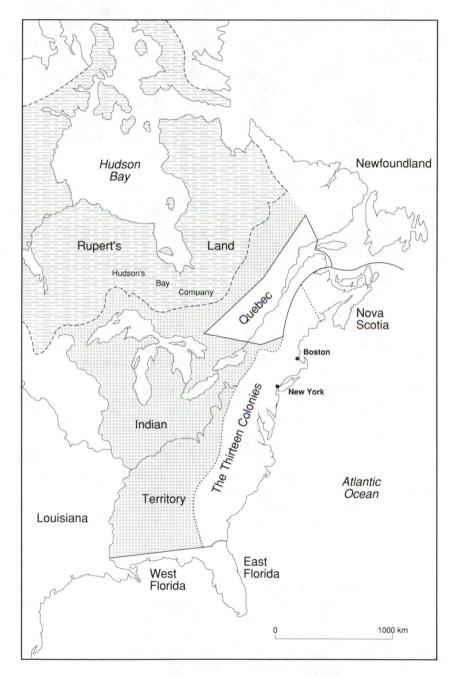

SOURCE: Adapted from J. R. Miller, *Skyscrapers Hide the Heavens*, p.72.

The Proclamation was vehemently opposed by the land-hungry colonists. With the 1763 Treaty of Paris that ended the French and Indian War (Seven Years War), France ceded its land east of the Mississippi River to the British. The colonists anticipated that this land would soon be 'opened' for settlement (Figure 10.2), but their expectations were not fulfilled. Contrary to the colonists' wishes, the British prohibited settlement on the lands west of the thirteen colonies, beyond the Allegheny Mountains, and withdrew the power of purchasing Indian lands from the colonial governments (Price, 1972: 13). Intended to curb the excesses of greed and rampant exploitation on the part of the colonists, this new British land policy would prove to be one of the key frustrations that, along with the issue of taxation without representation, led to the 1776 American War of Independence.

The Northwest Territory Ordinance, 1789
The decades following the American Revolutionary War are generally known as the treaty-making period, 1789-1871 (Price, 1972: 15). The new Republic embarked on this flurry of treaty-making for a number of reasons. Foremost among them, however, was the constant resistance to expansion that took the form of border disputes. In short, it was hoped that peace treaties would in fact bring peace. The Northwest Territory Ordinance of 1789 adopted the provisions of the English Royal Proclamation of 1763 as the policy of the United States of America (Steiner, 1968: 319). This document was lofty in its rhetoric:

> The utmost good faith shall always be observed toward the Indians, their lands and property shall never be taken from them without their consent . . . laws founded in justice and humanity shall from time to time be made, for preventing wrongs done to them and for preserving peace and friendship with them (cited in McNickle, 1973: 51).

Nevertheless, the Northwest Ordinance proved to be no more effective in protecting aboriginal land than the Royal Proclamation had been. The treaty-making period is viewed by Cornell (1988: 41-2) as simply a return to the philosophy of the 'discovery doctrine'. When Congress ended the treaty-making period in 1871, the era of government-to-government negotiation with aboriginal peoples ended as well.

The 'Domestic Dependent Nations' Ruling, 1831
By 1830 the Cherokees facing removal from their traditional lands in the southeast were attempting to assert their sovereignty as a nation above the authority of the state of Georgia, which was pressing for their relocation. In the Cherokee Nation v. Georgia case of 1831, the same Chief Justice Marshall who had earlier delivered the Johnson v. McIntosh decision articulated the 'domestic dependent nations' thesis, which

flowed from the same assumptions underlying the three documents discussed above. The Marshall decisions upheld the principle of tribes as distinct political entities whose inherent self-governing rights are largely unaffected by treaty or trading acts, and derive from original occupancy (Royal Commission, 1992). Marshall concluded that 'a weak state, in order to provide for its safety, may place itself under the protection of one more powerful, without stripping itself of the right of government, and ceasing to be a state' (cited in Deloria, Jr, and Lytle, 1984: 17).

In the following year, another Marshall decision (Worcester v. Georgia, 1832) further strengthened the notion of Cherokee sovereignty by ruling that Georgia did not have the legislative authority to supersede Cherokee law. (Worcester was a missionary who deliberately violated Georgia law in order to test the relative strength of Cherokee law in a bid to help the Cherokees legally retain what was theirs; see also p. 140 below.) In the next section we will examine selected examples of resistance movements mounted successfully by the aboriginal nations prior to the twentieth century.

ABORIGINAL NATIONAL RESISTANCE PRIOR TO THE TWENTIETH CENTURY

In attempting to make distinctions between historical periods in the broad sweep of aboriginal–European relations, we have called the initial era, from 1600 to the 1763 Royal Proclamation, the contact period. As outlined in Figure 10.3, conflict was by and large a post-colonial phenomenon. But this is not to suggest that conflict was not present in the early period. For example, a full century before the War of Independence, in 1675-76, the Wampanoag Indian King Philip formed an alliance among various New England tribes in an abortive attempt to contain the colonists (Josephy, 1976: 35). And, as noted above, in the southwest the Pueblos successfully united to drive out the Spanish in 1680. Thus collective resistance did occur in this early contact period, although in comparison with the later period such conflict was relatively rare.

The fur trade was at its pinnacle in the early years of contact, and this factor alone accounts in large measure for the relative absence of conflict between the Europeans and the Native North Americans. Among aboriginal peoples themselves, however, there was competition, and conflict—often leading to inter-tribal warfare—was common. For instance, it is thought that the Huron were annihilated by the Iroquois in 1648-49 in a dispute sparked by the desire to exert control over the fur trade, which inflamed old enmities (Cornell, 1988: 23).

The commerce in pelts was profitable to both parties. The trade goods (e.g., tools, weapons, cooking utensils) that the aboriginal people

Figure 10.3
Key Events and their Impact on Aboriginal Nations (1600–present)

Period	Geographical Area	Event	Effect
contact 1600–1763	southwest; east coast to Great Lakes and Allegheny Mountains	Spanish exploration; British and French settlement; fur trade; King Philip's War; Peace of Paris; Royal Proclamation;	Pueblos revolt; military alliances are formed; Indian as 'broker'; economies are enhanced; aboriginal groups that survive are strengthened
conflict 1763–1819	east coast to Mississippi River	Treaty of Paris; Start of treaty-making period between Americans and Indians (1789–1871);	treaties are violated by Americans, but recognize aboriginal peoples as 'nations'; forced expropriation of land
		Northwest Ordinance; Louisiana Purchase; War of 1812; First Seminole War; Spain cedes Florida	
assimilation 1819–1934	west of Mississippi River	Trail of Tears; California Gold Rush; Wounded Knee; Allotment Act;	Indian genocide through forced relocation and massacres; reservation land given to non-Indians;
		Oklahoma statehood;	Indian state of Sequoyah becomes 'lost cause';
		Indian citizenship;	detribalization
limited autonomy 1935–present	US mainland plus Alaska	Indian Reorganization Act (IRA); termination leads to urban migration;	'tribes' are reconstituted; opposition to termination develops; pan-Indian movements form;
		limited attempts at developing reserve economies; self-determination becomes the 'official' federal policy	Indians are co-opted into federal agencies; 'radicalism' is repressed by the federal government

received greatly improved their standard of living, while fur such as beaver was a valuable commodity on the European market. This period of contact has been called the Golden Age. 'While the trade flourished, both Indian and European—with some important exceptions—flourished as well' (Cornell, 1988: 19). It was only when the fur trade in the United States waned, at the end of the eighteenth century (much earlier than in Canada), and agricultural interests replaced it that would-be farmers and ranchers came into serious conflict with Native people over land.

The Royal Proclamation of 1763 represented an attempt to regulate relations between indigenous inhabitants and invaders, but it was in effect for only twenty years and was often grossly violated. After the Treaty of Paris in 1783, the newly formed American Republic was no longer bound by the Royal Proclamation's land policy. The conflict between the aboriginal peoples and the European intruders increased quite radically with the founding of the American Republic. The victory of the Americans was viewed with disfavour by most Indian nations— if not immediately, at least within a few years of the British defeat. For example, the Oneida nation, a member of the Iroquois Confederacy, attempted to remain neutral, but eventually fled to Canada to join the other Iroquois peoples who had been granted land there by Britain in recognition of their assistance during the American Revolutionary War.

Prior to 1783, the aboriginal nations tended to ally themselves with either the French or the British as overseas powers, but not with the soon-to-be-independent colonists (Patterson, 1972). In the case of the French there was no fear of land theft, for it was the French pattern to build trading posts along water routes rather than to establish agricultural settlements. And while the British did have agricultural interests, they at least took some (admittedly ineffective) steps such as the Royal Proclamation to safeguard aboriginal rights. With the new Americans, by contrast, there would be no such restraints. On the contrary, American legislation and treaties in the next decades would be designed to strip the Indians of their more valuable lands, leaving them only worthless acreage of no agricultural or settlement value.

At the formation of the first American congress in 1789, 'Indian affairs' were put under the direction of the War Department, and soldiers who had fought in the war were paid handsomely with land west of the Alleghenies (Price, 1972: 15). In short, Indian land was available for what we today call 'development'. A new expansionist phase had begun and, with the expansion, an escalation in conflict.

Military Alliances and Diplomacy

While in some cases aboriginal nations took direct action against the Europeans (e.g., King Philip's War), in others they formed military alliances with the imperial powers from the beginning, attempting to play one off against the other to their own benefit. England's success among the Iroquois, for instance, resulted in part from the price advantage of English manufactured goods at Fort Orange (Albany) over French goods at Montreal. Native peoples were also key players both in the War of Independence and in the War of 1812, in each case siding with the British. Analysts stress that aboriginal peoples were not exploited as pawns by the Europeans, but were sought after and valued as allies (Cornell, 1988: 17). Consistently the aboriginal peoples saw the imperial power—whether French or English—as more likely to protect their interests than the settlers or their New World governments. This perception accounted for the strategy behind aboriginal collective resistance.

Not only did the aboriginal nations engage in direct combat against some European nations and form alliances with others, but they also engaged in diplomatic efforts to resolve disputes. To illustrate this diplomatic form of resistance, we will focus on the concerted attempts of the aboriginal statesmen Pontiac and Tecumseh to secure their lands in the Ohio Valley and southern Great Lakes area.

Pontiac (1720-69)
Pontiac, an Ottawa chief, was a master strategist who between 1763 and 1765 successfully united eighteen aboriginal tribes from Lake Ontario to the Mississippi River to resist British encroachment in 'Indian country' (see Figure 10.2 above). Trading furs at Fort Detroit, the Ottawas had been dismayed to see the British flag raised over the Fort in 1760. Pontiac thought that since the French were still in the Louisiana territory west of the Mississippi, they could, even after the fall of Quebec, be encouraged to come up the Mississippi and retake Detroit. With this objective in mind, Pontiac laid siege to Fort Detroit. But his efforts were to no avail. The French refused to support his daring military adventure, and when he finally realized the folly of this plan, he negotiated peace with the British in 1765. It is reported that he dictated the following to the British commanding officer: 'The word which my father [the French] has sent me to make peace I have accepted; all my young men have buried their hatchets. I think you will forget the bad things which have taken place for some time past. Likewise I will forget what you have done to me. . . .' (cited in Josephy, 1976: 125). Because Pontiac was instrumental in bringing peace, he was resented by some of his own people and was killed by a Peoria Indian near St Louis in 1769—six years after the signing of the Royal Proclamation of 1763.

Tecumseh (1768-1813)
Born in the Ohio Valley one year before Pontiac's death, Tecumseh,

a Shawnee, had the same goals: containment of the settlers and establishment of an Indian homeland. Under the Royal Proclamation of 1763, the Indiana territory had been protected as 'Indian country', but by the early nineteenth century American settlers were encroaching on it. Thus, just as Pontiac had allied himself with the French against the British colonists in the years leading up to the American Revolution, so Tecumseh joined with the British against what were now the Americans in the years prior to the War of 1812.

In 1804 the Louisiana Purchase was enacted, ending French influence in North America and expanding the territorial sovereignty of the United States to lands west of the Mississippi River. Two years later, the explorations of Lewis and Clark in the American northwest signalled that a new frontier was 'opened' to settlers. Now the moving frontier had shifted from the east to the west, and Indian leaders like Tecumseh were anxious about the future.

Coming a generation after Pontiac, Tecumseh felt an even greater sense of urgency: this would be the last chance to protect aboriginal land from encroachment and establish an 'Indian state'. His strategy was twofold. On the one hand, he endeavoured to prevent the sale of land, and on the other, he attempted to ignite a pan-Indian consciousness, using as his example the powerful union that the United States had achieved in their battle for independence. In articulating the belief that land belonged to all in common, and that no one chief had the right to sell, Tecumseh tried to counteract the piecemeal alienation of land that was becoming rampant, especially as individual chiefs attempted to undercut one another in order to make deals.

A colourful and effective orator who travelled widely in his efforts to win converts to his position, he was also a successful military leader who, with British General Brock, managed to retake Detroit, only to lose it later when General Proctor replaced Brock. By the time of his death on the battlefield in 1814, he had achieved the 'greatest military alliance in native history' (Josephy, 1976: 153), extending from Lake Superior to the Gulf of Mexico. His dream of an 'Indian state,' however, proved elusive.

Of the Native leaders who arose in the next generation, none had the national vision of Pontiac and Tecumseh. The aboriginal peoples east of the Mississippi were fragmented and demoralized; west of the river, massive population transfers from the east and the establishment of reservations loomed tragically on the horizon.

Cherokee Court Challenges

With the defeat of Tecumseh, the lands east of the Mississippi and north to the Great Lakes were open to settlement, but territory to the south was still disputed. A first war with the Seminoles was fought in 1817, two years before Spain ceded Florida to the United States. To secure 'law and order' along this southeastern frontier, a plan was devised to remove—forcibly, if necessary—the Cherokee, Creek, Chickasaw, Choctaw, and Seminole peoples of the Creek Confederacy and relocate them on land west of the Mississippi acquired by the 1804 Louisiana Purchase:

> Under the Removal Bill, which President Jackson signed . . . on May 28, 1830, the southern Indians were offered the privilege of exchanging their ancestral homelands . . . for territory west of the Mississippi River in . . . present-day Oklahoma, but they were given no alternative other than death to escape the forced exile (Josephy, 1976: 179).

Also referred to as the Five Civilized Tribes, the members of Creek Confederacy were labelled 'civilized' inasmuch as they governed themselves in a manner understandable and acceptable to Europeans; they were agriculturists, and they were literate. A Cherokee newspaper, the *Cherokee Phoenix*, was first published in 1828 in Georgia, and the Seminoles imitated Europeans by holding African slaves. Florida under the Spanish was a haven for runaway slaves whom the Seminoles both protected and exploited; intermarriage between the two groups was common (Bennett, Jr, 1966: 269; Wright, 1986: 80). Black people were well integrated into the social and economic life of the Creeks and Seminoles. Their knowledge of agriculture was valuable to their new masters, and those who knew English or Spanish acted as interpreters—a role that often expanded to that of counsellor or political adviser. Nevertheless, while not all Blacks were slaves, they 'bore the brunt of racial discrimination in the Southeast at the hands of both whites and Indians' (Wright, 1986: 78).

Further evidence of the Cherokees' European style 'civilization' was their use of the courts in an attempt to oppose the removal legislation. But the Marshall decisions in Cherokee Nation v. Georgia and Worcester v. Georgia, addressing the question of Cherokee sovereignty and the limits of the legislative authority of a state, proved Pyrrhic victories, for President Jackson ignored these rulings and allowed the Cherokees to be forcibly removed from Georgia.

The Cherokee 'Trail of Tears' in 1838 was 'one of the greater official acts of inhumanity and cruelty in American history' (Limerick, 1987: 194). As Price (1972: 16) recounts the events, 'The Americans dragged [Cherokees] from their homes . . . ; drove them to concentration camps at the point of a bayonet, and abandoned their dwellings and possessions to white plunderers and thieves.' Price estimates that of the 12,000 Cherokees who commenced the forced march to Oklahoma along the Trail of Tears, only 8,000 survived. More recently, scholars like Thornton (1984) have put the death toll closer to 8,000.

The Ghost Dance

Messianic religious movements, in a general sense, have been observed prior to the development of full-blown nationalistic ones. Worsley (1967: 227) noted that such movements may tend to arise in societies that have no overall unity or government. Rather than acting collec-tively to resist invaders or oppressors, people may tend to rally around a charismatic religious figure. Such was the case on the Great Plains. The Ghost Dance messianic movement, marking the transition from sporadic military resistance to pacification, 'arose under conditions of society-threatening stress' (Cornell, 1988: 64).

While variations of the Ghost Dance were found in various dislo-cated tribes, principally in the west, the ritual is thought to have orig-inated with a Paiute named Wovoka in Nevada in 1889. It was performed by men and women dancing to exhaustion in a circle with hands clasped, chanting to the music of voice or drum (Spicer, 1962: 528). According to Mooney (1965: 777), 'The great underlying princi-ple of the Ghost Dance is that the time will come when the whole Indian race, living and dead, will be reunited upon a regenerated earth, to live a life of aboriginal happiness forever free from death, disease and misery.' It prophesied a distinctive aboriginal renaissance and 'fostered intertribal linkages and brought diverse groups into common frameworks of action and belief' (Cornell, 1988: 110). Specif-ically, followers of the cult believed the new dawn would be ushered in when 'dirt would fall from the sky and bury the white man and his railroads and mines. . . . Jesus . . . would return as an Indian' (Burnette and Koster, 1974: 148).

The messianic vision was not a new phenomenon for Native peoples. Messianic (or millenarian: the terms are used interchangeably) religion had played a supporting role in helping to unite various tribes behind Pontiac and Tecumseh; in fact, Tecumseh's brother was called the Shawnee Prophet. What was new about the millenarian religion sweeping the Prairies was its stoic resignation coupled with rejection of any intertribal military effort akin to the united resistance launched by Pontiac and Tecumseh. The Ghost Dance relied upon supernatural, not military action: 'Wovoka told his followers explicitly to abstain from violence and to wait for the Second Coming' (Burnette and Koster, 1974: 148). Although it was potentially a unifying force, it did not take hold among all groups. In the case of the Navajo, for instance, the imagery was not compatible with their cosmology, in which the dead were to be feared.

Over the years, the Ghost Dance has become most closely associated with the Sioux. Perhaps the most hostile to whites, the Sioux version prophesied the annihilation of non-Natives and the return of the buffalo on which Great Plains cultures depended. Ultimately, the panic the Ghost Dance caused among the settlers led army troops to suppress the new religion at the 1890 massacre of the Sioux at Wounded Knee (Burnette and Koster, 1974: 148). Looking back at the Ghost Dance phenomenon and attempting to interpret it within its historical context, Cornell (1988: 67) observes that 'resistance had moved from the political arena . . . to the ideological: long after the war had retired from the field, the battle continued on the terrain of ideas, identity and interpretation.'

The end of the nineteenth century was truly the end of an era. As the period of the moving frontier drew to a close, the aboriginal peoples' attempts at self-determination collapsed as well. Suffering from disease, their ranks decimated, their land alienated, the survivors were corralled on barren reservations often far removed from their original hunting grounds.

By the beginning of the twentieth century, the Native peoples were reduced to dependent wards of the government and subjected to federal government policies of assimilation and acculturation aimed at detribalization, or the 'systematic destruction of tribal organization' (Cornell, 1988: 56). How this process was set in motion, its devastating effect on the social organization of the aboriginal peoples, and the subsequent attempts to stop its momentum and eventually reverse its direction will be considered in the following section.

DETRIBALIZATION:
THE DESTRUCTION OF ABORIGINAL NATIONS

By the end of the nineteenth century, the Indian population had been reduced to fewer than 250,000 (Marger, 1991: 161) from the 850,000 estimated to have lived in the United States at the time of the first contact with Europeans in the fifteenth century (Price, 1972: 6). Disease, alcohol, forced relocation, neglect, and armed resistance had taken their toll, as had the practice of intermarriage. (According to the Swedish sociologist Gunnar Myrdal, some of the smaller Native groups in the southeast intermarried with runaway African slaves to the point of becoming 'untraceably lost' in the Black population [Bennett, Jr, 1966: 268].)

Inasmuch as a frontier existed, it was now in the west. Gold had been discovered in California in 1848. In Limerick's opinion (1987: 257) the ensuing rush of white prospectors was 'even more devastating to the population than the Spanish missions had been'. Enslavement of non-Christian Indians had been permitted under Spanish law (Spicer, 1962: 28), and Indians had been slaves on Mexican *rancheros*. With the discovery of gold, however, there was 'slave raiding among the yet unsubdued tribes in the interior and targeting Indian women and children as potential servants' (Limerick, 1987: 257).

Apart from those enslaved, thousands of aboriginal people lost their lives and lands in the flood of white prospectors; in California, for instance, Indians were hunted down and murdered (Horsman, 1981: 278). The racism that condoned such behaviour was rife in the 1850s. The generally accepted view that Indians were an 'inferior race', and that their extinction was inevitable, was clearly stated by California Governor Peter H. Burnett in 1851:

> That a war of extermination will continue to be waged between the two races until the Indian race becomes extinct, must be expected; while we cannot anticipate this result but with painful regret, the inevitable destiny of the race is beyond the power and wisdom of man to avert (cited in Horsman, 1981: 279).

It is estimated that the aboriginal population in California fell from 100,000 to 35,000 in the decade following the discovery of gold, 1849-60 (Price, 1972: 19). By 1906 it had dropped to less than 20,000 (Heizer et al., 1971).

Observers of the 'Indian problem' thought the crisis to be ultimately self-limiting, as the projections showed many tribes, especially the smaller ones, becoming extinct. By the beginning of the twentieth century, Native morale and will to live were at an all-time low (Witt, 1965: 98). Increasingly, the American public thought the Indians a 'vanishing race'; 'if this occasioned regret,' according to McNickle (1973: 3), 'it was no more deeply felt than that expressed for the extermination of the passenger pigeon and the buffalo. Such losses were accepted as part of the cost of taming a wilderness world.'

With the settlement of California, the European robbery of aboriginal land was complete. Americans began to realize that their policy of 'manifest destiny' had had dire consequences for the aboriginal peoples. In this regard, it is Horsman's opinion (1981: 207) that 'Americans transferred their own failure [to create an enlightened policy] to the Indians and condemned the Indians racially. By 1850 only a minority of Americans believed that transformed Indians would eventually assume a permanent, equal place within American society.'

The Dawes Act (General Allotment Act), 1887

The mid-nineteenth century had seen the emergence of a humanitarian movement preoccupied with abolishing slavery. After gaining a successful resolution to the Civil War, however, this movement turned its attention to the plight of Native people. The Dawes Act (or General Allotment Act), supported by do-gooders of the social-gospel bent, was a well-intentioned, liberal piece of legislation designed to uplift the Natives by giving them individual property rights. According to the ethnocentric thinking of the day, the impoverishment of the aboriginal people could be traced to their communal (tribal) social organization; they would not be able to progress as individuals as long as they were weighed down by the millstone of tribal status. Furthermore, individual title to their lands would free them to develop and prosper in the manner of other Americans.

It is truly ironic that the liberal reforms envisioned by Senator Dawes, in effect for less than fifty years, wreaked more havoc on traditional Indian social organization than all that had transpired in the previous two centuries. A classic example of assimilationist policy, the Dawes Act was the first piece of legislation explicitly intended to destroy indigenous social organization. By removing social structural supports, it denied the tribe any firm foundation on which to build. Providing for the allotment of 160-acre parcels of reservation lands to heads of households, the Act stipulated that lands 'surplus to the allotment requirement would be put up for sale to White settlers' (Cornell, 1988: 42). In this way 2.75 million hectares—more than 60 per cent of the remaining Indian land base—passed into non-Indian hands between 1887 and 1934 (Cornell, 1988: 44). It is apparent from these data that the Dawes Act was of interest to more than the reform element in society: it also benefitted white land speculators and commercial interests. Its passage can be attributed to a political marriage between the reform interests of the east, seeking social justice, and the land developers of the west, craving new terrain. The marriage proved satisfying only to the latter.

The Dawes Act is significant both for the amount of land it made available to non-Indians and for its weakening of tribal social organization. In fact, however, the erosion of the aboriginal peoples' status as 'nations' had already begun in 1871, when Congress declared that 'hereafter no Indian nation or tribe . . . shall be recognized as an independent nation, tribe, or power with whom the United States may contract by treaty' (cited in Cornell, 1988: 49). Henceforth the Indians were wards of the federal government; they were no longer seen or dealt with as separate nations. Any power that they might exercise as wards would be delegated—not inherent (Deloria, Jr, and Lytle, 1984: 203). Inherent powers accrue to sovereign states by virtue of their sovereignty; delegated powers may be removed at Congressional whim. This fundamental shift in the power relationship between Washington and the aboriginal nations moved the latter from a position of relative power to one of complete powerlessness. The Dawes Act, enacted sixteen years later, was simply the final nail in the coffin.

It was between the 1871 institution of aboriginal wardship and the 1887 Dawes Act that the reserve system was set in place. At the core of the reserve policy was the Bureau of Indian Affairs (BIA), the agency responsible for implementing and enforcing Congressional Indian legislation. It was thought that the Indians could best be assimilated by segregating them on reserves and subjecting them to a strict period of tutelage in American ways. But the corruption of the Indian agents and the under-funding of the health, economic, and social programs doomed the reserve policy to failure. Indeed, this was apparent by 1887, when it was hoped that the Dawes Act would remedy past mistakes. Instead, the Act compounded them. According to Witt (1965: 99): 'The Act produced internal tribal schisms unlike any previous governmental deed. Detribalization was concomitant with personal demoralization and disintegration. Inter-tribal communication was slight. The struggle for continued existence inhibited political development.'

The Indian Territory of Oklahoma

The political activities in the Indian Territory before it became the state of Oklahoma in 1907 constituted the one significant exception to Witt's observation concerning the absence of intertribal communication during the period of the allotment policy. Such communication did occur among the Five Civilized Tribes (a sizeable component of the general relocated aboriginal population), who preserved the self-governing structures in place before their forced relocation; in fact, this was a guarantee they secured before their removal. Thus, as Deloria, Jr, and Lytle (1984: 23) point out, 'Self-government was not "given" to these Indians; they preserved their own version of self-government though innovation.'

The acid test of American good will and the ability of the Cherokee, Creek, Choctaw, Chicasaw, and Seminole to communicate in an innovative way both within their own ranks and with the federal government came at the time of negotiations concerning the entry of the Indian Territory into the Union. The Five Civilized Tribes argued that the Indian Territory should enter the Union as an Indian state, which they proposed to call Sequoyah, after the revered Cherokee leader. Their proposal gained indirect support through the 1892 Talton case.

The Talton case is significant because it reinforced the Cherokees' right to self-government as an inherent power. Talton, a Cherokee, had killed two other Cherokees. What was in question was not the killing itself, but whether the powers the Cherokee exercised were delegated or inherent. When the Supreme Court ruled that 'the crime of murder is . . . not an offense against the United States, but an offense against the local laws of the Cherokee nation' (cited in Deloria, Jr, and Lytle, 1984: 202), it bolstered the legitimacy of the Cherokees in their bid for the establishment of the State of Sequoyah.

The decision in the Talton case was markedly at odds with previous judgements regarding other tribes. For example, the Sioux Crow Dog murder case in 1882—a decade before Talton—had led Congress to pass the Seven Major Crimes Act, which removed major criminal jurisdiction from aboriginal peoples in such crimes as murder (Deloria, Jr, and Lytle, 1984: 4). While this self-governing status meant that the Five Civilized Tribes were exempt from the provisions of this Act, it was not known until the Talton case exactly how the exemption would be interpreted in terms of sovereignty issues. However, the victory for the principle of Native self-government was short-lived, for 'within a decade of the Talton decision, there were no tribal courts functioning with the exception of the Iroquois . . . and the practices of the Pueblos' (Deloria, Jr, and Lytle, 1984: 204).

This fragile experiment with self-government within the framework of 'dependent nation status' came to an abrupt halt in 1907, when Oklahoma joined the Union as a non-Indian state. Consequently, all tribes in Oklahoma were subject to the Dawes Act and allotment proceeded, against their will, at such a pace that by the 1960s tribal land in the state consisted of only 23,744 hectares, as compared with 663,636 hectares of allotted land (Steiner, 1968: 326). More to the point, it resulted in the loss of 5.26 million hectares and produced 72,000 landless Indians (Philp, 1977: 151).

Most analysts believe that the greatest stumbling block the Five Civilized Tribes encountered in their campaign to have Sequoyah admitted as a state was their absolute commitment to communal or tribal property. They could not negotiate this point, for to do so would run counter to their sense of peoplehood. 'Congress rejected the Indian efforts to create a suitable constitution for the Indian Territory because no provision was made for the allotment of tribal lands following admission to the Union' (Deloria, Jr, and Lytle, 1984: 24). Indeed, even without the Dawes Act it is doubtful that Washington and the Five Civilized Tribes could have reached an agreement. As it was, the Dawes Act ended the Sequoyah State dream and systematically demolished the aboriginal people's last hopes to protect their land and culture from encroachment.

The Federal Bureau of Indian Affairs (BIA)

When, in 1849, the BIA was transferred from the War Department to the Department of the Interior—an appropriate move, as the period of armed conflict had ended—the next major phase in aboriginal–white relations, acculturation (or detribalization), began. The process of detribalization was to be managed by the BIA in the context of the reserve system. By the end of the century its success was evident; the reserve system had effectively destroyed the cultural, social, economic, and political systems of the aboriginal peoples. The BIA had the mandate to fill this vacuum—to acculturate and govern the Native people. The scope of such a mandate is overwhelming, even if sensitivity and intelligence could be brought to the domination of one culture by another. The result in this case was a continuation of the greed, incompetence, and exploitation that had already come to characterize the behaviour of the larger American society towards the aboriginal people. Corruption was rife in the ranks of the BIA agents, especially before bureau employees obtained Civil Service status in 1894 (Josephy, 1971: 345; Deloria, Jr, and Lytle, 1984: 32), and even the better-intentioned agents shared the enthnocentric assumptions of the era.

At this juncture in history—the decades following the Civil War—the US was not noted for its generosity to minority peoples. The Jim Crow code segregating the Black community was in full force, and lynchings in the American south were commonplace. Nor were Blacks the only minority subjected to brutally inhumane treatment; the Ku Klux Klan was in its heyday, directing its venom against Jews, Catholics, and 'foreigners' as well. The Indians were one group in this larger racist landscape.

The BIA had two major functions. In addition to its role as paternalistic care-taker, filling the void created by the destruction of Native social structures, the BIA considered itself bound to suppress any 'anti-social' behaviour that might inhibit the success of acculturation programs. Cultural activities such as feasts and dances, as well as various religious practices, were defined as 'Indian offenses' by the commissioner of Indian Affairs in 1883: 'Courts of Indian Offenses, composed of Indians appointed by the agents, were set up to enforce these rules . . . replacing . . . traditional forms of dispute resolution' (Cornell, 1988: 57).

Very early on, attempts were made to ridicule and prohibit traditional religious expressions such as the Ghost Dance and the peyote rites that feature in the services of the Native American church found in the southwest. Full religious freedom did not apply to the aboriginal peoples until the mid-1930s; citizenship was not extended to all Indians until 1924, even though many had fought for their country in the First World War; and an Indian Civil Rights Act was not passed until 1968 (Deloria, Jr, and Lytle, 1984: 210).

It is clear from this recital of events that the Native Americans were second-class citizens until well into the twentieth century. The BIA gained momentum over the decades, implementing policies of acculturation and assimilation. If the aboriginal people were to make any progress towards recovery of their former status, either they would have to throw off the yoke of the BIA—an impossible task, given the bureau's monopoly power—or the BIA would have to be reformed. The first serious efforts at reform from within the structure of the BIA occurred in 1933, when John Collier was appointed the Commissioner of Indian Affairs in the New Deal administration of President F.D. Roosevelt.

The Indian Reorganization Act (IRA), 1934

The Indian Reorganization Act marked a turning-point in federal–Indian relations, not only for what it strictly accomplished, but also for the legal groundwork it put in place, upon which later aboriginal generations would build.

The IRA (also known as the Howard Wheeler Act), was an outgrowth of the 1928 Merriam Report. Based on the first systematic survey of reservation conditions, this report recommended substantial reforms in health, education, and welfare; these were never acted upon, as the US was in the midst of the economic chaos of the Great Depression and the political will for implementation was weak. In addition, however, the report harshly criticized the General Allotment Act: 'the government assumed that some magic in individual ownership of property would in itself prove an educational civilizing factor, but unfortunately this policy has for the most part operated in the opposite direction' (Merriam, 1928: 3).

Collier, the new commissioner, had some sympathy for the plight of the Indians before his appointment, and thought their salvation rested in self-government. He was not advocating the dissolution of the BIA, but a new role for it. In his view, the unit of community organization should be the band or the tribe, and the BIA should encourage the Indians to draw up their own constitutions under its guidelines. His philosophy of reform took final shape as the IRA.

Collier did not consult with the aboriginal peoples prior to passage of the legislation (Deloria, Jr, and Lytle, 1984: 102), and their reactions to it were mixed. The more assimilated Indians saw no need for the IRA. Those who owned the title to their land thought it was a trick to take it away and return land to tribal holdings. For the most part, though, Collier found support for the IRA, if for no other reason than that the majority of Indians could only stand to profit from change. Collier's IRA and other programs became known as 'the Indian New Deal' (Kelly, 1983).

In evaluating this Act, two considerations come to mind. First, even though advocating self-government, the IRA was still an instrument of assimilation. The version of self-government that it deemed acceptable was dictated to the Native Americans and superimposed on any vestiges of traditional decision-making that might remain. The objective of so-called self-government was the ultimate incorporation of Native Americans into the social structures of the larger society. As defined by the BIA, aboriginal self-government was simply a means to achieve assimilationist ends.

Second, under the IRA the basis of organization was not the traditional aboriginal unit, but the reserve. Anomalous situations had developed in which more than one group of aboriginal people were living on the same reserve. With the reserve as the unit, new 'tribes' were formed. These newly created tribes bore no necessary relation to the social organizations of pre-contact times. Between 1935 and 1945, 93 tribal governments were established under the IRA, of which only 31 could be classified as tribes by the usual cultural criteria (Taylor, 1980: 68). Rather than strengthening aboriginal political and cultural structures, it made a mockery of them, further eroding their integrity. Thus while the IRA may have advanced reserve self-government, as was its intent, it did not further aboriginal self-determination or nationalistic revival.

Yet nationalistic revival did occur in the following decades. If the origins of the revival cannot be traced to the IRA, what policies or social forces were responsible? The following section will examine the rebirth of aboriginal nations.

THE REBIRTH OF ABORIGINAL NATIONS

The government-to-government negotiations that characterized the treaty-making era ended in 1871, when the aboriginal peoples became wards of the state. In addition to losing any semblance of political self-determination, they twice suffered the brutal alienation of their land— once when they were herded onto reservations, often far from their true homelands, and once again when the 1877 allotment policy reduced their reserve holdings. At the same time, the BIA's policy of assimilation prohibited aboriginal religious expression and supported English-language residential schools for the young, systematically eroding traditional cultures. Even the IRA of the Roosevelt era, promising a 'New Deal for Indians', was fundamentally a sham, for although it trumpeted self-government and encouraged tribes to write their own constitutions, these constitutions had to follow a format dictated by the BIA. Equally absurd from an aboriginal perspective was the equation of the reserve with the tribal unit, since any one reserve might contain Natives from a variety of groups.

Given the very bleak picture of Native American life in the first half of the twentieth century, few would have predicted the reversal of fortune that has occurred in recent decades. The forces of assimilation that had been set in motion appeared irreversible. Even the extension of the franchise and full citizenship rights to aboriginal peoples in 1924 was an assimilatory gesture that further eroded the special legal status implicit in their treaties with the federal government.

How can we explain the rebirth of aboriginal nations? At what point did aboriginal peoples regain their footing and begin to organize on their own behalf? While no one event or leader can be singled out as the cause of this turn-about, a series of dramatic political initiatives, especially in the late 1960s and early 1970s, had a significant impact on federal–aboriginal relations. These political initiatives had their origins in Operation Relocation.

Operation Relocation (1952)

Operation Relocation was one of many federal policies in the 1950s that stemmed from a 'terminationist' philosophy. Usually members of the Republican Party in the US Congress, the terminationists represented a reaction against the massive spending policies of the former Democratic administration's New Deal policies, including the IRA. Critical of the BIA's costly efforts to strengthen reserve economies and expand critical services in health and welfare, these conservatives wanted to terminate the special relationship, based on the treaties, that aboriginal peoples had with the federal government. Termination was to take place on a tribe-by-tribe basis since some tribes were better prepared for cutting all ties to the BIA than others. Ultimately, however, all tribes would be terminated; the BIA would be defunct, and the US government would be out of the 'Indian business'. To this end, the House passed Concurrent Resolution 108 in 1953:

> it is the policy of Congress, to make the individuals within . . . the United States subject to the same laws and entitled to the same privileges and responsibilities, to end their status as wards of the United States, and to grant them all the rights and prerogatives pertaining to American citizenship (cited in Limerick, 1987: 209).

Relocation was one aspect of termination. The goal was to move Native Americans from the reserves, which were not capable of sustaining them economically, to urban areas where—in theory—they could join the workforce and live like ordinary Americans. First articulated in 1952, Operation Relocation supported the commonly held thesis that poverty on the reserves stemmed from 'surplus population' (Burt, 1982: 7). From this diagnosis it followed that the solution was to relocate the surplus to the cities, as it was fruitless to attempt to accommodate them all under adverse conditions on the reserves. The relocation policy backed by the terminationist philosophy was highly assimilationist in both intent and effect.

According to two Native American analysts, the 'forced assimilation into the urban ghettos of the nation . . . [was] the final solution to the "Indian problem"'(Kickingbird and Ducheneaux, 1973: 211). But while assimilation rates did increase, relocation had some unforeseen consequences. In cities such as Kansas City, Denver, Seattle, and San Francisco an urban proletariat developed. Prejudice and discrimination on the part of the larger society were serious barriers to assimilation; instead of melting into the American pot, urban Native Americans lacking a land base became aware of themselves for the first time as an ethnic group. In fact, their landless condition was the issue around which they eventually would organize. Their diffuse, supra-tribal ethnic consciousness was created by the day-to-day experiences they shared as outsiders in a hostile, alien, urban milieu.

Aboriginal Initiatives in the 1960s and 1970s

The 1960s in the US was a decade of social ferment. The Black civil-rights movement to end racial segregation and achieve equality of opportunity was in full swing; there were protests against the Vietnam War; the women's movement was gathering steam; and the gay rights movement, though in its infancy, was growing in such cities as New York and San Francisco. Society was being called upon to broaden, at the very least, its human-rights base. Not content with minor reforms, the more militant counter-culture activists questioned the moral correctness of the acquisitive, materialistic society rooted in capitalism. President Lyndon Johnson's response was a War on Poverty—social and economic programs designed to elevate the poor and change the social structures of society.

The more militant wing of the Black civil-rights movement was the Black Power faction. More than a social movement, Black Power was also an ideology that went beyond the goals of racial integration to focus on the building of self-esteem through pride in Black history and culture. The nationalistic activism that developed among the aboriginal nations was called Red Power. It would be inaccurate, however, to assume an exact parallel with Black Power with respect to either aspirations, goals, or ideology.

The fundamental difference between Red Power and Black Power was clear: whereas the civil-rights movement in general was seeking equality within the framework of individual rights and freedoms, the Red Power movement was reacting *against* the terminationist ideology that strove to put aboriginal peoples on an equal footing with all other Americans. In other words, Red Power was engaged in a struggle to regain a land base for aboriginal peoples and have their collective rights as nations acknowledged alongside their individual rights as citizens.

Just as there were many factions within the Black civil-rights movement, so too Red Power was composed of various groups with competing aspirations, strategies, and goals. Among the protest action groups falling under the more general Red Power rubric were the Indians of All Tribes. Focusing, as their name implied, on the necessity of transcending local, tribal loyalties, this group was most prominent in urban areas on the west coast. Decades of relocation efforts, coupled with increasing numbers of aboriginal students and Native veterans of the Second World War seeking job opportunities and a better quality of life, meant that by the late 1960s a sufficient number of Natives were living in urban areas to launch protest action. Their grievances included not only the prejudice and discrimination commonplace in such areas as health care, education, employment, and housing, but also the refusal of the larger society to recognize their treaty rights and other entitlements—a rejection that was an ever-present source of anguish.

The Indians of All Tribes: Alcatraz (1969)

The Indians of All Tribes decided to focus their efforts upon the land issue that is so central to aboriginal identity. The island of Alcatraz in San Francisco Bay was the site of a federal penitentiary that had recently been abandoned. To draw attention to the land robbery that Native people collectively had suffered, the Indians of All Tribes decided to occupy the island, demanding that Alcatraz and all other surplus federal land be returned to them as partial compensation. While their occupation ended with their removal by federal marshals in the summer of 1971, Alcatraz became both a symbol and a potential solution to the land grievance. In this sense, Kickingbird and Ducheneaux (1973: 215) judge the occupation of Alcatraz to be 'the most important event in the twentieth century for American Indian people'. Other events were soon to follow.

The Trail of Broken Treaties (1972)

In 1972, Washington, DC, was the site of a national protest march known as the Trail of Broken Treaties. To rally support for this action, Sioux leader Robert Burnette gave a speech calling for national unity and activism:

> it has been my dream to take 200 Indians into the capital and stay there until the government takes action to correct the abuse, discrimination and injustices. I have dreamed that . . . all Indians would [have] pride and dignity instead of being ashamed of tribal government that will eventually lead to termination (Burnette and Koster, 1974: 198).

Two issues—(a) tribal government and (b) termination—feature prominently in this rallying call. The 'tribal government' to which Burnette referred was the result of the IRA tribalization policy. Not only was the structure of tribal government antithetical to traditional aboriginal political organizations, but many of these governments did the bidding of the

BIA, and were cut off from the aspirations and realities of the grassroots. While termination was no longer an active policy, the philosophy behind it was still present in some Congressional circles, and its effects were still painfully evident among those tribes, such as the Menominee and Klamath, that had been terminated.

The Washington march was not the first attempt at nation-wide Native activism. The earliest efforts can be traced back to the 'fish-ins' in Washington State in the mid-1950s, when conflict arose over Indian fishing rights, guaranteed by treaties, on the Puyallup River (AFSC, 1970: 107). These 'fish-ins' were organized by the National Indian Youth Council (NIYC) (Lurie, 1970: 302), the first national aboriginal group to organize outside the aegis of the BIA or IRA. (For example, the National Congress of American Indians [NCAI], in which Indians opposed to termination voiced their concerns, was formed in 1944 as part of the federal–Indian consultation process under the IRA [Burnette and Koster, 1974: 157].)

The Trail of Broken Treaties was organized by another national group, the American Indian Movement (AIM). Founded in 1968 by George Mitchell and Dennis Banks, Chippewas living at the time in Minneapolis, Minnesota, AIM had previously engaged in such urban guerrilla theatre as the 1970 capture of the replica of the *Mayflower*—the ship that transported the Pilgrims from England to Massachusetts in the seventeenth century—and in 1971 had demonstrated at Mount Rushmore, a mountain in the Dakotas on which are carved the faces of several American presidents. Thus when it came to the Washington protest action, neither AIM nor the aboriginal people were entirely inexperienced at peaceful social protest.

In a tremendous show of strength, thousands of Native people, including elders, religious leaders, and students, converged on the American capital during the election week in November 1972. Even more significant than their numbers, however, was the program of change they carried with them, called the Twenty Points.

The first eight points dealt with a return to government-to-government relations between the federal government and aboriginal nations and reaffirmation of the treaties. Later points included a detailed proposal to restore the aboriginal land base to the dimensions it had attained prior to the 1887 allotment policy. Kickingbird and Ducheneaux (1973: 228) describe the original Point Ten as it was worked out in Minneapolis in the days prior to the Washington demonstration:

> Simple justice would seem to demand that priorities in the restoration of land bases be granted to those Indian nations who are landless by fault of unratified and unfulfilled treaty provisions; Indian nations, landless because of congressional and administrative actions reflective of criminal abuse of trust responsibilities; and other groupings of landless Indians, particularly of the landless generations, including many urban Indians

and non-reservation Indian people—many of whom have been forced to pay, in forms of deprivations, loss of rights and entitlements, and other extreme costs upon their lives, an 'emigration-migration-education-training' tax for their unfulfilled pursuit of opportunity in America—a tax as unwarranted and unjustified as it is unprecedented in the history of human rights in mature nations possessed of a modern conscience.

The central importance that the aboriginal peoples attach to their land is clearly evident here, as is use of the rhetoric of 'nation' to articulate and politicize their struggle. At the same time, far from confining their efforts to those land-based groups that constitute nations, the drafters of this document deliberately included landless and urban Indians as well. Although the Twenty Points never received a real hearing from federal authorities, they marked the end of the era in which Indians were seen as 'just another minority'. American Indians—if only in a symbolic sense—had once more emerged as 'nations within'.

The Oglala (Sioux) Nation, Wounded Knee (1973)

In 1890, Wounded Knee, South Dakota, was the site of a massacre in which 146 Sioux men, women, and children were slaughtered by the US Seventh Cavalry. The second confrontation at Wounded Knee, in 1973, was also highly significant, though for different reasons. First, the cast of characters had changed; no longer were there only two sides. In 1973 the Sioux people themselves were divided between those who supported the tribal government established under the IRA guidelines and recognized by Washington, and those who supported a rival government set up along traditional tribal lines. The issue came to a head in the months following the Trail of Broken Treaties, as the American Indian Movement had a strong presence on the reserve and supported the traditional tribal government (Burnette and Koster, 1974).

Second, the 1973 incident at Wounded Knee marked the first time in the twentieth century that an aboriginal group had taken a politically self-conscious stand as a nation. The Oglala (Sioux) Nation—including, under the Treaty of 1868, the Brule, Oglala, Miniconjou, Yanktonai, Hunkpapa, Blackfeet, Cuthead, Two Kettle, Sans Arcs, and Santee bands—stood in opposition not only to the American government, but, as importantly, to the IRA-constituted reserve government in which fellow Indians held positions of power. The Oglala argued that the IRA violated the Sioux Treaty of 1868: 'The Treaty of 1868 is silent on the form of government, which means that the right to self-government is reserved to the Sioux Nation. . . . the leaders called attention to the petition, with fourteen hundred signatures, requesting a referendum to rescind the tribe's constitution' (Burnette and Koster, 1974: 252).

The Oglala Nation was not acting alone. It had the support of AIM, which, composed of aboriginal people from all over North America, was still basking in its political success in Washington the previous year. Moreover, unlike the Indians of All Tribes who took Alcatraz or the National Indian Youth Council that supported the Washington State 'fish-ins', the Oglala Nation was acting as a specific nation residing on its traditional homeland.

Finally, Oglala nationalism reached the proportions and intensity of a full-scale social movement. The political aspects of this movement were perceived as threatening by all levels of established government. Following an armed confrontation at Wounded Knee, the leadership of AIM was severely harassed and discredited by the FBI. With the media emphasizing the armed aspect of the struggle, public opinion in the larger society swung towards the criminalization of aboriginal nationalism. (Parallel developments were taking place with respect to the Black Power movement.) As a result, in the following decades AIM had a much lower profile (Cornell, 1988: 203), and activism on all fronts— Native and non-Native—seemed to taper off with the end of 1970s.

The International Treaty Council
Extra-institutional activism, however, was not the only political action in which Native Americans engaged in the 1970s. In addition, the national movement was furthered by the creation of the International Treaty Council in South Dakota in 1974. The founders of this Council stressed 'the importance of acting as a nation, and they emphasized the necessity of taking their case to other nations, with the hope that by creating a favourable image of American Indians in the larger world, the United States would be forced to respond to some of their requests' (Deloria, Jr, and Lytle, 1984: 241). The International Treaty Council's legitimacy was acknowledged the following year when the United Nations accorded it the status of a non-governmental organization with observer rights. In 1980 an International Treaty Council 'delegation made statements concerning several well-documented cases of deprivation of tribal rights by the United States to the UN Commission on Human Rights and the Subcommission on Prevention of Discrimination and Protection of Minorities' (Deloria, Jr, and Lytle, 1984: 242).

Federal Responses to the Aboriginal National Movement

How did the federal government respond to the aboriginal self-determining initiatives of the 1960s and 1970s? We have already mentioned the suppression of 'radical' elements. At the same time, some efforts were made to understand and accommodate Native demands for tribal or national legitimacy. For example, in 1975 two notable pieces of federal legislation boldly proclaimed a new era of self-determination.

The Indian Self-Determination and Education Assistance Act (1975)
According to Cornell (1988: 205), the Indian Self-Determination and Education Assistance Act was a 'genuine return to bilateral relations'. Intended to promote the 'orderly transition from Federal domination of programs for and services to Indians to effective and meaningful participation by the Indian people in the planning, conduct, and administration of those programs and services' (US Congress, Public Law 93-638),·the Act envisioned Native self-government in the areas of education, economic development, and social services. In addition to being encouraged to take over such programs and services from the BIA, the tribes would be empowered to contract with outside sources (Cornell, 1988: 204).

By 1979, nineteen tribally-organized colleges had been established, and between 1978 and 1986, Indian enrolments at publicly-supported colleges and universities increased from 78,000 to an estimated 90,000 (Dinnerstein et al., 1990: 326). Bilingual instruction and Native history in elementary-level tribal schools are an attempt to strengthen and link self-determination with education. While it is impossible to say what changes are directly attributable to the Act, Native self-determination in the field of education clearly made great strides forward. As Burt (1982: 129) notes, the Act 'gave tribes a significant role in setting policy goals and in administering all federal programs affecting them'.

The American Indian Policy Review Commission (AIPRC), 1975
Following on the heels of the Trail of Broken Treaties and Wounded Knee, the American Indian Policy Review Commission submitted 206 recommendations that were designed to appeal to and bolster Native moderates. According to Deloria, Jr, and Lytle (1984: 238), the AIPRC 'did not seek to advocate a new institutional framework in which future Indian progress could take place. Rather it suggested tightening the rules and regulations governing existing institutional arrangements, hoping to make them more efficient so they would deliver services faster.'

In Cornell's assessment (1988: 203), the AIPRC recommendations were 'largely ignored'. Nevertheless, the Commission had symbolic significance, as it marked the first time that a federal government Indian policy study had been heavily staffed by aboriginal people and sought input from them. (Earlier reform policy efforts, such as the 1923 Committee of One Hundred, had been composed of non-Native activists and celebrities [Deloria, Jr, and Lytle 1984: 41].)

Thus some progress was being made towards self-government and self-determination. But it was not unimpeded. Native resources—mineral deposits, land, water—were coveted by corporate and agricultural interests. While Native people were making some gains with respect to mineral royalties and control over development, including environmental protection and preferential hiring on reserve business enterprises, the attitude of the larger society—especially in the west, where resource competition was greatest—tended to be actively hostile and exploitative. Among the many anti-Indian lobbies constituting a backlash to aboriginal assertiveness (Morris, 1988: 741) was the Interstate Congress of Equal Rights and Responsibilities, formed in 1976 'to agitate on issues ranging from the status of certain lands to political control of areas with heavy Indian population and the nontaxable status of Native American property' (Burt, 1982: 130). In addition, various bills seeking to revive the termination policy were presented to Congress (which rejected them).

Land Claims
Some aboriginal people also made significant strides in the area of land claims in the 1970s. In 1971 the people of Taos Pueblo, New Mexico, regained their sacred Blue Lake and surrounding forest area after years of struggle (in 1965 they had rejected a proposed cash settlement from the Indian Claims Commission). That same year in Alaska a major land claim involving aboriginal title to 16,200,000 hectares was successfully negotiated with the federal government and 'the Indians, Aleuts, and Eskimo people' (Dinnerstein, 1990: 326). Although the Alaska Native Claims Settlement was similar to other treaties in earlier centuries in that it reached an accommodation between the original occupants of the land and an invader, it differed significantly inasmuch as this time the aboriginal people themselves actively proposed and negotiated the final terms and conditions of settlement. McNickle (1973: 158), in fact, assesses the Alaska settlement as the first instance in 'more than four hundred years [in which] a native people and a colonizing power had come to terms'.

Elsewhere in the United States a fundamentally different land-claims process was underway in the 1970s. Unlike the Alaska claim, these claims sought both reinstatement of tribal status and compensation for lost land and damages. In Maine, for example, the Passamaquoddy—like many aboriginal nations in the east, where European settlement occurred early and population density is high—had been thought to have assimilated totally into the larger American society; as a result of their claim, the Passamaquoddy won a judgement against the Department of the Interior in 1975 and negotiated a settlement worth $81.5-million. Following the BIA's 1978 announcement of guidelines for the reinstatement of tribes with treaty rights, over 100 tribes applied. However, 'by 1988 only 11 had been successful, while the claims of an equal number were rejected' (Dinnerstein, 1990: 327); the rest remain trapped somewhere in the bureaucratic maze.

The Conservative Era: 1980-present
Despite the progress cited above, the political climate in the 1970s remained generally unreceptive to change. With the election of presidents Ronald Reagan, in 1980 and 1984, and George Bush, in 1988, the larger society became even less sensitive and committed to reform than in the previous decade. The 1980s saw a series of budgetary proposals aimed at severely reducing social services of all types, and these cuts extended to Indian programs. The phrase 'termination by accountants' was coined (Morris, 1988) to describe the effect the cut-backs were having throughout the aboriginal nations.

The conservative era got into full swing with the now notorious budget of 1982, which recommended the total elimination of funding for the public-service employment portions of the Comprehensive Employment and Training Act; the Economic Development Administration; the Community Service Administration; and the Legal Services Corporation (Select Committee on Indian Affairs, 1981: 14-15). All subsequent budgets 'provided ample evidence of the extraordinary lengths the Reagan Administration' (Morris, 1988: 734) would go to in pursuit of its policy objectives. For example, in 1987 the Administration's proposed Indian education budget of $217.3-million represented a cut of $65-million from the 1982 figure (US Department of the Interior, 1986).

Needless to say, the quality of Native life declined in all aspects associated with health, education, employment, and housing. Morris (1988: 735) notes that the tribes were fearful that the extensive cuts would lead to the federal government's abandonment of Indian education and human services entirely, and 'in effect "terminate" the content of the federal trust'. The aboriginal peoples rallied against the cuts, but their concentration on fiscal policy made it difficult to focus on mounting new initiatives of their own.

In addition to health, education, and welfare, another aspect of federal policy of concern to aboriginal people is the protection of tribal lands and natural resources. In the 1980s the conservative philosophy of 'privatization' was to be extended to reserve economies. The jewel in the crown of the federal privatization program as applied to Native people was the 1984 Presidential Commission on Indian Reservation Economies, which reported that the major obstacle to economic development on reserve lands was government, both tribal and federal. Its analysis was reminiscent of the rationale behind the 1887 Allotment Act, which sought to break up communal land holdings in favour of private enterprise and individual ownership.

Three years later, however, President Reagan supported the federal regulation of tribal gaming operations. While the justification was to protect the tribes from organized crime, it was commonly believed that the Indians were seen as 'too successful' at minor gambling operations like bingo, and posed a threat to competition including charities and

churches. Thus, ironically, the market forces worshipped by the conservative economists as the final regulator of economic activity were
not permitted to operate when open competition favoured aboriginal
peoples (Morris, 1988: 742).

The federal regulation of gambling is one of many examples that
could be used to illustrate a more general point: that contemporary
federal Indian policies are 'created to control, direct, limit, then finally
defeat Indian economic initiatives which might threaten private, state
or federal interests' (Morris, 1988: 742). The same is true of self-determination, which has been paid lip-service by every American administration since 1960 (Nagel, 1982: 40). The conservative regimes have
not sought to end self-determination; they have simply chosen to
under-fund the programs needed to strengthen the ideal, and to ignore
treaty provisions in favour of state and private interests (Lacy, 1982:
27). The lack of effective leadership on the part of the Reagan and Bush
administrations has meant that the treaty-based trust relationship of the
federal government with the aboriginal nations has been jeopardized.

In sum, federal Indian policies and funding practices have belied the
government-to-government rhetoric that has permeated speeches from
the White House in the last two decades (Cornell, 1988: 209). Perhaps
the only progressive achievement from the Reagan years was the 1982
Tribal Government Tax Status Act, which permits tribes to raise their
own taxes and gives them the same status as states under the Internal
Revenue Code (Native American Rights Fund, 1986: 7). Although it is
widely feared that this power will be used by federal authorities to
argue for yet further cut-backs and termination of services, the symbolic importance of the Act cannot be denied. As the only legislation
from the 1980s that firmly supports the concept of Indian nations as
nations, it is highly significant, whatever its long-term effects.

Another hopeful sign is that aboriginal gains realized over the
years with respect to case law, treaty rights, and self-determination
have not been irrevocably eroded during the present era of conservative policies, even if specific programs have been terminated or
under-funded. The challenge facing aboriginal people is to go beyond
the rhetoric of government-to-government relations and arrive at the
substance of nationhood without being shunted into a dead-end
minority status. In recent years, higher-court challenges have tended
to favour the aboriginal peoples.

In addition, much political activity is occurring on the tribal level. In
Arizona, for example, the Papago—so named by the Spanish—have
dropped this colonial vestige, returning with pride to the former name
of their people: the Tohono O'odham nation (Dinnerstein, 1990: 323).
Other tribes such as the Chippewa have formed grassroots organizations
dedicated to non-violent resistance and upholding the treaties. They
recently rejected a $50-million offer from Wisconsin for a ten-year lease

on their usufructuary rights. While the tribal council had unanimously approved the offer, the grassroots rejected it as one more short cut toward treaty abrogation (Maulson, 1991). Such action shows both the vitality of the grassroots and the continuing lack of legitimacy that has plagued the tribal councils since they were first organized under the aegis of the IRA.

Overall, then, the aboriginal nations within the United States remain in a political limbo characterized by Vine Deloria, Jr, in the 1970s as 'expectant nationhood':

> Indian tribes . . . maintain a quasi-independent status vis à vis other nations . . . they are in a state of expectant nationhood. One judge of the . . . Supreme Court likened them to the Hebrews wandering in the Sinai Wilderness—a nation among nations, disenfranchised in part but capable of becoming cognizable owners of land (Deloria, Jr, in Kickingbird and Ducheneaux, 1973: x).

That this is still the case in the 1990s points to the lack of political will in the larger society to redress historical wrongs.

In the concluding section we will examine what social and legal changes would have to occur in order to more fully recognize the legitimacy of the 'nations within'.

CONCLUSION: IMPLICATIONS FOR THE FUTURE

Aboriginal nations have experienced more than two centuries of political interaction with the United States government. One aspect of that history is their increasing inclusion—as tribal nations and as individuals—in the institutions of American life. This conclusion will attempt to summarize the ways in which this incorporation has taken place, beginning with an overview of the demographic and legal status of aboriginal peoples and moving on to take a brief look at major policy thrusts on the part of the federal government in its efforts to balance on the one hand its management of relations with aboriginal peoples, and on the other the legitimacy of the state. Native issues challenge the fundamentals of democratic theory—especially the notion of the 'consent of the governed'—as well as international law and cultural survival (Chaudhuri, 1982: 19). Finally, aboriginal responses and initiatives are considered with an eye towards the future status of the 'nations within'.

Demographic Status

As noted at the beginning of this chapter, the aboriginal population in the United States is estimated to be less than one per cent of the total population (Jaimes, 1988: 785). More precise calculations by tribe or region, or indicating growth or decline, are beyond the scope of this book for several reasons. First, the aboriginal peoples have not been permitted to enumerate themselves using their own membership criteria. Second, census definitions have changed from 'blood quantum' requirements to a subjective self-definition, making comparisons over time difficult. The aboriginal people have never been consulted on this subject, and support neither the definitions nor the process by which they were established (Jaimes, 1988: 787). Third, as noted by the American Indian Policy Review Commission (1977): 'The Federal government, State governments and the Census Bureau all have different criteria for defining "Indians" . . . and even Federal criteria are not consistent among Federal agencies'.

Demographic data and their interpretations have political and cultural implications for the 'nations within'. The Reagan administration, for example, not only cut programs and entitlements, but also reduced the eligible number of aboriginal people (Morris, 1988: 735). In response to this change in eligibility requirements, a 1985 court case successfully challenged the constitutionality of 'blood quantum' as the sole eligibility criterion. The case involved Dianne Zarr, a registered Pomo band Indian of less than one-quarter blood who was initially ruled ineligible for a higher education grant because she did not meet the blood quantum requirement. A court of appeal ruled in her favour, stating that it is unconstitutional to base decisions solely on race (Zarr v. Barlow, 1985). Aboriginal people are looking to the Zarr case as a possible breakthrough in their struggle to determine their own identity (Jaimes, 1988: 794).

An even more serious issue related to identity is the use of demographic data to determine the viability of the tribe itself. Some tribes such as the Juanero were defined out of existence by the federal government in the late 1970s when their total numbers fell to a low level, even though new members were still being born into the tribe (Jaimes, 1988: 788). Striking at the core of group survival, such unilateral decisions on the part of the federal government are potentially a matter of genocide.

For all of these reasons, therefore, it is important that the aboriginal peoples themselves state their own criteria for membership in their group and be responsible for their enumeration. In fact, some groups have already taken steps in that direction. In defiance of the federal government, nations such as the Oglala and the Haida in Alaska have instituted naturalization procedures whereby they may accept non-Indians as citizens of their nations (Jaimes, 1988: 791); such self-definition—the prerogative of independent nations—has direct implications for their morale, health, and ultimate survival. Whether or not other groups follow their example, the present federal enumeration policy is paternalistic, inaccurate from a Native point of view, and in some instances may be genocidal. The last reason alone is more than sufficient reason for immediate change.

Legal Status

Like their demographic status, the legal status of the aboriginal nations has been obscured, disregarded, violated, and placed at the bottom of the federal agenda. Throughout this grim history, however, the existence of distinct and unique tribal societies has never been fundamentally challenged. What has been repeatedly questioned is the extent of tribal authority. The process by which this authority has become limited is the subject of this section.

Contemporary legal understanding of the 'nations within' in the US stems from three court cases in the nineteenth century involving Chief Justice Marshall. Judicial notions of inherent sovereignty are traced to Worcester v. Georgia, 1832 (see p. 135 above), in which tribal authority was protected from state encroachment. 'The highpoint of Indian sovereignty', according to Chaudhuri (1982: 16), the Worcester decision is thought to have provided much of the rationale behind the 1959 ruling that 'Indian tribes are not states. They have a status higher than that of states' (Native American Church v. Navajo Tribal Council, 1959).

The other two Marshall opinions—Cherokee Nation v. Georgia and Johnson v. McIntosh—also relate to the nature of tribal sovereignty and the limits to tribal authority, but in these cases the aboriginal people did not fare so well. The Johnson v. McIntosh case (1823) had its philosophical and legal roots in the seventeenth-century 'doctrine of discovery' (Williams, 1990). Involving a land dispute over whether aboriginal people, specifically the Illinois and Piankeshaw tribes, could sell land directly to individual speculators, the case was decided in favour of the state on the grounds that the aboriginal people were 'occupants . . . incapable of transferring the absolute title to others' (cited in Chaudhuri, 1982: 15). Therefore aboriginal people could not sell land, and a settler could not claim title to any land purchased from an Indian. Although in retrospect it is thought that Marshall's intent was to bolster the power of the federal government, the decision had the unintended consequence of weakening the inherent sovereign powers of aboriginal peoples.

Perhaps the best-known Marshall opinion was presented in the 1831 Cherokee Nation v. Georgia case (see p. 134 above), which established the aboriginal peoples as 'domestic dependent nations'. Although the term 'nation' occurs in the decision, it is qualified by the words 'domestic dependent'. It is a tragic irony that although the court ruled in favour of the Cherokee people's sovereignty and against the authority of the state of Georgia to relocate them, President Jackson ignored the ruling and allowed the relocation. Nor did the Marshall court issue any injunction to prevent it (Chaudhuri, 1982: 15).

Two points are relevant when assessing these cases. First, a coherent legal perspective is non-existent. What we have are a series of apparently contradictory rulings based on such dubious grounds as the 'doctrine of discovery'. Second, these decisions were not made from the perspective of what was fair and just for the aboriginal peoples. Rather, each decision is best understood within the political context of the day and the institutionalized tension between each branch of the government—the legislative (Congress), judicial (Supreme Court), and executive (President)—with the other (Chaudhuri, 1982: 20).

Nevertheless, throughout history it has been the courts that have been the most sympathetic to the legitimate concerns and aspirations of the aboriginal peoples. Congress, by contrast, has consistently tried to limit, deny, and terminate treaty rights, from the General Allotment Act to the termination policy. The executive branch of government has tended to occupy a middle ground, and speak with the proverbial 'forked tongue'. While duty-bound to uphold the trust relationship with the aboriginal peoples, the executive has been cross-pressured by the interests of the states and the electorate. Such conflicts of interest have typically been resolved in favour of the states. History abounds with examples, ranging from President Jackson's support for Georgia's policy of aboriginal removal to the sins of omission in the present era, in which a lack of presidential leadership in support of treaty rights has meant that 'after the mid 1970s little architectural work has occurred in program development. Indian policy has been . . . shunted aside' (Chaudhuri, 1982: 20).

American history bearing upon the 'nations within' is little known by non-Indians. Ignorant of aboriginal legal status and immersed in the broader cultural ideology of individual rights, even the more liberal segment of the American population that supports aboriginal causes tends to do so on the basis of broad humanitarian grounds rather than aboriginal status as 'nations within'. The history of the aboriginal peoples tends to be either omitted, distorted, partially recounted, or told from the biased perspective of the majority society, while Washington's tendency to call them 'Native' or 'First Americans' serves to homogenize their diversity and treat them on the same plane as other minority groups in the American melting pot. (Aboriginal leaders wishing to stress their government-to-government standing firmly oppose these terms for this reason [Witt, 1965: 122].) As a result, their true entitlements are denied and their nationalistic cause is not advanced. The American people cannot be full-fledged allies with the aboriginal peoples in their nationalistic cause unless the complete legal history of federal–Indian relations is known.

Federal Policy: Summary and Analysis

Assimilationist policies have characterized federal–Indian relations since the founding of the American Republic, especially after 1871 when the government 'often attempted to avoid recognizing Indians as members of tribal nations' (Lacy, 1982: 27). The supporters of assimilation have differed in the extent of their chauvinism, paternalism, and racism (Morris, 1988: 731), and since 1960 federal Indian policy has not been explicitly assimilationist—on the contrary, some policies have even had the term 'self-determination' in their titles. But assimilation and economic colonialism are still rife. Aboriginal people are still under the thumb of Washington; their treaty rights are still denied; their land base grows smaller each year; their resources flow out of their communities to the benefit of non-Indians; and the government that rules them does so without their consent. Even when they technically own their land, they frequently lose the profits to outsiders (Lacy, 1982: 27).

In the contemporary era, federal authorities have relied heavily upon a strategy of co-optation. In this strategy, the power-holder intentionally extends some form of political participation to actors who pose a potential threat to the legitimate order (Lacy, 1982: 23). One example of co-optation is the appointment of high-profile aboriginal people to government positions involving very little real power. The idea is to make it appear as if aboriginal people are part of the decision-making process, for such a perception will tend to give the programs and policies a legitimacy they might otherwise lack. Co-optation is also a way of ensuring that the shortcomings of the policy fall on the shoulders of the token Indians, who can be seen as accountable for their people's situation.

Lacy (1982: 32) points out that the result of co-optation has been to legitimize the federal Indian bureaucracy primarily in the eyes of non-Indians. So-called white liberals are assuaged of guilt because it is possible to point to aboriginal participation in the bureaucracy. Two prime examples of this strategy were President Reagan's appointment of Kenneth Smith, a Wasco businessman from Oregon, to the second highest position in the Department of the Interior (Morris, 1988: 732), and the 1985 appointment of Ross Swimmer, a Cherokee chief, as Assistant Secretary of the Interior.

Earlier administrations under such presidents as Roosevelt and

Nixon used the Indian Preference policy, a precursor of today's affirm-ative-action policies, as a means to achieve the appearance of aborigi-nal participation. By 1933 one-third of the positions in the Bureau of Indian Affairs were held by Indians, although it was not until the Nixon administration that the policy was aimed at training and pro-motion in addition to initial hiring (Lacy, 1982: 32).

Co-optation is seen by aboriginal people as at best window-dressing. At worst it is a conscious federal strategy that goes hand in hand with repression, rewarding the 'good Indian' while the 'bad' is punished. An example of this strategy was evident in the 1970s, when the FBI-led repression of the American Indian Movement (Matthiessen, 1983) was in force alongside the Indian Preference Policy and another co-optation effort, the National Council on Indian Opportunity (NCIO).

The NCIO was established by an executive order from President Johnson in 1968. Six Indian leaders appointed by the President were to join relevant cabinet officials and the Director of the Office of Economic Opportunity with a mandate to 'review Federal programs for Indians, make broad policy recommendations, and ensure that programs reflect the needs and desires of the Indian people' (Johnson, 1968). President Nixon increased the number of Indian members to eight, but aside from the symbolic importance of the NCIO and its potential to influence federal agencies and policy, very little legislation was passed that could be attributed to its recommendations (Josephy, 1976: 204). Figure 10.4 summarizes selected federal policy initiatives in terms of their consequences—co-optation and assimilation—for Indian peoples.

Finally, to understand the 'self-determination' policies of the federal government it is important to remember that in this context self-deter-mination is defined by the government, not by the aboriginal nations. In government terms, self-determination denotes nothing more than a federal promise that local Indian concerns and wishes will be consid-ered in the design and implementation of Indian policies (Morris, 1988: 743). It is not to be confused with a broader definition in which aboriginal people themselves would truly determine their own fate. As self-government is an extension of self-determination that embraces autonomy and sovereignty, one might argue that the Native peoples will not be able to achieve self-government until the prior condition, self-determination, is realized.

The high point of explicit assimilation legislation was the 'termina-tion' policy that flourished in the 1950s, in blatant violation of the federal trust relationship. Indeed, Williams (1990) argues that the termination legislation was unconstitutional as well as a moral breach of that relationship. In giving Congress the power to decide that certain tribes were self-sufficient and no longer in need of federal protection,

Figure 10.4
US Incorporation of the 'Nations Within':
Twentieth Century Federal Initiatives (Selected)

| Period | | Federal Initiative | Consequence | |
year	president	policy or legislation	co-optation	assimilation
1924	Coolidge	Indian citizenship	symbolic extension of rights, but no real control over lives or property	Indians become Native Americans
1933	Roosevelt	Indian Reorganization Act (IRA)	tribal governments formed;	organized by federal government;
		Indian Preference Policy (within the BIA)	Indians recruited to lower levels of BIA	no decision-making power
1946	Truman	Indian Claims Commission (ICC) (1946-60)	preparation for termination	tribal status denied
1956	Eisenhower	Indian Vocational Educational Act	preparation for off-reserve migration	urban ghettos form
1968	Johnson	National Council on Indian Opportunity (NICO);	advisory body;	no decision-making power;
		War on Poverty	economic development on reserves	treated as a minority, not a distinct society
1972	Nixon	Indian Preference expanded to Affirmative Action	rewards for conformity	repression of radicals legitimated
1982	Reagan	Tribal Government Tax Status Act	tribes able to tax members	government cuts justified

this policy was the most striking example in US history of the denial of the government-to-government relationship—a denial that is integral to federal aboriginal policy.

Treaties involve the principle of negotiation between two parties. By unilaterally declaring the treaties null and void—which is what the termination policy did—the United States was breaking the rules of the game. The official termination policy lasted only about a decade; however, unofficial termination continues unabated today. It takes the guise of under-enumeration in the census, 'extinction' of tribes whose numbers fall (Jaimes, 1988), and cutting or under-funding of essential programs. In addition, aboriginal land continues to be diminished in total holdings; Native people are forced to move off their reserves in search of work; and they do not receive adequate compensation for the mineral wealth on their land.

Termination was preceded by a brief period of indirect rule under the Indian Reorganization Act (IRA) of the 1930s in which Washington controlled Indian puppet regimes, called 'tribal councils', constituted to federal specifications. This assimilationist arrangement permitted the aboriginal peoples to have their own governments as long as they went through the election process and otherwise abided by the rules set down by the Bureau of Indian Affairs (BIA); in general, it did not permit indigenous tribal forms of political organization. These tribal councils are still in existence today and on many reserves are a constant source of conflict between traditional leaders and elected officials (Maulson, 1991).

Nevertheless, destructive of indigenous political organization as the IRA was, it is commonly conceded that without it the aboriginal peoples might have been totally incorporated as individuals into the American melting pot. Certainly this 'New Deal for Indians' represented an improvement over the blatant and brutal assimilationist policies, typified by the residential schools, that preceded it, when Native language and religion, customs, and culture were prohibited and systematically debased.

Considering the era before 1960, therefore, it is tempting to say that 'progress' has been made. But has it?

The 'Nations Within' in the Future

As Felix Cohen, an authority on the legal status of aboriginal peoples, wisely noted (1982: v): 'Like the miner's canary, the Indian marks the shifts from fresh air to poison gas in our political atmosphere; and our treatment of Indians, even more than our treatment of other minorities, reflects the rise and fall in our democratic faith.'

What would be indices of this 'rise and fall'? First, if democracy were on the rise, co-optation would be replaced with legitimate representation and participation on the part of aboriginal peoples, who would engage in government-to-government dialogue with Washington. In the place of the current pattern of colonial exploitation would be a recognition that the aboriginal nations are entitled to social and economic justice, whether they live on reserves or in cities. Outstanding land claims would be settled to the satisfaction of aboriginal peoples, and the provisions of the 371 formally ratified treaties (Jaimes, 1988: 778) would be upheld.

Second, democracy depends upon such notions as the consent of the governed and an informed electorate. Yet the Indian Citizenship Act of 1924 (to take only one example) was proclaimed unilaterally by the federal government, and even now the American public is kept in the dark about the legal status and history of the 'nations within'. It is convenient for politicians not to have to acknowledge the theft of land and resources, as such actions go against the grain of the democratic ideal (Lacy, 1982). A knowledge of aboriginal history would not only further empower the aboriginal people, but would also help to mobilize the progressive element in American society that is not sufficiently aware of present and past injustices. Likewise, education would remove the cloak of legitimacy from the anti-Indian lobby that denies any special status, national or otherwise, to Indians and refuses to recognize their distinct tribal identities.

The anti-Indian lobby uses the rhetoric of equality to deny aboriginal people their just entitlements as set out in the treaties. Using conservation arguments, for example, interest groups argue that special hunting and fishing rights for Indians are not only detrimental to the environment but 'anti-American', as all Americans should be treated equally under the law. The only hope of countering this unjust use of the ideology of equality rights lies in education regarding the concept of 'nations within'.

Finally, if the American faith in democracy were to be put into action, the definition of self-determination would be broadened to include aboriginal self-government. Native people would define their own group membership criteria and control their geopolitical and ethnic boundaries. The tribal councils set up under the IRA would be replaced by political organizations and structures determined by the tribes. The fundamental American commitment to the principle of the 'consent of the governed'—the people's right to determine how they will be governed and by whom—would be restored to the country's first inhabitants (Barsh and Henderson, 1980).

Especially since the 1960s, the aboriginal peoples' hope that American democracy might be extended to include them has led them to mobilize in an effort to correct the injustices they face. However, as Nagel (1982: 39) explains, this effort has been divided 'between tribally-based mobilization and mobilization on the basis of the larger Native American identity'; at the root of this split, she argues, is a federal policy that has 'vacillated between 1) recognition of tribes as . . . the foci of various government programs and legislation and 2) insistence that Indianness was the relevant ethnic distinction for political policy purposes'.

In effect, these two dimensions to federal Indian policy have meant that, in order to achieve their rightful entitlements, American Indians have had to organize on three levels: tribal (Sioux, Hopi, Cherokee, etc.), pan-tribal (Sioux with Hopi and Cherokee), and ethnic (Native Americans)—a level at which their actual tribal identity is irrelevant. Such multi-tiered mobilization is costly for a sector of society that is small in numbers and has the lowest per capita disposable income of any group in the US. In addition, there are the costs of what is essentially a divide-and-conquer strategy on the part of the larger society. The cleavages between aboriginal peoples—tribal, socio-economic, regional, political, demographic—are exacerbated by the federal government's strategy, which requires that they wage simultaneous battles on many fronts. Nevertheless, they have demonstrated their commitment to work within the democratic system. If the larger American society is to renew its own commitment to that system, it must learn first to recognize and then to live responsibly with the nations in its midst.

Working within the legal system, Williams (1990), a Lumbee Native scholar, points to one way in which the US and its aboriginal nations could place the legal status of the 'nations within' on a sounder constitutional footing. Quite simply, Williams is suggesting that the aboriginal nations be legally considered 'divergent groups'. As such they would be granted the specific legal protection extended to certain groups to ensure the right of expressive association.

There is ample precedent for treating aboriginal people in the United States not as individuals, but as a collective. The Cherokee Nation case, for example, established the concept of aboriginal peoples as 'domestic dependent nations'. Williams is of the opinion that just as the Cherokee case was used in the past to limit tribal authority, so in the future it may be used to guarantee or extend that authority.

The key, Williams argues, is associational rights. With the constitutional protection ensured through this 'back door', a policy like termination would no longer be allowed, as such legislation would violate expressive association rights. It is clear that the future of aboriginal nations in the United States would be enhanced through successful application of this argument. Without such constitutional protection, the 'nations within' may be more accurately termed the 'colonies without'.

PART III

THE MAORI OF
AOTEAROA/NEW ZEALAND

E L E V E N

Devolving Maori–State Relations

INTRODUCTION

Canada's aboriginal peoples are hardly alone in their struggle to define and shape the society they live in. Indigenous peoples in countries such as Australia and Norway are also primed to establish sovereignty and land rights as a basis for cultural renewal and economic development. In Australia, for example, the dominant policy framework for managing state relations with Aboriginal people has evolved from a paternalistic commitment to protection and assimilation to one of Aboriginal self-determination and community self-management over cultural and economic affairs (Standing Committee, 1990). Response to Aboriginal demands for greater consultation and involvement in decision-making has resulted in government moves to replace the Department of Aboriginal Affairs with the Aboriginal and Torres Strait Islander Commission, consisting of 60 Regional Councils grouped into 17 zones whose representatives comprise a Board of Commissioners (Aboriginal and Torres Strait Islander Commission, 1991). To date, however, the implementation of policies and programs that focus on community affairs, land and economic development, and improved service delivery has been a disappointment for the 230,000-strong Aboriginal population (Tonkinson and Howard, 1990). Until Aboriginal communities are supplied with the resources and the power to take control of their destiny, the 'devolution' of Aboriginal–government relations will continue to flounder for lack of direction and political will.

Pressures for revising the aboriginal agenda are no different in New Zealand. Maori–government relations are undergoing a period of unprecedented change and reassessment, in many ways consistent with upheavals across the country's public-service sector. A rethinking of Maori policy and administration along bicultural lines is a central component in this restructuring process. It includes (a) recognition of Maori structures as vehicles for development; (b) dismantling of the Maori Affairs Department in 1989 and its replacement by the Iwi Transition Agency (Te Tira Ahu Iwi); (c) the creation of a Ministry of Maori Affairs (Manatu Maori) as an advisory-monitoring agency; (d) increased public-service responsiveness to Maori values, needs, and aspirations; (e) a proposed new 'distributive ideal' (Sharp, 1990) based on a bicultural allocation of power and resources; and (f) growing acceptance of the Treaty of Waitangi as a policy blueprint for reuniting the founding partners of New Zealand.

Of foremost concern in the reconstruction process are moves to restore Maori tribal (*iwi*) structures to their rightful place in the design, delivery, and monitoring of government services. Widely heralded as a bold venture in the management of Maori–state relations, the emergence of *iwi* authorities as catalysts for self-empowerment speaks eloquently of New Zealand's decolonizing commitment. Yet this process is susceptible to containment and control. One problem is the interpretation of principles, policies, and practices; another consists in the limitations inherent in the decolonization process, reflecting competing visions of devolution and power-sharing. Evidence suggests that the proposed overhaul in Maori relational status—from colonialist dependency to limited sovereignty—will be a protracted affair, for it entails fundamental shifts in status, structure, and entitlement.

Beginning with an examination of the social and cultural characteristics of Maori society (with particular emphasis on the gradual decline of Maori sociocultural status and political salience) and current Maori aspirations, this chapter moves on to a brief historical overview of Maori policy: from assimilation and integration to the current focus on biculturalism and devolution. A highly political process, subject to manipulation, this restructuring of the Maori agenda is consistent with the 'partnership perspectives' implicit in the Treaty of Waitangi.

The following section considers political and state responses to Maori demands for recognition of their status as the *tangata whenua*, or original inhabitants, of New Zealand. Government initiatives in this regard dovetail with wider state moves for devolution and deregulation, but grave doubts persist about the realities of implementation. Despite good intentions, political and bureaucratic constraints continue to distort Maori aspirations for power-sharing and decision-making input. As often as not, although the Te Urupare Rangapu

('Partnership Response') policy of the Labour government (1984-90) conveyed the illusion of power-sharing, it remained embedded within an assimilationist/integrationist agenda. These paradoxical tendencies were evident in the administration of state policy by the Department of Maori Affairs and its successor, the Iwi Transition Agency. The proposed new superministry of Maori Development under the National Party government's Ka Awatea ('New Day') policy is likely to encounter similar problems. In short, recent efforts to retribalize Maori–state relations are fraught with ambiguity and deception. But these initiatives also hold out promise for more culturally-sensitive, tribally-based development in line with Maori aspirations for *tangata whenua* status.

The final section examines Maori resistance to state efforts at domination, absorption, and control, from nineteenth-century uprisings and religious movements to the highly politicized activism of the twentieth century. The recently created Maori Congress is the latest in a series of initiatives to capitalize on Maori resources as a basis for renewal and reform. Particular attention is devoted to one expression of Maori renewal that reflects and reinforces a working partnership between aboriginal people and the state in pursuit of a common goal. The establishment of Maori-language preschools (Te Kohanga Reo) is a prime example of Maori resolve to exercise self-determination through traditional community structures and cultural values. The politicization of Maori-language preschools is advancing the restructuring of Maori–government relations, and their success suggests that New Zealand is on the right path, not only towards decolonizing its society, but also towards asserting its identity as a bicultural country.

THE POLICY CONTEXT: MAORI SOCIETY

Contrary to what many of us have been led to believe, New Zealand is not a model of racial tranquillity. Relations between the indigenous Maori tribes and the Pakeha (whites of European descent) are prone to suspicion and doubt, in large part because of inequities within the system (Reynolds, 1990). The Maori are over-represented on the negative side of the social economy (e.g., unemployment and imprisonment), and under-represented on the positive side (e.g., income and education). The loss of land (Maori own 5 per cent of New Zealand's land) has contributed to the Maori's poverty, and makes it difficult to secure a base from which to overcome their powerlessness. This material impoverishment is compounded by the gradual erosion of language and cultural identity that has left many Maori youth uneasily suspended between competing value systems. As part of the struggle to correct these imbalances, some Maori groups are working to restore the Maori heritage to its former status in society. Others have reasserted Maori claims for coastal fishing rights and the repossession of lands illegally taken by the Crown. In this climate of competition between unequal partners, the absence of overt interracial violence can be attributed largely to good fortune and self-deception rather than to deliberate design or compassion on the part of central authorities. If we are to appreciate the sometimes perilous status of Maori–state relations in New Zealand, we must first examine who the Maori are, where they stand in society, how they came to occupy their place in the queue, and why.

Traditional Maori Society

New Zealand is a small liberal democracy in the South Pacific with a largely urbanized population of just over three million, of which the indigenous Maori comprise about 13 per cent. The majority in both the numerical and the political sense are the non-Maori, non-Polynesian Pakeha, many of whom trace their ancestry back to Britain or Northern Europe. Racial minorities such as the Chinese and East Indians are included in this loose designation, but, as might be expected in light of New Zealand's once-restrictive immigration laws, their numbers are relatively small and their impact insignificant. Perceptions of New Zealand as an egalitarian society notwithstanding, the Pakeha continue to predominate politically, economically, and culturally.

The various tribes collectively known as Maori represent the indigenous inhabitants of Aotearoa, having occupied that territory for up to a thousand years prior to European contact. The Maori tribes shared much in common with their Polynesian ancestors, despite certain cultural differences created by historical and environmental circumstances. Like most Polynesians, they lived in relatively self-sufficient communities of related families (*whanau*). They derived their subsistence from agriculture and foraging. The unit of political reality rarely extended beyond the tribal (*iwi*) level, although on occasion a group of related tribes would collaborate for military or economic reasons. As was common in pre-capitalist societies, Maori social organization was communal and organized around the dual principles of kinship and residence. Formal hierarchies of status and rank were important, though less so than in Polynesian kingdoms such as Tonga or Hawai'i. In interpersonal relationships the most prized qualities were personal honour, generosity, and readiness to take revenge. These virtues were often defined, expressed, and consolidated through inter-community warfare and the staging of large-scale feasts (Parsonson, 1981). Spiritual agents and the transcendental forces of *mana* (power) and *tapu* (prohibition) pervaded the Maori cosmos, reinforcing the prevailing distribution of power and authority (see Metge, 1976, and Davidson, 1981, for an overview).

This sociocultural design persisted relatively intact until the early part of the nineteenth century when, in the wake of wholesale European settlement, an inexorable decline set in. Early relations were characterized by reciprocity and co-operative self-interest. Later, however, as the white settlers imposed an alien system of authority and values at odds with Maori tribal interests, interaction was marred by hostility and violence. Progress, civilization, paternalism, and protection were the rallying calls of early government policy and administration. As in Canada, the goal was anglo-conformity—to absorb the Maori into the mainstream by undermining the cultural basis of Maori authority. Competition over land, status, power culminated in the Land Wars (now known as New Zealand Wars) of the 1860s, which further weakened the Maori presence and provided an excuse for the state to confiscate large expanses of Maori land as punishment for rebellious tribes. By the turn of the century the Maori population had dropped to about 46,000 (from a high of approximately 250,000), in part because of disease and in part because of assimilationist pressures that left many Maoris poorly equipped for modern society. The twentieth century has not substantially altered the peripheral status of the Maori, although recent developments show some promise.

Contemporary Maori Society

Evidence suggests the Maoris have suffered from their status as dependent wards of the state. Modest improvements in recent years notwithstanding, they are beset by major disparities in all measurable areas (Ministerial Planning Group, 1991): education, employment, crime, incarceration, morbidity, and mortality. Numerous urban Maori youth have lost any ability to speak or think in their ancestral language, much less to identify with their cultural background. Despite recent efforts at linguistic and cultural renewal (Fleras, 1987a, b; 1989b), it remains to be seen if the dead weight of assimilation can be lifted in time to avert open hostility.

The underclass status of the Maoris is borne out in statistics pertaining to demography and socio-economic characteristics. Although pastoral images continue to circulate, by 1981 80.3 per cent of the Maori were living in cities. They constitute a younger population than the Pakeha, with a median age of 20.5 years; 42 per cent are under 15, compared with only 22 per cent for the rest of the population. They also earn less than the Pakeha. Among males, the median income in 1981 was $9,148, versus $10,978 for non-Maori men; among females, the medians were $3,472 and $4,337. Only 3 per cent of the Maori workforce earned annual incomes above $20,000, compared with 11 per cent of their non-Maori counterparts. In 1986, only 3.3 percent of

Pakeha males were unemployed. Maori then comprised 7 per cent of the workers but 11.2 per cent of the unemployed—a figure that had skyrocketed to 20 per cent by 1991 as the Maori continued to bear the brunt of economic restructuring and a downturn in the New Zealand economy (Ministerial Planning Group, 1991). Among women the Maori rate of unemployment stood at 17 per cent in 1986, versus 5.7 per cent for non-Maori women. As well, there is considerable job ghettoization. More Maori (67%) than Pakeha men (43%) were employed in production, manual labour, transport, and equipment operation. Sixty per cent of Maori women worked in service and production— more than double the figure for non-Maori women (26 per cent).

The Maori still lag behind in educational qualifications, whether measured by formal credentials or by advancement into tertiary levels, although the gap is closing (*Dominion*, 23 July 1990). With respect to health, the life expectancy for Maori males stood at 65.2 in 1980—a big improvement over the 1926 figure of 46.6, but still behind non-Maori males' 72.0. For Maori women life expectancy had also improved, to 68.3 in 1980 from 44.7 in 1926, but again this was well below the 76.8 years expected for Pakeha women. Mortality rates have also improved; however, infant deaths among the Maori population outnumbered those in the rest of society by a factor of two.

Finally, the Maori find themselves disproportionately at odds with New Zealand's justice system. Between 1961 and 1984, the number of Maori charged in the criminal justice system increased six-fold, whereas among the Pakeha the figure merely doubled. Maori at present account for 7 per cent of the population over 15 but 39 per cent of those indicted and charged in courts. Maori accounted for 49 per cent of juvenile court appearances in 1981; 71 per cent of these cases involved crimes against property. Maori are also over-represented in the prisons, representing nearly 49 per cent of those confined in 1984. With 361 people per 100,000 in prison, the incarceration rate of the Maori stood second only to that of the Aborigines in Australia (726.5 per 100,000). Little wonder, then, that Maori leaders speak of a pervasive disillusionment among Maori youth and a profound sense of alienation from society—Pakeha and Maori alike (Ministerial Planning Group, 1991).

Maori Aspirations

In their overall concerns and aspirations, the Maori are typical of many encapsulated indigenous populations. Although details vary with tribal affiliations, socio-economic status, age, gender, degree of urbanization, and level of education, in general these aspirations focus on protection and preservation of culture and identity, removal of barriers to social equality, procurement of a sustainable economic base as a basis for self-sufficiency, and revision of formal status within the state. Among the social, cultural, economic, and political and goals are these:

1. to restore Maori social patterns and collectivities as the basis for a tribal renaissance; to redesign Maori institutions according to Maori objectives;

2. to reinstate Maori language, culture, and identity to their former status in society; to encourage Maoris to aspire to *be* Maori in thought and outlook;

3. to reclaim Maori ownership over land and resources as a basis for a tribally-generated renewal; to reinforce aboriginal rights apart from the rights of non-Maori; to decolonize Pakeha attitudes and institutions;

4. to reinforce self-determination by way of power-sharing and decision-making at institutional levels.

These aspirations are varied but consistent with a commitment to *tangata whenua* status, *iwi* development, and recognition of the Treaty of Waitangi. Together they point to a common desire among Maori for full incorporation as integral parts of society, without loss of their distinctiveness as a people.

Tangata Whenua o Aotearoa

Maori appeals for self-determination have emerged as a potent political force in challenging the agenda for Maori–government relations (Awatere, 1984; Greenland, 1984; Levine and Vasil, 1985; Kelsey, 1986). The protest activism of the 1970s has been transformed into political action, much of it aimed at overturning the monocultural bias of government policy in favour of one that is accepting of Maori self-determination and aboriginality as well as control and ownership over Maori resources. Land remains at the centre of protest: the reduction of Maori tribal estates from 27 million hectares to 1.3 million has not only diminished the Maori economic base but also contributed to the decline in the Maori cultural and linguistic heritage (Rice and James, 1987). The impact of this protest is clearly manifest. Judging by recurrent demands to (a) protect Maori culture and language, (b) promote development of Maori initiatives, and (c) settle past grievances in line with the Treaty of Waitangi, even moderate Maori sectors now appear concerned over issues of power-sharing, resource allocation, and restoration of what rightfully belongs to them (Ministerial Planning Group, 1991).

The Treaty of Waitangi

Evolving in conjunction with broader changes in society, Maori demands have become increasingly politicized and directed at restructuring Maori–state relations. This is especially evident in the rapid ascent in formal status and legal standing of the Treaty of Waitangi as a 'binding compact' of moral and legal significance (Pearson, 1990). Now at the forefront of debate over New Zealand race relations, this Treaty has been viewed by the Maori as a starting point for a bicultural society (Department of Statistics, 1990). From the peripheral position of a 'legal nullity', as it was called in an 1877 ruling, the Treaty of Waitangi has evolved to become a social contract calling on both Maori and Pakeha to conduct themselves 'reasonably' and in 'good faith' for fulfilment of mutual obligations (Kawharu, 1989; Walker, 1989). The recent Labour government inserted Treaty principles into several laws, including the State-Owned Enterprises Act that inhibited the privatization of Crown assets if Maori groups had some claim (Vowles, 1991). Entrenchment of the Treaty provides a rationale for the Maori to assert their right, as *tangata whenua*, to a distinct status in New Zealand society with guarantees of cultural integrity and social equality.

Maori responses to the Treaty are varied. Some see it as a fraud and deception, not to mention an embarrassing vestige of New Zealand's colonial past. Others regard it as a sacred, living covenant that upholds bicultural principles and partnership arrangements. Legal interpretations of the Treaty also vary (see Binney, 1989; Cleave, 1989; Tauroa, 1989), but many now accept a version that upholds rather than detracts from Maori sovereignty. While ceding legal authority to the Crown in exchange for British imposition of law and order, the Treaty is now generally interpreted as reasserting some degree of Maori political sovereignty and control over resources (McHugh, 1989). The significance of the Treaty for Maori aspirations cannot be underestimated. It symbolizes and legitimizes the status of Maoris as partners in and constitutional contributors to the reconstruction of a post-colonialist society.

Iwi Development

> The other great object was the detribalisation of the Maoris—to destroy if it were possible, the principle of communism which ran through the whole of their institutions, upon which their social system was based, and which stood as a barrier in the way of all attempts to amalgamate the Maori race into our social and political system.
>
> —Minister of Justice, New Zealand Parliamentary
> Debates 1870: 361.

The Maori are eager to take control of their destinies by developing a sound economic base for renewal and progress. Their demands during the 1980s focused on reclaiming Maori land and access to resources as promulgated in the Treaty (Reynolds, 1990). Development is now clearly driven by Maori sensitivities and priorities rather than those of the dominant sector. Thus the preferred channels for Maori development are traditional kinship structures such as the family and tribe. That the government concurs with this direction marks a significant departure from the detribalization policies of the past, as described in the excerpt above.

This commitment to tribal identity and affiliation constitutes an integral component of Maori culture, enabling the *tangata whenua* to establish a 'sense of place' and a basis for supportive interaction and communication. Tribal structures are seen as the ideal channel for capitalizing on the resources, enthusiasm, and commitment of local communities, since they operate in a Maori context with a cross-section of Maori opinion. Such systems allow decisions to be made as close as possible to those who are served, by people who are knowledgeable about the area and local concerns, and who can be held accountable for their actions. It also reflects a perception that tribal authorities must assume control of state spending and priorities as part of the partnership arrangement between the founding nations of New Zealand.

GOVERNMENT MAORI POLICY:
FROM ASSIMILATION TOWARDS BICULTURALISM

'He iwi kotahi tatou' ('We are all one people')
— Captain Hobson at the signing of the Treaty of Waitangi, 1840.

Maori tribes lived in relative isolation for many centuries. Then, following the explorations of James Cook and others, a variety of Europeans—from whalers and traders to adventurers—arrived in hopes of striking it rich. In time these interlopers were dislodged by the systematic colonizing efforts of missionaries and settlers. The ensuing patterns of interaction between Maori and Pakeha were not altogether different from those that evolved in other colonies such as Canada (Armstrong, 1987; also Fisher, 1980), moving from an initial phase of co-operation to increasing competition for land resources, escalation of conflict to the point of open skirmishes, and eventual withdrawal of the vanquished aboriginal sectors from involvement in society.

Early European Contact and Settlement (1840-65)

The signing of the Treaty of Waitangi in 1840 established a 'blueprint' for Maori–Pakeha relations that has prevailed into the present. A relatively enlightened social contract for its time, the Treaty provided the Maori with British citizenship and rights to their resources in exchange for British sovereignty over New Zealand. Maori–Pakeha relations were to be guided by the lofty slogan *he iwi kotahi tatou* ('we are all one people'). However, it quickly became apparent that the one-people ideal was grounded on the primacy of Anglo-Saxon values and institutions. Although they granted the Maori a relatively high position on the evolutionary scale, the Pakeha remained resolutely opposed to any social order that did not recognize their own racial and cultural superiority (Sinclair, 1971). The spirit of accommodation that had characterized early Maori–Pakeha relations disappeared in the face of settler greed for land and control. The ensuing New Zealand Wars of the 1860s consolidated settler control over much of New Zealand at the expense of the Maori.

Smoothing the 'Dying Pillow': Assimilation as Policy (1865-1945)

> Our plain duty as good compassionate colonialists is to smooth down their dying pillow. Then history will have nothing to reproach us with.
> —Dr Isaac Featherston, Superintendent of Wellington, 1856.

For nearly a century, government interaction with the aboriginal population was defined by a commitment to assimilation. The principles of assimilation framed New Zealand's race relations by defining what was normal, acceptable, and desirable in the societal scheme of things. As in Canada, the aboriginal people were regarded for the most part as a 'social problem' who either 'had problems' because of cultural differences or 'created problems' in competition over power and resources. Early British policy conceded the need to protect and assist the Maori on their way towards assimilation into the mainstream. The objective was to establish government control by phasing out as humanely as possible the cultural basis of Maori society. By law, all legislation concerning the Maori was to concentrate on achievement of this objective:

> Resolved: That in the adoption of any policy, or the passing of any laws, affecting the Native race, This House will keep before it, as its highest object, the entire amalgamation of all Her Majesty's subjects in New Zealand (New Zealand Parliamentary Debates 1862: 483-4).

While the imposition of liberal-capitalist values at odds with the communal principles underlying Maori culture was gradually marginalizing the Maori's social status, passage of the Native Land Act (1865) and the Native School Act (1867) accelerated their cultural demise. Nowhere was the irrelevance of Maori culture more evident than in the wholesale dismissal of Maori language as a tool of daily communication. Following New Zealand's assumption of responsible government during the 1860s, when English emerged as the sole language of instruction at school, Maori was downgraded to the status of a rural folk language for use at home and on ceremonial occasions (Dewes, 1968). In effect, both the cultural and linguistic bases of Maori society were dismissed as irrelevant to nation-building in New Zealand.

Few disputed the desirability of assimilation. Then as now, government Maori policy was constrained by the need to retain power without alienating the Maori to the point of outright rebellion. The assumptions underlying this policy were perceived as too obvious to require defence or analysis. Only questions related to the means, pace, and scope of absorption—whether rapid or gradual, piecemeal or comprehensive—were open to debate. When assimilation proved more difficult than anticipated, special measures such as the system of separate Maori seats in Parliament (see Part I) were instituted. At the same time, as a result of the introduction of disease and alcohol, the Maori population declined to a level where its demise was widely accepted as unfortunate but inevitable in the face of relentless evolutionary progress. All that remained was for the Pakeha to 'smooth the dying pillow' as one last compassionate gesture towards a doomed race.

Integration as Policy: Old Wine in New Bottles? (1945-78)

'Let's integrate!' the shark said to the kahawai, and opened its
mouth to swallow the small fish for breakfast.

—A Maori saying

Under assimilation, Maori–government relations reflected the one-people ideal. Tacitly justifying government actions, this commitment to assimilation continued to play a prominent role in New Zealand's racial affairs until the end of the Second World War. By the late 1950s, however, in response to increasing international awareness of minority rights, a different principle was assuming growing lustre. In contrast to assimilation, which sought to absorb the Maori with complete loss of culture, the new principle of integration centred on retention of diversity within a single overall framework (Hunn and Booth, 1962).

Integration as policy was formally launched in 1961 with the publication of what came to be known as the Hunn Report. Consolidating in a concise manner what was already practice in policy and administrative circles, this report envisioned integration as ensuring equal rights and opportunities for the Maori, but not at the expense of their right to cultural pursuits of their own choice. The ideal was to combine Maori and Pakeha elements into one New Zealand culture without destroying the cultural distinctiveness of either.

In reality, there was much in the practice of integration to suggest that assimilation remained the true ideal. Maori leaders, in particular, saw little appreciable difference in style or objectives. As far as they were concerned, the policy of integration served merely to disguise the government's assimilationist goals in the same way that earlier appeals to assimilation had concealed the intent to appropriate Maori land. Nor did a commitment to integration resolve Maori claims for retention of their cultural aspirations, as noted in this excerpt from a Maori response to the Hunn Report:

> Let it be understood that, while we are willing to join with the Pakeha in becoming New Zealanders, we have no desire whatsoever to become Pakehas. There is much in the Pakeha way of life which is admirable, and much that we are willing to learn and adopt from it. Above all, we wish to live in harmony and equality with our Pakeha brethren. But this means cooperation from both sides. For our part, we are willing to give as well as to take, but we strongly oppose the assumptions that we must forget our history, our culture, our racial origins—all that is involved in the word Maoritanga. Only when this is clear to all will there be any true basis for lasting harmony. We are people proud of our heritage, and attempts to destroy that, however disguised by expressions of good will, can only result ultimately in serious disturbances (Maori Synod, 1961).

To Maori leaders, the conclusion was inescapable: both assimilation and integration shared a single political objective: the creation of a uniform society, united under a common set of political and social values. Maori culture was devalued except as decoration.

That the government had overplayed the relevance of integration as a solution to the Maori 'problem' became clear as Maori activism exploded during the 1970s. Maori politicization arose out of the interrelated dynamics of post-war Maori urban migration and the emergence of a Western-educated Maori intelligentsia (Pearson, 1991). To draw attention to their grievances, a number of activist groups resorted to American-style civil-rights protests in pursuit of cultural identity and social equity. A milestone in such activism was the Land March of 1975. More than any other event, this march from Cape Reinga to Wellington symbolized the growing assertiveness of Maori *mana* (power) and the resurgence of Maori pride and identity as a distinct people (Butterworth, 1990). This protest and the confrontations that followed at Waitangi, Raglan, and Bastion Point highlighted the Maori's resolve to decolonize their relations with New Zealand.

'Tu Tangata': Community-Based, Culturally-Sensitive Development (1978-88)

In an effort to reassert control, the government undertook a series of commissions and consultations that led to the creation of a new policy in 1978 entitled Tu Tangata ('Stand Tall'). The primary goal of Tu Tangata was 'the development of the Maori people and their resources' (Puketapu, 1982). It aimed at nothing less than the re-emergence of the Maori as a culturally unique people, willing to 'stand tall' and capable of overcoming institutional dependency when properly equipped with resources by the state (Fleras, 1984; Butterworth, 1990). Promotion of socio-economic equality, particularly for those at the bottom of the ladder, lay at the heart of this philosophy. In contrast to conventional policies, Tu Tangata embraced not only Maori cultural values but a spiritual dimension as a catalyst for growth. Expressions of Maori culture were promoted not as a problem for the government to solve, but as a resource for enhancing the effectiveness of locally based projects. Kinship structures and various traditional forms of reciprocity and support were no longer disparaged as detrimental to advancement; instead they were embraced as inherent strengths and instruments of adaptation in improving the performance of Maoris at school and in the workplace.

Community-based development entailed new commitments. To overcome apathy and negativism, members of the community were encouraged to participate in the design and implementation of programs. Community-based solutions to local problems were promoted as preferable to those depending on the infusion of more funding or expertise. Tu Tangata was directed at eliminating the sources of the 'problem', not merely at treating its symptoms. Prevention, not treatment, became the motto as the Department of Maori Affairs envisioned long-term solutions to recurrent problems through the collective utilization of community resources and resourcefulness (Fleras, 1985a).

The effects of Tu Tangata were evident in areas as diverse as (a) public service staffing (b) formal recognition of Maori as an official language (although not equal to English), (c) increased funding and support for Maori services (especially Maori-language preschools), and (d) increasing reliance on bilateral consultation and government by consensus. Of particular importance was the creation of specific government programs and commissions. The convening of the Hui Taumata (a national gathering on Maori economic prospects) in 1984, followed by the establishment of the Maori Economic Development Commission, drew public attention to the inadequacies of 'negative' Maori spending (money spent on welfare, prisons, etc.) (Report, 1984). The Maori Resource Development Corporation, a state-sponsored concessionary 'bank' for small commercial projects known as 'Mana' (Rice and James, 1987), was instituted, in addition to 'Maccess' (a tribally-based training program for the unemployed). The willingness of tribal authorities to assume responsibility for the implementation of the Mana Enterprises and Maori Access schemes contributed to a shift in public perception of Maori structures as forces for advancement.

Politicians and the state sector responded positively to Tu Tangata initiatives. The new policy's emphasis on community-driven solutions to the Maori 'problem' mollified those dissatisfied with Maori dependence on state spending and paternalistic support systems. In addition, its 'anti-bureaucracy' bias appealed to those who favoured openness, direct action, and non-hierarchical networks over formal structures. Finally, successive National and Labour governments enlisted this philosophy as a convenient platform from which to address the growing crisis in Maori–government relations (Fleras, 1985a; also Martin, 1982).

Sectors of the Maori community were equally supportive of Tu Tangata. The proliferation of action-oriented programs demonstrated clearly the strength of public enthusiasm. Among these were home-work centres for Maori secondary pupils, vocational and trade training projects for school leavers, and alternative juvenile justice procedures. Few, however, so captured the public's imagination as the Department-inspired Te Kohanga Reo program, establishing immersion Maori preschools (Fleras, 1983; 1987a, b; 1989). From its inception in April 1982, this program expanded to the point where nearly 700 centres had been established throughout New Zealand by the end of 1990. As we shall see later, it typified the Department's commitment to culturally-specific and community-focused development by upholding the principles of *whanau* (extended family values) and Maori language renewal. It also illustrated the extent to which the Maori community was willing to assume responsibility for a social movement that allowed a considerable degree of local input and control.

But this and related success stories did not insulate the Tu Tangata policy from criticism (Tainui Report, 1983). Resentment grew among the ranks of the bureaucracy, where the swiftness of reorganization confused and angered many officials. Applying Tu Tangata philosophies outside the main urban centres of Wellington and Auckland proved impossible in the face of entrenched tribal interests. District and subdistrict offices displayed indifference and hostility to Head Office overtures. Many were sceptical of the Department's motives in revising its relationship with its client groups. As often as not, the Department resorted to the time-honoured practice of imposing priorities without adequate local consultation, leaving the community with little room for input except in 'fine-tuning' the implementation of already specified local programs. Others dismissed the shift towards people-powered development as a shrewd exercise in transferring the burden of responsibility, costs, and accountability to the local community (see also DiTamasco, 1984). For many activists, failure to promote Maori collective and land rights, much less sovereignty and power, confirmed the essentially conservative agenda of Tu Tangata. That the reality of these reforms fell short of their promise gave rise to a credibility gap that was later exploited by activists as justifying additional change.

Contemporary Maori Policy: 'Te Urupare Rangapu'

Whereas the Treaty of Waitangi symbolizes the special relationship between the Maori people and the Crown: And whereas it is desirable that

the spirit of the exchange of sovereignty for the protection of rangatiratanga [chieftainship] embodied in the Treaty of Waitangi be reaffirmed:
And whereas rangatiratanga in the context of this Act means the custody
and care of matters significant to the cultural identity of the Maori people
of New Zealand in trust for future generations: And whereas, in particular, it is desirable to recognise the special relationship of the Maori
people to their land and for that reason to promote the retention of that
land in the hands of the owners' descent groups, and to facilitate the occupation and utilisation of that land for the benefit of the owners' descent
groups: And whereas it is desirable to establish agencies to assist the
Maori people to achieve the implementation of these principles. . . .

— Preamble to the Maori Affairs Bill, 1988.

In 1984 a fourth Labour government came to power with a resounding
majority. The party had campaigned diligently in defence of Maori
interests, stressing the need to renew Maori relations with the state
through improved consultation, power-sharing, and local self-determination. It sought to augment Maori influence over limited jurisdictions and decision-making spheres through traditional tribal (*iwi*) units
and the justificatory rhetoric of devolution (McLeay, 1991). The government's Maori policy agenda was set out in the 1988 publication 'Te
Urupare Rangapu' ('Partnership Response'). Among the key provisions were promises:

1. To honour the principles of the Treaty of Waitangi. Protection of
   Maori interests had to reflect the exercise of government powers
   in a manner that was reasonable, in good faith, and consistent
   with Treaty provisions.

2. To eliminate the socio-economic gaps between Maori and non-
   Maori. Primary attention focused on removing discriminatory
   barriers that were not derived from individual or cultural prefer-
   ences.

3. To provide economic opportunities. A sound economic basis
   rooted in Maori ownership of land and control of resources was
   necessary if Maori were to eliminate dependency and impoverishment.

4. To deal expeditiously and fairly with Maori grievances arising
   from breaches of the Treaty.

5. To foster Maori language and culture as positive contributors to
   the development of a distinctive New Zealand identity.

6. To promote Maori involvement in policy formulation and service
   delivery, in addition to implementation and monitoring of
   various programs.

7. To encourage Maori participation in the political process.

These provisions continue to underlie government policy and administration despite a change in government in October 1990. Some changes in emphasis and administration are expected, but all indications suggest a 'business as usual' approach by the National Party government.

The Treaty of Waitangi: Cornerstone of Maori Policy
The Labour government's Maori policy drew its inspiration and legitimacy from the partnership ethos inherent in the Treaty of Waitangi. Signed in 1840 between the British and numerous Maori tribal chiefs, the Treaty is now firmly established as a founding document of New Zealand society and the basis of constitutional authority. Public recognition and endorsement is escalating: a Heylan Poll in February 1990 (reported in the *Project Waitangi Newsletter* [1990]) revealed a sharp increase in public support for the principles of the Treaty. Nearly 60 per cent of the respondents (compared with only 44 per cent in September 1989) saw the Treaty as important. It was viewed as a foundation stone of society by 65 per cent (52 per cent the previous September). Another 72 per cent endorsed the Treaty as a system of unity and understanding (compared with 61 per cent the year before).

A modern reconstruction in English of the Maori version of the Treaty, used by the New Zealand Court of Appeal in 1987, reads in part as follows:

> . . . The First,
> The Chiefs of the Confederation and all of the chiefs who have not joined that Confederation give absolutely to the Queen of England forever the complete government of their land.

> The Second,
> The Queen of England agrees to protect the chiefs, the subtribes and all of the peoples of New Zealand in the unqualified exercise of their chieftainship over their lands, villages and all their treasures . . .

> The Third,
> For this agreed arrangement therefore concerning the Government of the Queen, the Queen of England will protect all the ordinary people of New Zealand and will give them the same rights and duties of citizenship as the people of England. . . .

Nevertheless, the terms of the Treaty continue to be disputed, in part because of differences in the Maori and English versions of the document (Orange, 1989; Temm, 1990; Mitchell, 1990). In the English version, article one appears to extinguish Maori sovereignty by transferring authority and control to the Crown. The Crown acquired not only absolute ownership of the land, but the right to rule New Zealand in accordance with Western principles. The Maori interpretation, by contrast, suggests a transfer not of sovereignty (for which there was no Maori equivalent at the time), but rather of governorship (*kawanatanga*), implying something less than absolute authority. In article two, the English version confirms full, exclusive, and undisputed possession of land, forests, fisheries, and other assets, whereas the Maori version indicates that the Queen will protect the unqalified exercise of Maori chieftainship over lands, villages, and 'treasures' (*taonga*). Article three is less contentious, as both versions appear to extend Crown protection to the Maoris with corresponding rights and privileges as equal British subjects.

These variations in interpretation are not merely academic. They contribute to the Treaty's ambiguity as a source of moral guidance and social justice and as a guide to distribution of resources. In its English version the Treaty appears to legitimize Crown sovereignty over the land in exchange for protection of the indigenous population. By contrast, in its Maori version the Treaty appears to represent not a surrender, but a declaration of traditional Maori authority and a reaffirmation of (a) their sovereign status within Aotearoa, (b) the inalienability of their rights over land, language, and culture, and (c) their unrestricted access to natural resources (Armstrong, 1987). Not only does this version legitimize Maori social, economic, and cultural renewal, but it upholds their status as the *tangata whenua* and elevates their relations with the government to the level of partnership and biculturalism. In this solemn transaction, the British Crown acquired the right to pass laws for effective government in exchange for the obligation to protect and promote *tangata whenua* interests. The Maori, in turn, ceded 'governorship' to the Crown (that is, the right to make laws for maintenance of social order), but retained control of their possessions, interests, and customs.

At present, legal, public, and political opinion alike are veering towards the Maori interpretation. In this reading, the Treaty represents a fundamental constitutional fact that acknowledges the status of the *tangata whenua* as 'nations within', with a corresponding right of self-determination over physical or cultural resources. It recognizes that the Maori possess a special status as a founding people who entered into a contractual relationship with the Crown concerning sovereignty (McLeay, 1991). It also establishes a basis for genuine biculturalism, rooted in the principle of Pakeha legal authority and Maori political sovereignty (McHugh, 1989).

Between 1986 and 1990, the Labour government actively used the Treaty as a basis for government policy and administration (Labour Government 1988a, b; Kelsey, 1990). For the government, the Treaty of Waitangi has emerged as a linchpin in the bicultural restructuring of its relations with the Maori. As a powerful symbol with varied meanings, it establishes an overarching framework that legitimizes government initiatives for devolving Maori–government relations. At the same time, it furnishes (a) a guideline ('blueprint') for policy action, (b) a standard ('charter') by which to evaluate the effectiveness of government initiatives, and (c) a rationale ('ideology') justifying programs and practices in this area. Among the specific guidelines for government policy that the Treaty provides are the following:

1. The Treaty establishes the principle of two nations with two distinct cultures within a single overarching political framework.

2. The Treaty is interpreted as a declaration of *iwi* (tribal) independence and Maori sovereignty over Aotearoa, promotion of inalienable Maori rights over land and culture, protection of indigenous human rights, and unrestricted access to natural resources (Armstrong, 1987; Williams, 1989).

3. The Treaty extends the rights and privileges of British citizenship to the *tangata whenua*, including the rights to Maori language, identity, and culture. Recognition of the bicultural focus of the Treaty has conferred two sets of entitlements on the *tangata whenua*: namely, equality rights as partners and citizens of Aotearoa and special rights vested by virtue of the reference in article two of the Treaty to Maori control of their possessions, interests, and customs (see Temm, 1990).

4. The Treaty guarantees Maori rights and interests as well as authority to protect and promote those 'treasures' of concern to the *tangata whenua*. Neither Parliamentary nor regional laws may be passed if they violate the spirit of the Treaty or if they transgress Maori land holdings and natural environs. In effect, the role of the state is not merely to recognize these rights and interests; in light of its fiduciary role as trustee for special Maori interests (Macdonald, 1990), the state must become actively and positively involved in the protection and promotion of relevant cultural values (Ministerial Committee of Inquiry, 1987).

Following these policy guidelines, the Treaty has begun redefining mutual rights, reciprocal obligations, and intergroup entitlements. The bicultural 'distributive ideal' (Sharp, 1990) espoused by the Treaty provides a blueprint for restructuring Maori relations with the state, based in part on a partnership agreement, and in part on the state's awareness of its responsibility to advance equality and equity. As well, the elevation of the Treaty to a constitutional level has empowered the courts to make judgements upholding the legitimacy of Aotearoa as a bicultural state (Sharp, 1990). For example, passage of the State Ownership Enterprises

Act in 1987—already hailed by some as the country's single most important piece of legislation (*New Zealand Herald*, 26 Dec. 1987)—placed an injunction against government sales of Crown land to private interests in contravention of Treaty principles (Macdonald, 1990).

The Waitangi Tribunal

To put Treaty principles into practice, the government has agreed to incorporate them in any new legislation. More significantly, in 1975 it established a formal channel for Maori grievances and claims against the state. A 'quasi-judicial advisory body' (Rice and James, 1987), the Waitangi Tribunal was originally created to examine contemporary land disputes stemming from the Treaty, but its jurisdiction has been rolled back to include unlawful confiscation of Maori lands or resources since 1840. The main function of the Tribunal is to inquire into and make recommendations to the Crown for Maori claims or grievances relating to sections of the Treaty. With the expanded power and jurisdiction at their disposal, the Maori as a group now possess the right to press claims against the Crown for land or resources unfairly expropriated by previous governments.

To date, the Tribunal's rulings have drawn public attention (and dismay) to unlawful government activity in restricting Maori access to resources (cultural and material) as guaranteed in the Treaty. The Tribunal has been viewed as a major catalyst for Maori politicization, a spiritual and ideological focus for Maori politics, and a stimulant to discussion of New Zealand nation-building and Maori sovereignty (Pearson, 1991). But its success in addressing—let alone resolving—Maori grievances has been only moderate. Terms of reference are restricted. For example, the Tribunal cannot accept Maori claims for disputed land under private ownership; its authority is limited to applying the specific principles of the Treaty; and it must work with the knowledge that its decisions are binding on the government only where Crown land or state enterprises are concerned (Reynolds, 1990). Moreover, because of the unpredictability associated with judicial decisions, the National Party government has proposed to circumvent the Tribunal by way of an *ad hoc* fast-track system for political negotiation of Maori grievances.

Clearly New Zealand's experience with the Tribunal has been paradoxical. In a critique of the government's Treaty policy and the Waitangi Tribunal, Jane Kelsey (1991) criticized Labour government Treaty initiatives as self-seeking efforts to deflate Maori militancy and defuse Maori political/economic ambitions, without any disruption to the prevailing distribution of power. Debate over the Treaty was gradually reformulated to accommodate Maori demands within the political and economic structures of the New Zealand state. Maori challenges to the constitutional legitimacy of the state and restoration of economic resources were defused by the Waitangi Tribunal, which had become 'overloaded and under-resourced' and 'highly legalistic, with claimants dissempowered and dependent on costly lawyers' (Kelsey, 1991: 127). The Tribunal's organization grew increasingly bureaucratic while its personnel became Pakeha-dominated and marginalized by the government. Hearings proved to be a drain on the claimants' resources, with few prospects for tangible returns even in successful cases. In short, not only had the Tribunal ceded the symbols of Maori sovereignty to the Crown, but it had momentarily co-opted Maori interests in an act of 'legal imperialism' (Kelsey, 1991: 128).

Restructuring Maori Affairs

With the Treaty firmly established as blueprint and signpost, the Labour government embarked on a path to restructure Maori policy and administration. In many ways its policy initiatives were consistent with broader efforts to reduce state involvement in the delivery of services generally, by separating and privatizing various functions (policy, commercial, regulatory, and service) of state departments. In 1988, following a series of submissions to the discussion paper 'He Tirohanga Rangapu' ('Partnership Perspectives'), the government promised to modify the delivery of programs and services and to make the process more consistent with Maori priorities and structures. The appearance of the government's policy statement in 'Te Urupare Rangapu' ('Partnership Response') was an outcome of this commitment (Fleras, 1991).

Of critical importance was the passage of the Maori Affairs Restructuring Act in 1989, initiating a three-pronged devolution of Maori policy and administration. The first stage established a monitoring and advisory body to be known as the Ministry of Maori Affairs, or Manatu Maori, which came into effect on 1 July 1989. Its mission statement put it squarely under the Treaty as a blueprint for reconstruction:

> To give substance to the principle of partnership embodied in the Treaty of Waitangi by generating an environment which encourages Maori people to express their rangatiratanga [chieftainship] in ways that enhance New Zealand's economic, social, and cultural life.

In addition, the new ministry took on responsibility for advising government on policy and sought to monitor institutional and organizational responsiveness to the partnership provisions of the Labour government's Treaty policy. Freed of any operational responsibilities, it also assumed a watchdog role in reviewing all legislation pertaining to the Maori and the Treaty.

The second phase addressed the operational aspects of Maori–government relations. The formal inception of the Iwi Transition Agency (Te Tira Ahu Iwi) gave practical expression to the government's proposal for a tribally-based system of service delivery. The empowerment of *iwi* structures for the distribution of government goods and services served as the touchstone of the government's devolutionary Maori policy. A network of relatively autonomous tribal authorities was to be established; each would have some degree of functional independence, but all remained answerable to the government for use of funds. Central to the development process was the acknowledgement of Maori authorities as the *only culturally appropriate* mechanism for the planning and implementation of all government-funded social, economic, and cultural programs as they apply to the Maori. However, despite high hopes, by 1990 relatively few tribes appeared sufficiently organized to take over responsibility for delivering services.

The third phase in the devolutionary process saw passage of the Runanaga a Iwi Bill (initially called the Iwi Empowering Bill) in August 1990. The new Act sought to confer legal authority upon recognized tribal (*iwi*) structures, which would enable them to enter into formal contractual arrangements with government or private sectors. It also proposed to give these structures the legal power to determine the allocation of funds and resources to various groups. Hence the Act was intended to give full control of possessions, interests, and custom (*rangatiratanga*) to *iwi* authorities by clearing up a variety of administrative matters pertaining to the corporatization of *iwi* structures.

But implemention of the Act has been aborted. As promised in its election campaign, the incoming National Party has moved to repeal the Act on the grounds of excessive government interference in Maori affairs. While repeal of the Act may de-corporatize tribal structures, there is no indication of government plans to dismantle the *iwi*-based system of service delivery upon which Labour's Maori devolution policy was based.

Partnership Response/Institutional Responsiveness

In June 1986 the Labour government announced that Treaty principles would be incorporated in all future legislation, and that government departments were obligated to consult the appropriate Maori authorities in policy matters related to Treaty issues or 'partnership responses' (Macdonald, 1990). The 1988 government policy document 'Te Urupare Rangapu' ('Partnership Response') reiterated this commitment to make the public service more responsive to Maori aspirations, values, and concerns. The chief executive officers of all government departments were to be held accountable for the implementation of effective and proactive measures, not only to reflect Maori presence in society but also to improve institutional accommodation with regard to structure, procedures, and reward allocation.

The assumptions underlying the principle of 'partnership responsiveness' transcended the simple injunction to improve the effectiveness and universality of service delivery to the general public (Responsiveness Unit, 1989). By virtue of their unique status as a founding people, the Maori were entitled to active and meaningful input in the areas of policy-making, corporate planning, internal administration, and personnel. The goal of this policy was to overturn policies that in the past had contributed to Maori marginalization while reinforcing long-standing Maori antipathy to monocultural state agencies. Such a commitment meant revamping the focus of government services to the client through enhanced comprehensiveness, relevance, participation, consultation, and cultural sensitivity. In effect, the treatment of Maori clients was to be consistent with the (a) Treaty partnership provisions, (b) government responsiveness objectives as defined in Te Urupare Rangapu, and (c) the state commitment to improving public-service efficiency.

As a basis for restructuring Maori–government interaction at the level of service delivery (Responsiveness Unit, 1989; also Waitangi Tribunal, 1988) the government has adopted six principles: (a) the principle of partnership as established in the Treaty; (b) the principle of reciprocal obligations involving the mutual rights and duties that flow from recognition of the Treaty; (3) the principle of freedom to govern without unreasonably restricting Maori rights to land, resources, and culture; (d) the principle of tribal self-regulation, whereby tribal authorities retain a paramount right (in conjunction with state authority) to exercise control over Maori land and resources; (e) the right of redress for past breaches of the Treaty (subject to qualification by state priorities); and (f) the principle of equality reflecting the necessity for special measures if equity is to be achieved. Government performance in upholding Treaty rights was to be measured by institutional responsiveness to Maori concerns, values, and ambitions.

State service institutions are now under an obligation to implement 'partnership responsiveness'. For example, the Department of Inland Revenue is undergoing a series of institutional reforms, including (a) a name change to Te Tari Taake, adoption of a departmental *waiata* ('song') and Maori motifs on letterhead, and inclusion of a Maori elder as a patron; (b) emphasis on Maori involvement in corporate planning and training packages to inform senior and middle man-agement of the new policy shifts; (c) consultation and networking with Maori communities with regard to organizational matters and unmet Maori needs; (d) acknowledgement of Maori values in the length of leaves granted Maori employees to attend funerals; (e) creation of a 'partnership response' unit that is directly responsible to senior management; (f) review of Departmental policies by Manatu Maori; and (g) holding the Chief Executive Officer accountable for the implementation of measures to bring about Departmental responsiveness (Department of Inland Revenue, 1990).

To assess the scope of institutional responsiveness as a basis for future action, Manatu Maori has circulated a self-evaluation questionnaire to government departments. Among the questions it asks are (a) how well the organization reflects and reinforces a Maori dimension in line with Treaty and partnership principles; (b) what strategies are to be implemented to meet the government commitment of full responsiveness by 1994; (c) what resources are likely to be allocated and what outcomes they are expected to produce; (d) what measures are being implemented to ensure Maori involvement (participation and consultation) in decision-making as well as planning and operations; and (e) how organizations can assess Maori levels of (dis)satisfaction with current government services and interaction.

Preliminary findings indicate some unevenness in institutional responsiveness. Organizational accommodation to date has largely concentrated on sensitivity exercises through in-house training packages or sessions held at Maori ceremonial complexes (*marae*). Issues pertaining to organizational structure, operational procedures, corporate culture, working environment, and personnel are rarely addressed. Nor is there much activity around equity issues related to improved representation, training, and promotion of Maori employees. Broader issues outside the normal institutional discourse—such as entitlement of the *tangata whenua*, closure of the socio-economic gap, empowerment of tribal authorities, and enhancement of Maori language and culture—receive even less attention. In others words, Manatu Maori has concluded, much needs to done if state institutions are to reflect the partnership principles intrinsic to the Treaty.

'Ka Awatea': Old Policy, New Rhetoric?

Ka Ao, Ka Ao, Ka Awatea (It is dawn, it is dawn, it is daybreak).
— The National Party's slogan for its Maori policy, 1990

A change of government in October 1990 meant that it was only a matter of time before a 'new' Maori policy came into effect. Several months later, in March 1991, the National government unveiled its blueprint for the 1990s. Entitled Ka Awatea ('It Is Daybreak'), it represented a curious mixture of old and new, but in many ways continued along the same path as its Labour predecessor (Te Urupare Rangapu). Sixty-eight recommendations were proposed, with particular emphasis on improving Maori education, employment, and training programs;

economic development through more efficient land use and small business ventures; and health issues, especially prevention. A new Ministry of Maori Development was proposed that would combine the resources and staffing of the Iwi Transition Agency and Manatu Maori. As a superministry with advisory and monitoring powers, the new Ministry would handle policy, operations, auditing, and strategic planning, but on a smaller scale than the former Department of Maori Affairs (Ministerial Planning Group, 1991; *Nga Kauwae*, March/ April 1991).

The creators of Ka Awatea were shrewd enough to accept aspects of Te Urupare Rangapu that were consistent with National philosophies and integral to Maori aspirations. These included a continuing commitment to the Treaty of Waitangi as a 'founding document of New Zealand' that conferred on the Crown the right to pass laws, subject only to recognition of Maori needs for self-determination, control over land and resources, and social equality. The new policy also supported the concepts of institutional responsiveness and ministerial responsibility for the design and delivery of culturally-sensitive services to Maori clientele. As part of the ongoing commitment to restructure Maori–government relations, it also came out in favour of the principle of devolution at the level of 'tribal development'. Maori tribal structures developed under the Labour government would not be tampered with, and *iwi* would continue to be free to form corporate bodies and contract for services from the appropriate government agency.

In other points of emphasis and direction, Ka Awatea appeared to revert to more orthodox approaches in defining the 'Maori problem' and appropriate 'solutions'. The new policy has abandoned much of its predecessor's rhetoric both on tribally-driven development and on restructuring of Maori–state relations to reflect and reinforce Maori rights as the original inhabitants of New Zealand. Under Ka Awatea, the social and economic difficulties that have encumbered Maori progress would be dealt with through a combination of government resources and community skills operating in much the same way as the Maori preschool program, Kohanga Reo, has brought together local and government resources to avert the demise of Maori language. With its overwhelming economic focus, Ka Awatea appears less 'politicized' than Te Urupare Rangapu, and in many ways more consistent with the National Party's Tu Tangata initiatives (emphasizing community-based and culturally-driven development). Not unexpectedly, the Maori are once again depicted as an economic problem, or as having economic problems. To improve their socio-economic status and above all to reduce their dependency on the state, a certain degree of government intervention is proposed—albeit carefully targeted to ensure that market forces were not unduly hindered (see Ministerial Planning Group, 1991). Improving

Maori educational standards was singled out as especially important in taking New Zealand out of its economic doldrums and enhancing its international competitiveness.

The creation of a 'new' government policy (Ka Awatea), combined with the Ministry of Maori Development proposed for 1992, can be seen as part of an ongoing restructuring to deal positively with the Maori 'problem'. Services are to be provided on a predominantly regional basis, with *iwi* supplying representatives to ensure that delivery proceeds smoothly (McLeay, 1991). With its focus on enhancing Maori access to the services and resources of the public sector, the new ministry is expected to monitor government responsiveness to Maori needs and to provide advice as well as to initiate local programs in training, health, education, and economic resource development (*Nga Kauwae*, 1991). The proposed reduction of Maori staff to a policy advisory unit of about 200 is consistent with government efforts to devolve Maori affairs and foster community and tribal self-sufficiency, but may not coincide with Maori ambitions. At a time when the Maori are looking to restructure their relationship with the New Zealand state, the government is casting about for ways to 'get out' of the Maori business as part of a massive social restructuring. While it is still too early to gauge the full Maori reaction to Ka Awatea, the likelihood of rejection and further struggles to 're-politicize' the Maori agenda appears strong.

THE ADMINISTRATION OF MAORI AFFAIRS: FROM BUREAUCRACY TO DEVELOPMENT

New Zealand's Maori policy has undergone a significant overhaul in recent years in response both to Maori activism and to changes in the country's political economy. Once directed towards assimilation and, later, integration, it now incorporates a working commitment to the principles of partnership, biculturalism, and devolution. No less important have been the policy notions related to Maori self-determination and control over issues of relevance to them (local development, culture) and respect for Maori sensitivities rather than political or bureaucratic priorities. But putting such principles into practice has not always been easy. This certainly has been the case with respect to the Maori Affairs Department in its role as mediator between the New Zealand state and the Maori population.

For nearly 150 years, Maori policy administration and the implementation of government initiatives were conducted through various state agencies that collectively have come to be known as the Department of Maori Affairs (Butterworth, 1990). By the late 1980s, however, efforts to 'invert the bureaucratic pyramid' and put it under client control (Fleras, 1989a) were seen as insufficient, and in 1989 Maori Affairs was abolished, to be replaced by the Iwi Transition Agency (Te

Tira Ahu Iwi). This concept of tribal development sounds promising, yet several practical limitations have appeared that reflect competing views of 'devolution' and 'partnership' (Fleras, 1991). A reluctance to fundamentally redesign the relational status of Maori in New Zealand society has also proven problematic.

The Department of Maori Affairs: A History

As we have seen, initial Maori policy revolved around the principles of protection, civilization, and assimilation. The aim was to protect the interests of the Maori without ever losing sight of the need to civilize and absorb them for the greater good of the colony (Ward, 1974). In order to transform the Maori into loyal and self-sufficient citizens of the colony, the government instituted a series of Native Offices that collectively have come to be known as the Department of Maori Affairs. In theory, these Offices attempted to protect the Maori from disruptive influences without denying them access to the virtues of civilization and Christianity. In practice, however, they tended to concentrate on issues pertaining to the sale or development of Maori land. This paradoxical commitment—to protect both Maori and non-Maori interests within a bureaucratic framework—has been a central theme in the administration of Maori affairs.

The history of the Maori Affairs Department is complex and convoluted (Butterworth, 1989, 1990). For convenience, four eras can be discerned: Native Protectorate, Native Department, Maori Affairs Department, and Iwi Transition Agency. First was the Native Protectorate between 1840 and 1846. With its focus on mediating between the Maori and the Crown, the Protectorate sought to advise the government on how best to assist, protect, and advance Maori rights as stipulated in the Treaty of Waitangi (Reedy, 1990). These efforts proved to be its downfall, since they interfered with colonists' interests, and the abolition of the Protectorate in 1846 left a vacuum in policy and administration that was eventually filled by the creation of the Native Department in 1861.

Instituted largely to deal with an immediate crisis in Maori–Pakeha relations, the Native Department had a strong assimilationist mission: to incorporate the Maori into the political, legal, and social fabric of New Zealand society, as well as to foster limited government assistance in areas such as Maori education and policing. But, constrained by the racist and evolutionary ideologies of the day, the Native Department declined to little more than an administrative rubber stamp for transferring ownership of Maori land to settlers. When, by 1893, it appeared that the Maori were about to disappear through either absorption or attrition, the Department was abolished and its functions were transferred to the Justice Department and the Native Land Court.

Once again, however, the absence of a formal mediating institution highlighted the dangers of inaction, particularly with regard to land issues and Maori health. The establishment of Maori Councils (regional organizations of sub-tribes) in 1900 went some way towards improving Maori hygiene and sanitation, but, like other grassroots initiatives, they suffered from a lack of resources and political will, and were non-existent by 1929 (Fleras, 1981). Meanwhile, in 1906, the Native Department (the name was changed to Maori Affairs in 1947) had been reconstituted, largely as a land management agency. Its major functions were to assist the Maori to consolidate what was left of their land by way of Maori Land Boards; to ensure maximum use and administration of Maori lands under various Maori Land Administration schemes; and to improve the social and economic status of the Maori. The latter function become increasingly more important with passage of the Maori Social and Economic Advancement Act in 1946 (to deal with the post-war return of Maori service personnel), at which time the government began encouraging the Maori to leave rural lands and move into cities, an effort that created a wide range of adjustment problems.

Maori Affairs as Social Welfare
With the ascendancy of the Labour Party in 1935 came increased political awareness of the government's responsibility to assist the Maori (Orange, 1977; Love, 1977; Hanson, 1980). State involvement was justified on the grounds that it would accelerate the integration of tradition-bound Maori into modern society as productive and self-reliant citizens. Government resources flowed into Maori land-development schemes, while public funds were channelled into improving rural Maori housing (Grace, 1937). Responsibility for overseeing these programs of material rehabilitation resided with the reconstituted Native Department, which established a social-welfare division in 1944. Although initially directed towards assisting Maori in war-related industries, the Department's welfare operations expanded in size and scope to include job placement, education, and family relocation within urban settings (Hunn and Booth, 1962).

Emboldened by this wider mandate, the renamed Maori Affairs Department evolved into a bureaucracy of formidable proportions. Where once government authorities had dominated the Maori by threat of force, control was now achieved through the manipulations of a bureaucracy that reached into almost every aspect of its clients' lives. But expansion during the 1950s and 1960s failed to produce much improvement in Maori social and economic status, and by the early 1970s it was obvious that integration was no more successful in this respect than assimilation had been (Report, 1984; also Report, 1981, 1982). Worse still, Maori language and cultural identity were continuing to erode. Outbreaks of Maori activism in the late 1960s and the 1970s alerted political officials to deficiencies in the government's race relations policy. Alarmed by this breakdown in established responses to the so-called Maori 'problem', and fearing American-style urban race riots, the government had little choice but to reappraise the administration of its Maori policy (Fleras, 1985a).

Tu Tangata: Debureaucratizing the Bureaucracy
Under pressure from various groups both within and outside the Department, the Minister of Maori Affairs called for an extensive review of Departmental policies and practices. The resulting Community Services Report (Puketapu and Haber-Thomas, 1977) warned of the growing chasm between the Maori and the state as the Department drifted along, oblivious to its clients' cultural and developmental needs. Spiralling bureaucratization had created a top-heavy and paternalistic agency far removed from the people it was expected to serve (Puketapu, 1981, 1982). Clients were viewed as hapless victims, incapable of exercising control over their destiny and bereft of any inclination to do so unless prodded into action. Maori cultural values were generally regarded as impediments to modernization, to be purged from the agenda except when relevant in advancing Departmental objectives. Administrative solutions to Maori problems had emanated from desk-bound professionals who stipulated what was best for the Maori and stifled local initiative in the process. To break up this bureaucratic log-jam, in June 1978 the National ('conservative') government unveiled a new administrative program for Maori Affairs. Reflecting the assumption that excessive state dependency contributed to the Maori 'problem', this administrative policy, entitled Tu Tangata ('Stand Tall'), soon put into motion a chain of events that culminated in its demise a decade later.

The introduction of Tu Tangata as the basis for administrative action resulted in a partial realignment of the Department's objectives: to move from a relationship based on dependency, paternalism, and control to one grounded in the principles of development, partnership, and self-determination (Fleras, 1985a). To this end, the Department subjected itself to a series of far-reaching reforms in terms of its philosophy (culturally-based community development), structure (indigenization), style (decentralization in the design and delivery of social services), and commitment (delegation of power and responsibility to local groups). In making this transition from 'people administration' to 'people development', the Department abandoned its role as 'protector' or 'benefactor'. Embracing instead the role of 'joint decision-maker' and 'partner', it promoted itself as an enduring component in the total mix of people's efforts to 'stand tall' and advance with confidence into the future (Maori Affairs Position Paper, 1981). Central to Tu Tangata was a commitment to mobilize the community in pursuit of social and economic goals through self-initiative and local participation.

Achievement of this objective was contingent upon 'inverting the bureaucratic pyramid', a notion succinctly expressed by the last Secretary for Maori Affairs, Dr Tamati Reedy, in 1982:

> So, it is putting the decision making power back into the hands of the people. In another sense, one might say, it is inverting the pyramid so that the flat bottom of the pyramid is at the top which represents the people and we, the bureaucracy, are at the bottom of the pinnacle. . . . In other words, providing the resources, providing the advice when it is asked for and providing some stimuli in new and creative areas.

By fusing Maori cultural values and a community-based developmental ethos into a workable administrative program, the Department hoped to revise the agenda upon which Maori–government relations were structured. That, ultimately, it failed can be attributed largely to the pervasiveness of entrenched bureaucratic patterns and the lack of political will (and resources).

Beyond Bureaucracy: Te Tira Ahu Iwi
The fourth and final era began in 1989, when the Maori Affairs Department was replaced by the Iwi Transition Agency, Te Tira Ahu Iwi. In response to embarrassing financial disclosures and allegations of waste and mismanagement, the Labour government had decided to dissolve the Department and transfer its functions to other departments and local Maori authorities. But, faced with evidence of the need for an identifiable Maori presence in the public sector and an unprecedented display of Maori support (Labour Government, 1988c), the government relented and responded with an interim measure that left Maori administrative structures relatively intact. The Transition Agency was given a five-year mandate to strengthen the operational structures of Maori *iwi* in preparation for the transfer ('devolution') of responsibility for the management of government services (Reedy, 1990). As we shall see, the decision to replace the Maori bureaucracy with an *iwi*-empowering agency reflected and reinforced broader government moves not only to restructure the state itself, but to realign Maori–state relations on a partnership basis.

The goals of the Iwi Transition Agency were clearly articulated in several publications (Labour Government, 1988b; Iwi Transition Agency, 1990a,b). They included:

1. promotion of Maori cultural values of relevance to the identity of Aotearoa as a nation;

2. recognition of the *iwi* (tribe), not the individual, as the unit of Maori policy and administration (Williams, 1989);

3. assistance to *iwi* authorities for achievement of partnership as set out in the Treaty of Waitangi;

4. enhancement of *iwi* participation in national policy-making by strengthening *iwi* capacity to negotiate contracts with private or public sectors;

5. development of delivery mechanisms for the transfer of programs and services from the Transition Agency to *iwi* authorities when they are ready and properly resourced;

6. empowerment of the operational bases of *iwi* authorities along partnership lines (Iwi-Transition Agency, 1990b).

The concept of *iwi* structures and authorities is widely endorsed as a key element in the devolutionary process and the emergence of a bicultural Aotearoa. The essential premise behind this system is acknowledgement of Maori structures and values as (a) the source of Maori strength and resourcefulness (Fleras, 1987a, b), (b) the vehicle appropriate for negotiating government assistance, and (c) the solution for Maori survival and socio-economic renewal (Cabinet Social Equity Committee, 1986).

To some extent, these changes are in compliance with the government's aim of corporatization throughout the public sector. Government discourse is strongly supportive of *iwi* authorities as proactive business operations that, by contracting directly with government agencies for delivery of services, can be at once responsive to specific situations and accountable to central authorities (*Listener*, 13 Nov. 1989). *Iwi* authorities are expected to provide social, cultural, spiritual, and economic support for tribal members by linking financial and human resources with local concerns through contracts for services from government institutions. Joint ventures with the private sector are also widely encouraged. It remains to be seen, however, if the agency's resources and commitments are adequate to the task of truly retribalizing service delivery and local development. Moreover, the proposed establishment of a 'super' Ministry of Maori Development in early 1992 may render the Iwi Transition Agency superfluous to government ambitions.

STATE RESPONSES/MAORI ASPIRATIONS:
THE POLITICS OF REFORM

Just as Maori relations with the state are undergoing a fundamental change, so too the New Zealand state itself is experiencing a period of profound upheaval (Marshall, Peter, and Smith, 1990). Current government initiatives are driven by the principles of devolution and deregulation, and we cannot begin to understand the politics of Maori policy and administration without understanding the logic underlying this wider change.

The restructuring of the state along market lines is a salient feature of many modern capitalist economies. New Zealand is no exception (Walsh and Wetzel, 1990). Acceptance of free market principles and various monetarist policies has discredited the once inviolable doctrines of Keynesian interventionist economics (Kelsey, 1990). The five chief means towards this restructuring are (a) privatization and state divestment, (b) corporatization of government departments into relatively autonomous commercial enterprises, (c) deregulation of market products, (d) contracting-out for services, and (e) introduction of private-sector management and accounting procedures. Central authorities justify this uncoupling of the state from the economy as 'enhancing freedom':

> It also eases fiscal pressure, and is viewed as inherently more efficient than public provision, which is thought to elevate political considerations above market factors, and to make bureaucratic empires impervious to challenge. Assigning priority to commercial goals clarifies objectives for managers, and, it is argued, allows the efficient utilisation of resources for the first time (Walsh and Wetzel, 1990: 1).

Others denounce this market mentality as recipe for social disaster. Questions about the nature of ownership, the division of labour and resources, the exercise of authority, and the allocation of responsibility between public and private spheres continue to be shrouded in misunderstanding, and are often openly contested (Walsh and Wetzel, 1990).

New Zealand has now seen a decade of renewed faith in the virtues of the private sector, the efficiency of the market, and the benefits of corporatizing the public sector (Kelsey, 1990). Between 1984 and 1987, the fourth Labour government initiated a deregulation of the country's economy by exposing domestic industry to the realities of global competition and the demands of international markets (Jesson, 1988; Economic Monitoring Group, 1989). Having privatized state agencies such as Air New Zealand, the government turned its attention to deregulating the public sector. Some state-owned enterprises were dismantled and others were corporatized along private-sector management lines, while a commercial logic was imposed on remaining state functions (Marshall, Peter, and Smith, 1990).

Government efforts to pare away the bureaucratic centre did not encounter much resistance. As Kelsey (1990: 31) points out, the bureaucracy already faced 'trenchant criticism':

> state production of goods and services was inherently inefficient and

inflexible; decisions were made on political not economic grounds; executives were uncritically loyal to their political overseers; there were no effective accountability or performance measurements; interest groups succeeded in securing resources at the expense of those less powerful and more needy; and departments were dominated by inward looking institutionalised bureaucrats. There was a need for the decoupling of political and economic control.

Various organizational arrangements were made to ease and legitimize this transition away from centralized cores towards decentralized peripheries, with small policy units co-ordinating locally-driven services. Entire government departments such as Education were demolished and replaced by policy and advisory ministries. Responsibility for administrative and operational functions was delegated to local authorities on the grounds that (a) client needs should be central to social-service delivery, (b) clients should be involved in the design and delivery of programs that affected them, and (c) such an arrangement made service providers doubly accountable, both to Parliament and to clients (State Services Commission, 1988). What the restructuring process particularly needed, however, were intermediary mechanisms that would enable client groups to procure and implement required services. In the case of the Maori, the challenge lay in devising an arrangement that addressed their needs but did not veer outside the parameters of acceptable government behaviour: in other words, a culturally-sensitive and tribally-based delivery system rooted in and committed to the principles of devolution.

Devolution as Government Policy

Government commitment to the bicultural principles underlying the Treaty of Waitangi suggests that devolution is a concept whose time has come. Yet such a shift represents something of a departure in a country renowned for its centralization and standardization of services. It is equally evident that the concept is open to many interpretations, not all of which are compatible. Academics, politicians, bureaucrats, and clients use the term 'devolution' in ways that are often mutually exclusive. The range of meanings may extend from political partnership and power-sharing to (a) administrative debureaucratization and deinstitutionalization to (b) local autonomy and authority to (c) empowerment of community to (d) service reduction and cost-cutting ('service on the cheap') to (d) abdication of government responsibility ('pass the buck'), to (f) extension of organizational power and hegemony. This profusion of meanings has resulted in an outpouring of cynicism regarding the government's motives. It also has led Martin and Harper (1988) to attribute the popularity of devolution within political circles to its very ambiguity as a device for fostering the illusion of change without necessarily altering anything of substance. Adding to the confusion is a failure to make appropriate distinctions between 'devolution' and several closely related terms such as 'delegation' or 'decentralization' (Fleras, 1991).

Broadly speaking, we define 'devolution' as a mutually agreed-upon transfer of jurisdiction (whether power, resources, responsibilities, or authority) from a higher level of government ('the centre') to a lower ('the periphery') in an effort to bring decision-making closer to the people affected by it (State Services Commission, 1988; also Dacks, 1990). Ideally, the 'periphery' is not necessarily subordinate to the centre; nor are the powers so transferred subject to unilateral recall by the centre (Aucoin and Bakvis, 1988). What we have instead is a 'joint venture' involving two sets of authorities for the delivery of agency services that, together, should be more responsive, accessible, sensitive, and answerable to client sectors (Department of Maori Affairs, 1988). Taken to its logical conclusion, devolution is about power-sharing and restructuring, in an overall context of increased responsiveness to client needs (State Services Commission, 1988).

'Delegation', by contrast, refers to the transfer of duties and responsibilities from the centre to lower units. In the final analysis, *power remains in the centre* (Department of Social Welfare, 1989). Limited amounts of power are vested at local levels to improve client design, delivery, and evaluation of programs, while accredited community authorities have a say in expenditures according to local priorities. But levels of funding are centrally set, and the government establishes a framework that restricts the range of options to those consistent with political priorities. Central authorities also retain the prerogative to remove local representatives in cases of perceived negligence (Martin and Harper, 1988).

'Decentralization' is also different from devolution, at least in principle if not always in practice. Decentralization can be defined as geographical dispersal of administrative structures from an organizational centre to the peripheries. In breaking up the concentration of administration at the centre, decentralization focuses on the transfer of administrative units to local levels for the efficient delivery of social services. Thus decentralization is not about power-sharing or input into program design and delivery (but see Aucoin and Bakvis, 1988); rather, it is about bringing structures and delivery mechanisms closer to the clients who depend on them, while power and resources remain largely in the hands of central authorities (State Services Commission, 1988). As with delegation, the anticipated increase in community workload and responsibility is not necessarily matched by a corresponding increase in power.

Political Perspectives

Government policy administration is nominally committed to devolution. In June 1987, the Labour Cabinet endorsed the principle of devolving responsibility for Maori services as essential to a partnership perspective. In time, the government gave practical expression to devolution through: (a) dissolution of the Maori Affairs Department, (b) establishment of the Ministry of Maori Affairs and the Iwi Transition Agency, (c) transfer of existing Maori Affairs programs to mainstream departments (such as Justice and Housing), (d) stress on institutional responsiveness in the public sector, and (e) recognition of accredited *iwi* structures as the primary mechanism for service delivery. In government parlance, therefore, devolution consisted primarily in the *transfer* ('delegation') of state functions to 'appropriate' systems that were accountable to central authorities for allocation of resources. There was no intention to loosen up power and authority structures. This passage from the Minister of State Services is instructive:

> We do . . . regard it as essential that all parties understand very clearly from the outset that the Government retains ultimate responsibility in respect to the welfare and development of the people, to the machinery of Government, and indeed to the expenditure of public funds. Devolution does not allow us to abrogate these responsibilities. . . . We regard the Committee as an expression of our desire for real partnership in Maori development, for it will in practical terms be as much an agent of the people as of the Government. We certainly do not want to impose our version of Devolution, but we nevertheless believe *we have the responsibilities to set the basic course and to manage the overall process* (Minister of State Services, undated letter to the Devolution Implementation Committee; emphasis added).

In the eyes of the government, then, devolution became merely a mechanical device for 'delegating' authority and responsibility from one level to another. It involved the 'decentralizing' of delivery structures to the community level, without any substantial shifts in the prevailing distribution of power. Only the actors changed; the relationship remained the same.

Maori Perspectives

Maori perspectives on devolution, not surprisingly, differ from those of the political/administrative sector (Kia Mohio, Kia Marama Trust, 1989). Devolution based on political control of *iwi* delivery systems is spurned as paternalistic and regressive. In the words of the Devolution Implementation Committee (1987):

> The Government's objectives place emphasis on its articulation of policy and programs. If Devolution is to be truly meaningful, it must ultimately

strive to encourage Iwi authority and autonomy and not just be seen as a conduit for the allocation of funds . . . (emphasis in original).

Devolution for Maori leaders goes beyond the simple transfer of responsibility for the delivery of social services. Rather, devolution is about the *restoration* of power and authority to one of the co-signatories of the Treaty; *repossession* of resources that lawfully belong to the *tangata whenua*, which the government has unlawfully usurped; and *reclamation* of Maori power and control. This distinction is aptly phrased in a written submission (Labour Government, 1988c):

> Devolution in terms of the Treaty of Waitangi should mean, that the government shall ensure and protect Maori rights and privileges of citizenship, through the acknowledgement and upholding of Rangatiratanga. Specifically, this requires the Government to faithfully and dutifully *restore* a fair proportion of the power and resources it unjustly exercises and holds, in breach of both the Treaty and the equivalent rights of Rangatiratanga (emphasis added).

Differences are also apparent with regard to social and economic development. Devolution is perceived by the *tangata whenua* as the attainment of equal status through equal outcomes, reduced dependency, funding of positive initiatives, self-determination, and empowerment through *iwi* structures and Maori values. The government has countered with proposals for limited Maori administration of programs, minimal financing of commercial enterprises, and a market-oriented strategy for delivery of services (Kelsey, 1990). In other words, there is a serious communication problem, and as long as it continues, the two founding peoples of Aotearoa will continue to 'talk past each other'.

Summing Up: The Politics of Reform

Competing visions of devolution are a source of Maori–government conflict (Fleras, 1991). Regarding devolution as a means of increasing *iwi* autonomy and power, the *tangata whenua* perceive tribal use of resources as community-driven, with a strong commitment to collective accountability and operational freedom. In contrast, the government position emphasizes market-friendly resource use, ministerial accountability, integration into the overall political structure, and, as Ranginui Walker (1990a: 72) explains, control:

> The Government's present concern is firmer control and management of Maori affairs to ensure the success of its own social and economic goals. The objects of this policy, the Maori people, have their own agenda which is clearly evident in their submissions on the bill. It embraces affirmation of tino rangatiratanga, recovery of assets expropriated by the

Crown, establishment of an economic base, and maintenance of cultural integrity. Pursuit of this agenda which Maori have followed doggedly for the last 100 years, has increased in intensity with the current Maori renaissance. . . . For this reason conflict is bound to surface when the people make it clear to public servants what is expected of them.

Iwi authorities want to control the way money is spent with minimum intrusion from the government (Williams, 1989). Imposition of strict accountability procedures and 'eligibility criteria' for distribution of resources threatens to compromise Maori power and undermine the inherent partnership ethos of the Treaty. *Iwi* authorities, it is argued, should not be held answerable to the government for resource allocation any more than private owners should have to account for how they use their assets. Moana Jackson (1989: 19) writes:

> [T]he government has recently introduced its policy of iwi development. Its aim, according to government, is to encourage the reassertion of tribal rangatiratanga. However this policy illustrates the inherent incompatibility between claiming that indigenous people can have self-determination and control over their own lives, while at the same time subjecting them to an overriding power sourced in the political and social values of another, numerically dominant people. Such 'self-determination' is not rangatiratanga at all, and this is clear from the reality of the devolution policy. Tribes will be granted rangatiratanga by the Crown, a concept difficult in itself, only if they meet criteria defined by the Crown. They will then exercise only those powers which government sees fit to grant them.

In a nutshell, devolution for the government is synonymous with delegation and decentralization. The government accepts the legitimacy of Maori grievances over land and fishing rights—and a host of related social and cultural concerns—as set out in the Treaty. The difficulty lies in the solutions to these grievances. The government prefers to deal with problems through negotiations and consultation, institutional responsiveness, and inclusion of Maori perspectives. The Maori, on the other hand, see the solutions as lying in genuine reform through power-sharing and parallel institutions—proposals that the government regards as dangerous and separatist, and that are also inappropriate to the short-term interests of a party in power.

For the *tangata whenua* devolution encompasses a dialogue about power-sharing and resource allocation consistent with their status as 'nations within' with inherent rights and guaranteed entitlements. Devolution is rooted in the bicultural principles entrenched in the Treaty, coupled with the restoration of tribal authority and control over cultural and material resources. But while the *tangata whenua* talk about parallel development and separate institutions, the central authorities focus on tinkering with the existing system by way of Maori add-ons (Himona,

1989; Kia Mohio, Kia Marama Trust 1989). The clash of these paradigms is likely to aggravate the difficulty of restructuring Maori–government relations in a rapidly decolonizing Aotearoa.

MAORI RESISTANCE: POLITICAL RESURGENCE AND CULTURAL RENEWAL

Historically, in its relations with the Maori minority, the New Zealand State has been committed to assimilation through destruction of Maori tribal authority, marginalization of Maori language and culture, and absorption of the *tangata whenua* into the mainstream. In cases where conventional avenues have proved fruitless, from Parihaka in 1881 to Bastion Point in 1978, the state has resorted to physical force to obtain compliance.

Maori resistance to these efforts on the part of the state has been impressive. It has also become increasingly pan-tribal, and highly politicized as Maori have moved into cities. Although the goal of a bicultural partnership is a long way off, there is reason to believe that Maori activism will combine with established Maori organizations to further advance the process of decolonization.

Local Rebellion to Pan-Tribal Movement

Even with the might of the British Empire ranged against them, the Maori did not capitulate to the initial Pakeha intrusion without a struggle. Early resistance was localized, as groups separated by history and culture had little chance of mounting a concerted campaign. Occasional acts of civil disobedience and even outright rebellion marred the best-laid plans of central authorities for systemic colonization. Open confrontations were common during the New Zealand Wars of the 1860s, and by the end of the century various social movements were serving as outlets for Maori grievances (Clark, 1975; Webster, 1979), among them the Maori King movement, centred in the Waikato region, which refused to acknowledge Pakeha authority, land, or culture. The emergence of the Young Maori Party in Parliament (from the late 1890s to just before the First World War), with its dual commitment to improve social conditions and revive cultural practices, together with the political, religious, and social initiatives of the Ratana religious movement in the 1920s, kept Maori issues at the forefront. These collective responses to the loss of Maori power and land proved effective in improving local conditions in the short run, but were incapable of reversing the inexorable tide of assimilation and Maori decline.

The years following the Second World War saw the emergence of a nationwide system of local Maori committees aimed at exercising local control (through Maori Wardens) and dealing with urban problems related to employment and relocation (Fleras, 1981). A national voice was provided by the New Zealand Maori Council and the Maori Women's Welfare League, both of which continue to make their presence known through submissions and research reports (Fleras, 1986). As an alternative to the moderate stance of the latter groups, a more radical Maori activism appeared during the 1960s, gathering momentum into the 1980s. The net impact of this resistance has been considerable, and the restructuring of New Zealand race relations is a testament to the collective vision and sustained efforts of activists. But with the exception of the Kohanga Reo (Maori language preschools) movement during the 1980s, none of these groups was able to capitalize on Maori social structures as a basis for renewal.

In the middle of 1990, a large gathering of Maori tribes at Ngaruawahia, near Hamilton, declared the formation of the National Maori Congress. Critical of the gaps that remained in Maori policy and administration despite the proposed restructuring of Maori status in society, the Congress could trace many of its concerns to a four-volume set of submissions to the 1988 government discussion paper 'He Tirohanga Rangapu' ('Partnership Perspectives'):

1. Partnership uncertainties. Will the Maori continue to be the poor and dependent partners, lacking the resources and power to back up their demands and grievances?

2. Institutional response. While mainstreaming Maori concerns into the public sector is a fundamentally sound idea, are largely monocultural institutions realistically prepared for any partnership arrangement that entails 'cultural space' for Maori values, needs, and aspirations? Is there any guarantee that the Maori dimension will not be swallowed up or dispersed in the process of mainstreaming? Is the concept of institutional responsiveness part of the government's hidden agenda to assimilate the Maori, albeit in a more sophisticated fashion?

3. Devolution. The concept of *iwi* authorities managing government services is promising, but will the imposition of certain eligibility criteria infringe on *iwi* control over government funding and resources? Who will determine the eligibility criteria? On what basis? Will the resulting arrangement and structures be appropriate to the Maori people and consistent with their claim of inherent rights to self-determination? Will *iwi* authorities have to

compete with each other for the resources to do what is asked of them (*Dominion*, 18 July 1990)?

4. Restructuring Maori Affairs. Will government creations such as Ministry of Maori Affairs and the Iwi Transition Agency be answerable to the public sector or to Maori *iwi*? Will they have the power to make decisions and recommendations with teeth? Or will their roles be merely advisory? The fact that these questions remained unanswered has increased the pressure to devise tribally-based structures consistent with Maori desires to protect and enhance Maori power, land-holdings, and identity.

The Maori Congress is the latest in a long line of efforts to establish a unified Maori voice (*Dominion*, 18 July 1990). Numerous precedents had appeared over the last 150 years, but most suffered from lack of unity as tribes guarded their autonomy and succumbed to age-old rivalries. There were exceptions—notably the Kauhanganui and Kotahitanga unity movements around the turn of the century—but both were ignored and eventually lapsed.

The Maori Congress seeks to overcome the handicaps of its precursors in both structure and function. With the participation and commitment of up to 41 tribes, the Congress provides a representative base for a powerful Maori organization. Maori *iwi* are given a platform to debate and to articulate demands, but without diminishing the authority of member tribes. Leadership is provided by three high-profile Maori leaders whose collective stature as co-presidents will ensure power and credibility in both Maori and Pakeha eyes. Finally, the Congress has been created for and by Maori *iwi*, not government. This independence should allow the Congress to devise a system of organization and a policy statement that suit Maori rather than government interests. The Congress thus hopes to avoid the problems of the New Zealand Maori Council, whose credibility is constantly under scrutiny because it receives financial support from the government and its membership reflects government administrative convenience rather than Maori demographic realities (Fleras, 1986).

At this point, the structure, constitution, and objectives of the National Maori Congress need to be ratified and discussed. Nevertheless, the following objectives have been proposed by the Whakakotahi ('Towards Unity') Task Force (*Panui*, 21 June 1990): the exercise of tribal self-determination, provision of a national forum for tribal representatives to address a variety of issues, and promotion of constitutional and legislative arrangements to foster Maori development and self-determination. Among the Maori values that are to guide the way to these objectives are *whakakotahi* (shared unity and aspirations of Maori people), *Maori mana motuhake* (aboriginal rights), *tino rangatiratanga* (respect for *iwi* power and authority), and *paihere tangata* (strength of collective action). The articles of the Treaty of Waitangi will also serve as a basis for action. At present it is too early to tell whether the Congress will become a viable alternative in national politics; if it does, the decolonizing of Maori–government relations rights will have taken a major step towards realization.

Te Kohanga Reo: A Maori Renewal

Ko te reo te mauri o te tangata.
Ko te reo te mauri o te mana Maori

Language is the essence of human existence.
Language is the life principle of Maori vitality.

— Maori proverb

Around the world, aboriginal languages are disintegrating as systems of daily communication (see Hall, 1986a; Britsch-Devany, 1988; Teasdale and Whitelaw, 1981; Barman et al., 1987; Burnaby, 1982, 1984; Shkilnyk, 1985b, 1986). This crisis has precipitated debate over the concept of language renewal (Fleras, 1987a, b), particularly in New Zealand, where language and politics are inseparable. This section will examine Maori efforts at renewal through the establishment of culturally-sensitive and community-based Maori language immersion preschools.

The Maori of New Zealand are widely recognized—and admired—as innovators in promoting aboriginal interests and concerns. Nowhere is this more evident than in the establishment of a language renewal program, Te Kohanga Reo, for Maori preschool children. Reflecting their role as an essential component in Maori development, the Kohanga Reo ('language nests') have assisted in the revival of Maori language as a system of daily communication. More important, they have reinforced a sense of community through local collaboration and promotion of Maori social and cultural values—especially those pertaining to family and community—which themselves contribute to the program's organization, content, and style. As well, the Kohanga Reo program has politicized Maori cultural concerns and provided a political forum that has spearheaded the reordering of Maori status in Aotearoa.

The Crisis in Maori Language
The forced imposition of an assimilationist agenda brought about a gradual decline of Maori cultural values as an integral component of New Zealand's bicultural heritage. The deterioration of Maori language is a particularly graphic example of this decline. A wide range of pressures—from benign neglect at policy levels to outright repression in the schools—resulted in the restriction of Maori to private or ceremonial contexts (Dewes, 1968; Barrington, 1970). While language assimilation was not total, the failure of initiatives such as Maori

Family Preschools, bilingual schools, and Maori language courses served only to highlight the magnitude of the problem (McDonald, 1973, 1976; Benton, 1981). These programs did not capitalize on the enormous plasticity of young children, nor could they hope to duplicate the natural context in which language learning normally occurs. By the late 1970s, fluency in Maori was generally confined to middle-aged and elderly rural dwellers (Biggs, 1972). Without concerted action or reform, urban Maori youths and children were in danger of losing Maori as a symbol of their identity, let along as a language of everyday use at home (Benton, 1979).

In response to this concern, the first 'language nests' appeared in 1982. Drawing their inspiration from the Department's community-based Tu Tangata ('Stand Tall') development philosophy (Puketapu, 1982; Fleras, 1985a), these schools quickly appealed to the Maori grassroots. By 1984, a total of 262 centres with an average enrolment of 16 children were in operation. Each one was supported by a paid supervisor, trainees from the Labour Department, and an extensive network of parents and elders. By late 1990 nearly 700 languages nests were in operation, with a total enrolment of roughly 10,000, or nearly 45 per cent of Maori children under 5. By contrast, only a relatively constant 32 per cent of children attend state kindergartens, which suggests that the language nests are attracting many who otherwise would miss out on early childhood education (Ministerial Planning Group, 1991). Future projections show an enrolment figure of up to 75 per cent of all Maori preschoolers by the year 2000 (Report, 1988). Matching this growth has been the expansion of state support, in terms of both government funding (more than $26-million in 1990-91) and assistance from government departments such as Education, Social Welfare, Health, and Labour.

Objectives and Goals

The Kohanga Reo system is predominantly Maori in content, objectives, and style (Reedy, 1982). Using a community-based and culturally-sensitive approach to language education, it aims to foster a balanced ('holistic') development in children. Each centre consists of an extended family (*whanau*) group of elders and parents, situated within a deliberately created Maori cultural environment (Department of Statistics, 1990). The objectives of this movement appeal to a wide cross-section of the New Zealand community, ensuring broad support. Three goals predominate:

• *Language renewal.*   Although Maori language is central to the Kohanga Reo, the program is not necessarily geared towards language mastery. Rather, the emphasis is on language exposure through self-directed learning (see also Britsch-Devany, 1988). While fluency is promoted, the practical goal is for Maori children to identify with Maori language and culture as a way of fostering positive self-esteem.

To this end, preschool children are immersed in a Maori context. Maori is the only medium of instruction: children are spoken to in Maori, they are expected to respond in Maori, and daily activities are arranged to maximize exposure to Maori culture. The methods used are derived from traditional Maori practices in which teaching and learning become fused in a single process (Smith, 1987). Through interaction with elders the children learn basic vocabulary and phrases, simple sentence structures, and short conversational routines (see also Britsch-Devany, 1988). The success of the program depends in part on the home environment, but initial results are promising: many children have acquired some ability to speak and understand Maori by completion of the program (McTagget, 1986).

• *Cultural enhancement.*   An increasingly important goal is the promotion of Maori cultural values. In view of the powerful relation between language and culture, proponents of the Kohanga Reo have stressed the cultural dimension (Kerr, 1987). Children are saturated with elements of Maori culture through (a) daily operations, (b) activities and programs, and (c) learning styles appropriate to Maori sensibilities and tradition. Particularly relevant are those values underlying traditional Maori methods of child-rearing and socialization.

Of the diverse values endorsed by Kohanga Reo, none is promoted as vigorously as the *whanau* philosophy. On one hand, *whanau* conveys the idea of a traditional extended family arrangement wherein children grow up surrounded by grandparents, aunts, uncles, and cousins (Metge, 1976). The concept may also be extended, however, to denote a cluster of values including *aroha* (caring, sharing, empathy), *rangimarie* (peacefulness), and *manaaki* (kindness). In combining both applications, the image of a Kohanga Reo as a *whanau* centre is a powerful acknowledgement of the supportive role of the extended family within a rapidly changing urban context.

• *Community revitalization.*   Equally significant is the role of the Kohanga Reo System as an exercise in Maori community renewal. Each 'nest' not only capitalizes on existing community resources, but also helps to promote a revitalization in community organization. Community participation is regarded as crucial. Parents and grandparents are encouraged to become involved as part of their contribution towards the revival of Maori language. Some assume an active role in looking after children; others prefer to serve in a back-up or supplementary fashion. Parents too are encouraged to take advantage of the momentum created at the centre by speaking Maori both at home and in public. In some cases, they themselves have enrolled in Maori language classes as part of a broader commitment to their children. Elders are especially sought after; as 'authentic' educators, they are respected repositories of wisdom, experience, and tradition (Report, 1988). This sustained interaction among parents, children, and elders is critical in integrating the Kohanga Reo program into the community (also Britsch-Devany, 1988).

The spirit of community collaboration is fostered in other ways as well. In providing both a location and a purpose for drawing Maori together as partners working towards an ultimate goal, the Kohanga Reo centre serves as a focal point for parents and elders who might otherwise feel alienated in an urban setting. In 1984 a respected Maori elder wrote:

> It is a common fact that the urban scene becomes a nightmare for the solo parent. Hence you have a situation in many cities where young mothers are imprisoned in the impersonal and lonely constraints of the concrete jungle. That they never even get to meet other women of the same situation or older women who may add another dimension to their lives is an accepted fact. What we now have with the rise of TKR are situations where women can meet each other in a child care situation, a whanau situation and very often a cultural situation. So immediately you place TKR in the midst of the impersonal cold concrete city, suddenly you have a changed situation (Rangihau, 1984).

In short, by linking Maori together under the *whanau* umbrella, the Kohanga Reo program has instilled a sense of community, collaboration, and commitment. In focusing on the extended family, it enhances Maori community structures in a manner consistent with Maori cultural strengths and aspirations. At the same time, its emphasis on continuities with the past is helping to halt the fragmentation and alienation of Maori in rapidly changing urban environments.

Structure and Operations
A cultural dimension pervades the organizational structure of the Kohanga Reo. Although aspects of conventional preschool systems are incorporated, these are grafted onto a framework that is essentially Maori in structure, operation, and style (for a fuller discussion, see Fleras, 1983). Certain elements are common to all preschool centres. Most operate on a five-day schedule (Kerr, 1987); rules about nourishment, sanitation, and supervision are enforced; and children learn habits of personal discipline, order, and respect for authority, as well as how to pay attention, follow instructions, and get along with others. Beyond these features, however, the Maori component becomes increasingly manifest. For example, to foster a *whanau* learning

approach, most language nests are located at a Maori-owned site such as a *marae* (meeting place/ceremonial complex); in 1986, nearly 52 per cent of the centres were on *marae* property. With its antiquity and rich symbolism, the *marae* is ideally suited as a venue for language immersion.

Each language nest conforms to a basic daily routine that mixes formal sessions of learning and play. Learning sessions are kept informal: the emphasis is on language education through various repetitive actions in song, play, and instruction (Metge, 1984). Formal teaching methods are eschewed in favour of learning by exposure and verbal exchange between child and adult. To provide the optimal conditions for language learning, most centres cultivate as natural an environment as possible. Educational aids and equipment are generally downplayed in favour of resources within the Maori world. Even sophisticated computer and video technology has been retailored to capitalize on Maori cultural values and language expressions. Finally, a spiritual dimension is strongly emphasized, and prayers are conducted throughout the day to accentuate the inseparability of spiritual and temporal elements in Maori culture.

Kohanga Reo personnel comprise paid supervisors and trainees from the Labour Department in addition to the voluntary sector of interested parents and grandparents. All supervisors or *kaitiaki* (servants of the people) are selected on the strength of their Maori skills. Training is conducted through a certificate program leading to a licence (Kohanga Trust meeting, 31 Jan. 1984). The training package consists of practical work experience (400 hours) and five modules (100 hours each) on Maori cultural concepts: (a) Maori spirituality, including myth and genealogy, (b) concepts and celebrations, (c) health and related customs, (d) language skills and early childhood development, and (e) setting up and running a family-based preschool system. With these guidelines firmly based in Maori culture, control over the Kohanga Reo is likely to remain in Maori hands.

In keeping with the *whanau* principle, daily administrative work, budgeting, programming, and long-term planning for each language nest are the responsibility of a parent-controlled managing committee. Although Departmental community officers are expected to maintain some contact, each language nest is structured around community strengths, not bureaucratic imperatives. The Kohanga Reo program is carefully monitored by a National Coordinating Group comprising officials from a variety of government and Maori organizations (Kerr, 1987). To assist in co-ordination and promotion at national levels, a Te Kohanga Reo Trust composed of select Maori authorities and leaders is responsible for monitoring and shaping overall growth, but not to the extent of undermining the relative autonomy of each language nest. The Trust also acts on behalf of the program in making submissions to the government and state agencies for financial or political support. As a sign of political support, beginning in February 1990 the Kohanga Reo were to be funded on the same footing as Early Childhood Services, with a total allocation of nearly $26-million slated for 1990-91 (*Wellington Evening Post*, 15 Aug. 1990).

Impact and Implications of the Kohanga Reo

Standing at the forefront of Maori cultural rejuvenation (James, 1988), the Kohanga Reo System aims at producing bicultural and bilingual Maoris who can function in a modern context without losing their cultural identity (Report, 1983). In reasserting the primacy of selected Maori customs—particularly those based on obligations to kin (Fitzgerald, 1977)—the Kohanga Reo reinforces the value of traditional networks and community-based partnership for Maori achievement. Successful nests become centres of community interest, communications, and activity, as well as forums for the revival of Maori customs and knowledge (Yearbook, 1990).

The impact of the Kohanga Reo cannot be underestimated (Fleras, 1987b). A growing number of Maori children are now capable of speaking (or at least identifying with) their language, and many parents have acquired renewed confidence in their ability to advance Maori cultural interests. At the same time, by refusing to capitulate to assimilationist pressures, the Kohanga Reo system serves as a powerful symbol in promoting Maori aboriginal interests. As a catalyst for social change, it has (a) focused a critical mass of attention on the Maori language crisis, (b) united disparate Maori elements into collective action, (c) encouraged Maori grassroots activism, and (d) created conditions favourable for political reform. The Kohanga Reo has improved the self-esteem of Maori pupils by legitimizing the validity and power of alternative forms of knowledge (Smith, 1987). A growing number of Maori parents have become increasingly politicized over issues pertaining to justice and equality within education. In the process of linking education, knowledge, and empowerment, Maori parents have begun to question the role of education in a bicultural society. With its focus on empowerment, there is little doubt the Kohanga Reo system will continue to exert an impact on the redefinition of Maori–government relations within an emergent bicultural reality.

Maori Primary Schools

One of the more innovative offshoots of Kohanga Reo has been the growth of Maori immersion primary schools known as Kura Kaupapa Maori (Smith, 1990). Located primarily in Auckland and modelled to some extent after the Kohanga Reo, these schools are staffed by Maori teachers who rely exclusively on Maori pedagogy and language as channels of instruction. The predominantly Maori pupils are exposed to Maori philosophies and cultural values, although national curriculum guidelines are rigidly followed to ensure credibility and support. The premises behind these schools are relatively straightforward. They work on the principle that, in line with the bicultural ethos inherent in the Treaty of Waitangi, Maori people need to reclaim control over knowledge and education. Equally important is the need to overcome the multiplicity of interrelated factors that historically have contributed to Maori failure at school, including (a) the 'ownership and operation' of education by Pakeha, and (b) the highly Eurocentric content, style, and goals of the school system (Ministerial Planning Group, 1991). By contrast, the Kura Kaupapa reflect the desire of Maori parents for a school system that is sensitive to Maori needs, encompasses Maori styles of learning, respects language and culture, and ensures standards of academic excellence.

The government appears to have accepted the principle of Maori immersion within the primary system. In 1990-91, it increased the operational grant allocation to Kura Kaupapa (total enrolment was 155 pupils, with nine teachers in six schools) to $2.1-million, and an additional five schools are about to be funded (Ministerial Planning Group, 1991). But these small figures underplay the significance of Kura Kaupapa. As a symbol of Maori resistance, as well as a penetrating critique of education policy and an expression of Maori knowledge as a legitimate and viable alternative to Pakeha knowledge, this movement reflects the belief that Maori education is central to Maori cultural survival. In a country committed to bicultural principles, an educational system that fails to address that cultural imperative is likely to fail one set of partners.

BICULTURALISM: THE NEW DISTRIBUTIVE IDEAL

Liberal democratic societies throughout the world have tried in various ways to cope with the presence of culturally diverse minorities (van den Berghe, 1981). In New Zealand diverse strategies have been employed to impose a Pakeha solution on the 'Maori problem'. One of the more innovative sought to restructure Maori-Pakeha relations along the lines of devolution and delegation of responsibility. But the Maori have shown an intense dislike for such arrangements, and have proposed a bicultural alternative in hopes of accentuating their special status and unique entitlement. This biculturalism is reflected to some extent in the field of Maori education (with Maori language preschools and independent Maori primary schools) and in the delivery of government services through an *iwi*-based system.

Yet the obstacles standing in the path of partnership and biculturalism are formidable, reflecting competing visions of who should get what. For the government, biculturalism means including a Maori dimension in decision-making at local and national levels and delegating the powers required to take responsibility for the delivery of government services. For the Maori, biculturalism means nothing less than the full sharing of power and resources implicit in New Zealand's partnership ethos. In the past, Maori expectations were limited to what could be obtained by relying on Pakeha good will and sense of fair play (Vasil, 1988). Now Maoris demand fulfilment of all the inherent rights and guaranteed entitlements that flow from their status as *tangata whenua o Aotearoa*. Biculturalism entails the creation of a Maori 'nation' within the New Zealand state with corresponding control over internal affairs.

Relegated to the margins of New Zealand society, until recently the Maoris were little more than peripheral contributors to the nation-building process. Their culture was dismissed as quaint and decorative, hopelessly unsuited to modern existence. Similarly, Maori social and kinship patterns were denounced as self-inflicted discriminatory barriers that entrenched poverty and powerlessness. Central authorities approached the Maoris as a racial/ethnic minority whose impoverished status required active government intervention in pursuit of an egalitarian, English-style society.

The recent restructuring of Maori–state relations is nothing short of astonishing. In less than a decade, the Maori have moved from the margins of society into the mainstream—in large part because of activist and organizational pressure for redefining Maori status and relations with the state. Previous government policy (Te Urupare Rangapu) and administration (Te Tira Ahu Iwi) were focused around the Maori's status as aboriginal people with rights, entitlements, and powers consistent with a 'nations within' philosophy. The current government, under its Ka Awatea policy, appears less interested in addressing Maori political issues, but is equally committed to restructuring relations between government and the Maori. In theory, relations formerly based on welfare, dependency, and underdevelopment are now conducted within the framework of devolution, biculturalism, and Treaty rights. The Treaty of Waitangi has emerged as a central unifying force, providing a cultural frame of reference for renewal of Maori–state relations along lines of partnership and power-sharing. To be sure, the government's efforts to 'mainstream' the Maori people are riddled with ambiguity and manipulation, and there is ample evidence of government complicity in 'deflating' Maori political, economic, and cultural ambitions—at least to 'manageable' proportions. Few, however, will dispute the necessity of restoring the *tangata whenua* to their proper place as founding partners in the reconstruction of New Zealand as a bicultural nation.

PART IV

CONCLUSION

TWELVE

The 'Nations Within': Towards a Restructuring of Aboriginal–State Relations

Ka whawhai tonu matou (The struggle continues)

—A Maori expression

In this examination of the genesis, evolution, and contemporary status of aboriginal–state relations, we have looked at aboriginal status as it involves a struggle between the forces of the status quo and those of reform and redefinition. The primary focus has been Canada, but as the preceding chapters have indicated, certain common patterns are discernible in the experiences of other liberal democracies such as New Zealand and the United States.

Not all would agree with our use of the comparative approach as a tool for investigating the transformation of aboriginal–state relations. Historical and cultural differences do tend to cast doubt on the validity of common patterns and call into question the meaning of divergent findings. Yet to reject comparisons is to ignore the extent to which aboriginal peoples constitute a social type, occupying similar structural positions in society and facing similar challenges. Most importantly, aboriginal peoples in Canada, the United States, and New Zealand share a commitment to 'nations within' status (i.e., sovereignty) as a fundamental characteristic of their political culture. Such a commitment carries with it a dual objective to restructure their relational status in society and to secure the entitlements that derive from formal recognition of this restored status. In other words, aboriginal peoples share a common experience in terms of who they are, what they want, and how they propose to get it, through decolonization of their relations with the state and restoration of their once subjugated status to one consistent with the self-determining ethos of a nation within a state.

This commonality of experience and purpose justifies the comparative approach.

The Restructuring Process: Perils and Pitfalls

To conclude our examination of the 'nations within', we will analyse three areas in which efforts to redefine aboriginal–state relations in Canada, New Zealand, and the United States face serious difficulties. At the root of these difficulties are the competing interests involved in the introduction of any new paradigm within a conventional body of knowledge or practice. The three key areas of concern to be discussed here are (a) the new distributive ideal associated with restructuring of aboriginal status, (b) fiscal restraints, and (c) hidden agendas. Our primary attention is directed to the Canadian experience, with examples drawn from New Zealand and the United States as appropriate.

A New Distributive Ideal

Government policy responses to aboriginal demands are of a contradictory nature. On the one hand, political discourse in Canada is slanted increasingly towards recognition of the first nations as a 'distinct society' with special rights and claims against the state over and above those of citizenship. Government officials appear willing in theory to acknowledge the validity of aboriginal national demands, if only to avert a crisis in the legitimacy of the state or avoid international censure. Thus the principle of aboriginality is not dismissed outright; rather, debate focuses on the limits of aboriginal rights, the extent of jurisdictional boundaries, and how best to deal with aboriginal claims without destroying the social fabric of the larger society in the process.

On the other hand, misgivings are widespread among ordinary citizens regarding the concept of aboriginal status and the new ideal that it proposes with respect to the distribution of power and resources in society. Hence governments have sought by varying means to defuse, perhaps even to circumvent, aboriginal challenges to the prevailing social order, attempting to address aboriginal concerns within the liberal-democratic framework of central policy structures (Fleras, 1989a). For most, the very principle of aboriginality and inherent, collective aboriginal rights is at once vague and threatening, for such rights are often in conflict with the individualistic and universal values embedded within liberal-democratic societies (Weaver, 1984; Boldt and Long, 1984).

In assessing the relative progress that the 'nations within' have made towards their goal of institutionalizing the principle of aboriginality, it is necessary to keep in mind the starting points. In this respect, the Maori tribes of New Zealand were at first clearly in the lead, as their relations with the British settlers in the middle of the nineteenth century began as a partnership, albeit an unequal one, with formal equality. The Maori's task has been to force the dominant society to live up to the contract made in the Treaty of Waitangi. The Waitangi Tribunal was instituted in 1975 to do precisely this. While the Tribunal is moving at a snail's pace, it gives full recognition to the principle of aboriginality and has achieved some notable successes (Pearson, 1991: but see Kelsey, 1991).

For example, in the late 1980s the Tainui tribe claimed that its land had been taken in violation of the Treaty of Waitangi; it brought its claim to the Waitangi Tribunal asking that the Crown and Coalcorp (a coal-mining enterprise) be prohibited from further usurpation of its land and mineral rights. On 3 October 1989 the Court of Appeal issued a unanimous decision in favour of the Tainui. Ranginui Walker (1990: 283) states that this 'judgment puts New Zealand firmly into the post colonial era'. The country now possesses both the institutional mechanisms and the judicial backing to bring Maori–government relations to full maturity within the New Zealand state. Nevertheless, the lack of political will to abide by these decisions has made it difficult to put principles into practice.

Canada and the United States provide an interesting contrast to New Zealand, since their interactions with European society go back to the fifteenth century. The United States is similar to New Zealand, however, inasmuch as there too the legislative and legal groundwork that would determine the contemporary status of the 'nations within' was put in place in the mid-nineteenth century, when the Marshall decisions established the aboriginal peoples as 'domestic dependent nations' with limited sovereignty. As a result, the debate in the United States concerning the principle of aboriginality has been retrospective and defensive, not unlike that in New Zealand. After decades of destructive assimilation, the aboriginal nations are struggling to regain and maintain the powers that were assured them in the mid-nineteenth century, but that have in some instances eroded with time (Wilkinson, 1987).

The Canadian debate differs from those in the United States and New Zealand in three important ways. First, as Brock (1990) points out, Canada is not bound by nineteenth-century decisions to the same extent as the United States (and, we would add, New Zealand). Second, the debate is anticipatory rather than defensive, being politically, not judicially, shaped—although in time this may change. Third, the Canadian political system has the potential to accommodate the national aspirations of aboriginal peoples in much the same way as it has allowed the evolution of a partnership (however strained at present) between the French and the English 'founding nations'. In sum, the sovereignty aspirations of the 'nations within' and the assertion of their collective rights are 'not alien to Canadian political life, thought and discourse: they are both a product of and contributing feature of Canadian politics' (Brock, 1990: 32). Still as the struggle to entrench inherent aboriginal self-governing rights has demonstrated, political authorities continue to approach these issues in a cautious and compromising manner.

Fiscal Concerns

Fiscal concerns loom large in shaping government policy and administration. The cost of servicing the aboriginal sector is escalating yearly, and shows no sign of abating despite government efforts to curtail public expenditures. In the interests of fiscal responsibility, governments in Canada and New Zealand have focused on (a) down-sizing government agencies, (b) delegating administrative responsibility to local communities, and (c) decentralizing national structures. The basic aim is to phase out the separate structures that cater to aboriginal peoples and to incorporate them into the existing social, political, and administrative structures in society (see Boldt and Long, 1988).

In New Zealand the Maori tribes are expected to shoulder the cost of servicing the local population by organizing into corporate units that contract out for services on a market basis. In Canada, while aboriginal communities are anxious to accept increased responsibility, the provinces too have been called on to alleviate the federal financial load. In the United States, aboriginal nations have the power to tax and are encouraged to raise revenues for their own programs and services; at the same time, Washington has attempted to decrease the numbers eligible for aboriginal settlements.

Whether in Canada, New Zealand, or the United States, governmental objectives are similar. Political discourse regarding devolution and self-government is not about the transfer of power and resources to local authorities. It is about the delegation of responsibility and administrative duties. Powers that are surrendered do not undermine government control over the form and functions of self-determination. For central authorities, in other words, endorsement of aboriginal self-government constitutes a historic opportunity to reduce political obligations and costly legal commitments without conceding power or resources (Angus, 1990). In an effort to empower the first nations and to reduce both political and economic dependency on Ottawa, proposals for reconstructing aboriginal–government relations are conducted around the theme of community self-government (Weaver, 1990).

The contested nature of aboriginal policy and administration is evident in the contrasting views of self-government held by federal authorities and aboriginal groups themselves (Cassidy, 1990). Ottawa sees self-government as a community-based, quasi-municipal system of self-reliance, not as a distinct order of government that is constitutionally entrenched as an inherent right (Fleras, 1990). Self-government is merely a channel permitting the delegation of responsibility for local services while keeping aboriginal communities strictly accountable to DIAND or the Treasury. Under these circumstances, self-government is merely an exercise in *self-administration* in the design, delivery, and monitoring of local social services. This approach is consistent with the Canadian government's commitment to reduce the size of the Department of Indian Affairs and of the public sector in general (Morse, 1989).

Aboriginal leaders, by contrast, espouse self-government as a means of gaining control over activities, institutions, and financial arrangements. More than a channel for delivery of programs that comply with administrative priorities, aboriginal self-government reflects an *inherent* right to self-determination through self-rule. Self-governing powers may resemble those of either provincial or municipal authorities, but whatever level is chosen, it must permit maximum control over aboriginal affairs.

The Hidden Agenda
Policy discourse in New Zealand and Canada has shifted towards proposals for devolution of control over economic, political, and social institutions. In each case, a collective restructuring of aboriginal status is in the offing to move aboriginal people from a position of dependency and underdevelopment to one nominally commensurate with their aspirations for 'nations within' status (Fleras, 1990). Critics, however, see the proposed devolution as simply (a) an exercise in disguised assimilation and control (an indirect 'divide and rule' strategy); (b) an instrument by which to control tribal authorities through a host of requirements and accountability procedures; and/or (c) an attempt to diminish band integrity through excessive interference in local community affairs (Pearson, 1990). In this view, aboriginal concerns and demands are acceptable to government only as long as they fall within the parameters of the latter's priorities. Devolution is suspected as a smokescreen that has nothing to do with aboriginal empowerment and everything to do with denying aboriginal people the opportunity to exercise their rights as 'nations within'.

Political acceptance of aboriginality as a guiding principle for redefining aboriginal–government relations has been questionable. As Sally Weaver (1990) has argued, recent changes in Canada's aboriginal agenda are more symbolic than real. With the exception of the Constitution Act of 1982 (which entrenched aboriginal and treaty rights) there has been little appreciable gain with respect to aboriginal empowerment. A fundamental adherence to assimilation appears widespread, despite bold talk about the principles of self-government, aboriginal and treaty rights, and settlement of land claims (Cassidy, 1991).

A pervasive commitment to assimilate aboriginal peoples into Canada's institutional framework is also evident in recent initiatives to transfer federal responsibility to the provinces (Boldt and Long, 1988). Instead of the cultural assimilationist ethos that prevailed prior to the 1970s, we are now witnessing an era of 'institutional' assimilation. Among current assimilationist strategies are efforts to (a) phase out separate institutional structures, (b) formally rationalize aboriginal–government relations through the creation of formal land corporations and municipal governing structures, and (c) incorporate the first nations into the legal, administrative, and political structures of Canadian society (Frideres, 1990). In effect, government seems bent on destroying the traditional structures that distinguish aboriginal peoples, in one last-ditch effort to solve the 'Indian problem'. Thus it may well be argued that the changes in aboriginal policy over the past 150 years have been illusory, with major developments restricted to strategies and symbols rather than objectives and content (Boldt and Long, 1988). The 'unfinished business' of the 'Indian problem' remains uppermost in government policy and administration, precluding development of the political will to forge innovative relationships with the 'nations within'.

Central authorities have several options for responding to aboriginal demands. First, as Cornell (1988) notes, such demands may be stifled by actively suppressing radical aboriginal resistance to the status quo; for example, campaigns may be mounted to discredit activists or destabilize movements by belittling their demands as illogical, irrelevant, or non-representative. Second, central authorities can attempt to control and contain aboriginal demands through symbolic reforms that convey the appearance of change while maintaining the status quo and the prevailing distribution of power and resources. The appointment of radical sectors to advisory/policy consultation bodies represents one popular strategy for deflating aboriginal aspirations. Recent proposals to incorporate Canada's aboriginal people into the national political forum by way of guaranteed aboriginal electoral districts and representation in Parliament constitute a case in point. Similarly, aboriginal representatives within central bureaucracies may be increased without alteration to the institutional structure itself.

Third, political authorities may decide to relinquish some power through genuine concessions and substantial reforms. This need not, however, amount to actual power-sharing. Loss of control over the political agenda is kept to a manageable minimum, while the pace of reform is carefully monitored and regulated. Substantial changes are introduced that accommodate aboriginal demands to some extent, but simultaneously (perhaps even inadvertently) reinforce the status quo, often by co-opting aboriginal groups into the institutional structure of society. Even well-intentioned actions may have negative consequences, in large measure because they begin with faulty assumptions and improper assessment of the problem at hand. To date, for example, there have been substantial reforms in the economic field with the expansion of programs that deal with reserve resource utilization and reserve-based development. The same is true in the areas of education and politics, where demands for self-determination have paid off with limited reforms at local levels. But government does not grant such concessions for nothing. Not only are central authorities anxious to pry open access to aboriginal resources; they are likewise intent on 'normalizing' aboriginal involvement in society in the interests of social peace and fiscal restraint.

In short, although recent rhetoric about self-determination and self-government suggests a fundamental shift in state policy toward aboriginal peoples, no such change has occurred. Indeed, far from severing the bonds of dependency and underdevelopment, state initiatives may have had the effect, whether by design or by accident, of further incorporating aboriginal people into institutional structures (Cornell, 1988). All we have seen are changes in the strategies to achieve policy objectives that do not depart significantly from nineteenth-century assimilationist goals.

This essentially conservative policy agenda is maintained in several ways. First, state authorities agree to negotiate with aboriginal groups over reallocation of resources and power. But interaction is confined to officially recognized aboriginal bodies that are moderate in outlook and willing to comply with the system in return for funding or political status. Moderate organizations are upheld as legitimate representatives of aboriginal sectors. Central resources are directed to these bodies rather than to activist groups, enlarging their sphere of influence in decision-making. At the same time, these moderate aboriginal bodies that receive power and resources from the state become increasingly indebted to the institutional structure and political status in which they are embedded.

To point out the institutional assimilation of aboriginal organizations is not to imply a sell-out. Aboriginal bodies remain loyal defenders of their constituents' interest and are often vocal in their criticism of short-sighted government policies. However, as they play the political game, the actors and agencies begin to resemble other institutions both in their daily practices and procedures and in their latent objectives based on survival and self-interest. Even the representational basis of these organizations may be contested, or withdrawn, by central authorities if they fail to toe the line. The very act of participation in representational politics thus ensures that they are incorporated into the power structure and co-opted into the system as relatively isolated units, without much capacity for co-ordinated, pan-tribal action.

The distribution of power within the state is contested, but neither the institutions within the structure nor the institutional means of redress are openly disputed. Sustained aboriginal participation within the system, in other words, creates a situation in which aboriginal groups run the risk of becoming pawns in a bigger game, subject to the vagaries of bureaucratic rationality and political control.

From Colony to Nation: A Paradigm Shift?

Current aboriginal policy and administration in Canada, the United States, and New Zealand are constrained by paradigms that originated in the past and have persisted into the present. A policy paradigm can be defined as a system of relatively coherent ideas and assumptions that define a 'problem' in a particular way, along with a corresponding set of 'solutions' (Weaver, 1991). Since the paradigms operating in the United States are based on a different set of assumptions, we will briefly assess the situation there before turning our attention to Canada and New Zealand.

Aboriginal Nations in the United States

In the United States there has never been any question about the *inherent* sovereignty of aboriginal nations—the concept that currently dominates the aboriginal–state relations debate in Canada. As the noted legal scholar David Getches (1988: 197) has pointed out, tribal governments exercise legislative, judicial, and regulatory powers with their authority to do so 'derived from their aboriginal sovereignty, not from some grant of power by the federal government'. However, this sovereignty is limited inasmuch as aboriginal nations are 'subject to the overriding powers of Congress' (Wilkinson, 1987: 53).

Aboriginal nations have contested the restrictions imposed on their sovereignty by the federal government in the same way that states have resisted federal encroachments on their sovereignty or autonomy—the Civil War being an extreme example of a dispute over states' rights versus federal powers. The constitutional doctrine of 'residual powers' means that powers not ceded to the federal government are reserved by the states and aboriginal nations; in other words, the initial assumption is sovereignty. Hence, 'so long as Indian rights are not voluntarily ceded by the Indian tribes . . . or extinguished by Congress unilaterally, they continue to exist' (Getches, 1988: 198). If a treaty is silent on fishing rights, for example, the latter are in effect preserved, 'because the treaty does not take them away' (Getches, 1988: 198).

At the time of union, the states ceded to the federal government such powers as the right to declare war, issue currency, and regulate inter-state commerce. Likewise, aboriginal nations ceded the right to treaty with any power other than the US. Historically, having ceded these powers to the federal government, the states and aboriginal nations were pitted against each other with respect to the rightful exercise of their residual powers, which they jealously safeguarded and strove to protect. Since aboriginal nations are enclaves within the boundaries of states, jurisdictional disputes are ongoing today concerning the rights of non-Indians on Indian land, the right to tax, and the right to use land and consume resources. That jurisdiction itself is the prime issue is illustrated in the debate over water rights—a question of utmost importance in the arid areas of the west—which since 1908 has been 'not over the actual quantities to which Indians and non-Indians are entitled . . . but over which court will determine those quantities' (Getches, 1988: 204).

Clearly, co-operative strategies between the states and aboriginal nations are needed in such matters as conservation, taxation, and land use. The nineteenth-century Marshall case-law trilogy established a 'model that can be described broadly as calling for largely autonomous tribal governments subject to an overriding federal authority but essentially free of state control' (Wilkinson, 1987: 24). The modern era in federal Indian law, according to Wilkinson, was ushered in by the 1959 Supreme Court decision in Williams v. Lee. Essentially reaffirming the Marshall principles of aboriginality, the court ruled that a Navajo court had exclusive jurisdiction over a contract case involving a non-Indian. This decision promoted and protected tribal self-government and, at the same time, sharpened the conflict between state and tribal authorities, which continues to the present (Wilkinson, 1987). A further outcome of this ruling was a resurgence of tribal litigation after decades of inactivity resulting from federal assimilation policies, including termination.

What is needed to hasten the transition of aboriginal people from colony to nation in the US is not a new constitutional arrangement—as is being advocated in Canada—but the political will to implement the one already in place. Barriers to implementation run the gamut from the economic power of states to enforce their rights to the lack of understanding of collective (aboriginal) rights on the part of the general public, as well as lingering and all too pervasive racism. The profound ignorance of the constitutional basis of aboriginal people's 'nations within' status, coupled with racism, has consistently denied them their rightful place in American society. David Getches (1988: 198) sums it up this way: 'The struggle over jurisdiction is a struggle for power—a struggle that is *racial*. . . . Many non-Indians, taught . . . that all Americans are created equal, view the right of tribes to govern as evidence that Indians somehow have more rights. Indian rights may seem un-American to them' (emphasis added).

The aboriginal nations continue to struggle for justice. But in the absence of the political will to stop treating them as colonies, there is little indication that the 'domestic dependent nations' that Chief Justice Marshall envisioned will be fully realized. The shift in paradigms that would be the most advantageous to aboriginal nations would be towards one in which the American public graciously came to acknowledge the existence of collective as well as individual rights, and to value cultural pluralism and its protection to a significantly greater degree than is currently evident.

Aboriginal Nations in Canada and Aotearoa (New Zealand)
If the transition from colony to nation in Canada and New Zealand were to be realized, a different set of obstacles from those confronting the United States would have to be faced and surmounted. Canada, especially, is grappling with the need for a new constitutional paradigm that for the first time would acknowledge the *inherent* right of aboriginal peoples to govern themselves. New Zealand, for its part, has attempted to chart a middle course on sovereignty that has proved unsatisfactory to both partners. Although various interpretations exist concerning the status of Maori sovereignty (*mana Maori motuhake*) and the Treaty of Waitangi, a dominant Maori view is that *mana* (power) is equivalent to sovereignty. Since *mana* and *rangatiratanga* (chieftainship) are inseparable, it is argued that in guaranteeing *rangatiritanga* the Treaty effectively acknowledged the inherent sovereignty of the Maori, who would retain their *mana* without denying that of the Queen. The Crown would hold the *mana* of government while chiefs were confirmed in their authority (Walker, 1990: 266). In the Maori view, the Treaty was a reciprocal agreement 'which allowed for a sharing of authority, a partnership within the new nation' (Orange, 1987: 226). To date, however, there is no agreement concerning the constitutional parameters of this partnership; hence the need for a new paradigm.

In New Zealand as well as in Canada, the old paradigms reflect an outmoded analysis of state responsibilities to aboriginal peoples by emphasizing formal legal obligations and patterns of control. A paradigm shift in aboriginal policy and administration is gathering momentum in response to aboriginal demands and continued criticism of government initiatives by policy advisers and theorists. In New Zealand much of the impetus for the new paradigm originated in the politicization of Maori activism under the unifying symbol of the Treaty of Waitangi, with its promise of a partnership between two relatively sovereign nations within Aotearoa. In Canada the paradigm shift stems from the Penner Report on Indian self-government in 1983 and the Coolican Report on comprehensive land claims in 1985 (Weaver, 1991). While details vary between countries, the key themes in the two paradigms, old and new, reflect common patterns. Among these themes — (a) old and (b) new — are the following.

1. (a) Aboriginal–state relations are cast in stone with little or no possibility of transformation.
   (b) Aboriginal–state relations are ongoing and 'organic' as each party learns to adjust to the needs and demands of the other ('partnership').

2. (a) Government programs are special measures to assist a derelict and destitute population in need of state intervention.
   (b) Aboriginal demands are 'sanctioned rights' (not needs) in that they are acknowledged by the state as legitimate claims against its power and resources ('the new entitlement').

3. (a) Aboriginal cultures disappeared decades ago, and efforts to keep them alive are artificial and costly.
   (b) Aboriginal cultures are living and lived-in realities that must be encouraged to flourish and co-exist alongside dominant values and norms ('biculturalism').

4. (a) Government obligations are legally defined, and aboriginal relations must be based on a strict reading of the law and entitlements.
   (b) Aboriginal–government relations are to be based on a new 'political ethic' guided by principles of fairness, honesty, and generosity rather than by legalistic interpretations and 'sharp dealing' ('the new pluralism').

5. (a) Aboriginal claims to self-government are fine in theory, but impractical and unlikely to work in the larger society.
   (b) A stronger commitment to aboriginal self-governing structures — aboriginally designed and legitimated political structures — will promote cultural coexistence and economic self-determination. To achieve these goals, it is argued, the government must learn to recognize aboriginal authority in specific jurisdictions, ensure appropriate structures for exercise of that authority, and allocate sufficient economic resources to put these structures into practice ('self-determination through self-government').

6. (a) Government is eager to delegate responsibility to local communities (as long as the latter remain accountable to central authorities), ostensibly to bring decision-making closer to the people but also to reduce government commitments.

(b) Joint power-sharing and management systems must devolve real decision-making authority to aboriginal groups; mere delegation of self-administrating responsibilities is not enough ('devolution').

7. (a) The primary responsibility of the aboriginal affairs bureaucracy is to carry out the mandate entrusted to it by law and the legislative assembly.

(b) Administrative arrangements must move away from the previous emphasis on custody and control towards a new focus on culturally-sensitive development. The role of the administrative wing is to support and advance aboriginal political and economic interests while fulfilling negotiated agreements with central authorities ('development').

Much of the current turmoil in aboriginal–government relations reflects a conflict between traditional and evolving approaches to solving the 'Indian problem' (Weaver, 1991). In contrast to the old paradigm, with its emphasis on legalism and control, the new paradigm redefines aboriginal–government relations around the poles of justice, fair and equitable treatment, adaptation, and workable intergroup dynamics. To date, policy and administrative officials have been reluctant to follow through on the proposed paradigm shift. Such resistance is to be expected. But reform is inevitable as pressures escalate for fundamental change in the aboriginal agenda. Under these conditions, the chances are that competing forces will align themselves at opposite ends of the policy and administrative fields and only then work towards finding solutions. No doubt the transition period will be turbulent. A state of tension and conflict is likely to last until the conventional paradigm defers to the new in reconstructing aboriginal–state relations from our colonial past.

REFERENCE LIST

Abele, F.
    1990   'The Democratic Potential in Administrative Expansion: Assessing the Impact of the Transfer of Governing Responsibilities from the Federal Government to the Governments of the Yukon and Northwest Territories'. Pp. 295-316 in Dacks (1990).

Aboriginal and Torres Strait Islander Commission
    1991   *Annual Report.* Canberra: Government Publishing Services.

Aboriginal Justice Inquiry of Manitoba
    1991   *Report.* Vol. 1. *The Justice System and Aboriginal People.* A.C. Hamilton and C.M. Sinclair, commissioners. Winnipeg.

Ahenakew, David
    1985   'Aboriginal Title and Aboriginal Rights: The Impossible and Unnecessary Task of Identification and Definition'. Pp. 24-30 in Boldt and Long (1985).

Allen, Paula Gunn
    1986   *The Sacred Hoop: Recovering the Feminine in American Indian Traditions.* Boston: Beacon Press.

American Friends Service Commission (AFSC)
    1970   *Uncommon Controversy: Fishing Rights of the Muckleshoot, Puyallup, and Nisqually Indians.* Report prepared for the AFSC. Seattle: University of Washington Press.

American Indian Policy Review Commission
    1977   *Final Report.* Vol. 1. 17 May. Washington, DC.: US Government Printing Office.

Angus, Murray
    1990   *'And the Last Shall be First': Native Policy in an Era of Cutbacks.* Ottawa: Aboriginal Rights Coalition.

Armstrong, M. Jocelyn
    1987   'Interethnic Conflict in New Zealand'. Pp. 254-78 in J. Boucher, D. Landis, and K.A. Clark, eds. *Ethnic Conflict.* Beverly Hills: Sage.

Asch, Michael
    1984   *Home and Native Land: Aboriginal Rights and the Canadian Constitution.* Toronto: Methuen.
    1989   'To Negotiate into Confederation: Canadian Aboriginal Views on their Political Rights'. Pp. 118-37 in Wilmsen (1989).

Aucoin, Pierre, and Herman Bakvis
    1988   *Organization and Management in the Canadian Context.* Montreal: Institute for Research on Public Policy.

Awatere, Donna
    1984   *Maori Sovereignty.* Auckland: Broadsheets.

Axworthy, Thomas S., and Pierre Elliott Trudeau
    1990   *Towards a Just Society: The Trudeau Years.* Translations into English by Patricia Claxton. Markham, Ont.: Viking (Penguin).
Baker, Carol
    1990   In *Northern Perspectives* 18, 4 (Nov.-Dec.): 22.
Barman, J., Y. Hebert, and D. McCaskill, eds
    1987   *Indian Education in Canada: The Challenge.* Vol. 2. Vancouver: University of British Columbia Press.
Barrington, J.M.
    1970   'A Historical Review of Policies and Provisions'. Pp. 27-39 in J.L. Ewing and J.S. Shallcrass, eds. *Introduction to Maori Education: Selected Readings.* Wellington: New Zealand University Press/Price Milburn.
Barsch, Russel Lawrence, and James Youngblood Henderson
    1980   *The Road: Indian Tribes and Political Liberty.* Berkeley: University of California Press.
Barth, Frederik
    1969   *Ethnic Groups and Boundaries: The Social Organization of Cultural Difference.* Oslo: Universitetsforlaget.
Bell, Jim
    1991   'A Time for Candour: Could the NWT's Noble Experiment in Consensus Be in Trouble?' *Arctic Circle*, Sept./Oct.: 11-12.
Bennett, Jr, Lerone
    1966   *Before the Mayflower.* Baltimore: Penguin.
Benton, Richard A.
    1979   *Who Speaks Maori in New Zealand?* Wellington: New Zealand Council of Educational Research.
    1981   *The Flight of the Amokura.* Wellington: New Zealand Council of Educational Research.
Berger, Thomas
    1987   'Legal and Historical Perspectives'. In Ken Zeilig and Victoria Zeiling. *Ste Madeleine, Community without a Town: Métis Elders in Interview.* Winnipeg: Pemmican.
Bienvenue, Rita
    1985   'Colonial Status: The Case of Canadian Indians'. Pp. 199-216 in Rita Bienvenue and Jay Goldstein, eds. *Ethnicity and Ethnic Relations in Canada.* Toronto: Butterworths.
Biggs, Bruce
    1972   'The Maori Language Past and Present'. Pp. 65-84 in Erik Schwinner, ed. *The Maori People in the Nineteen Sixties.* Auckland: Longman Paul.
Binney, Judith
    1989   'The Maori and the Signing of the Treaty of Waitangi'. Pp. 20-31 in 1990 Commission. *Towards 1990.* Wellington: Government Printer.
Blauner, Robert
    1972   *Racial Oppression in America.* New York: Harper and Row.
Bodley, John H.
    1987   'Demographic Impact of the Frontier'. In Menard and Moen (1987).
Boldt, Menno, and J. Anthony Long
    1984   'Tribal Traditions and European-Western Political Ideology: The

Dilemma of Canadian Native Indians'. *Canadian Journal of Political Science* 17: 537-54.

1988   'Native Self-Government: Instrument of Autonomy or Assimilation?' Pp. 38-56 in Long and Boldt (1988).

Boldt, Menno, and J. Anthony Long, eds

1985   *The Quest for Justice: Aboriginal Peoples and Aboriginal Rights*. Toronto: University of Toronto Press.

Bressette, Shelley

1991   'Building the Road to Self-Government'. *Nativebeat* 1, 10 (June).

Breton, Raymond

1984   'The Production and Allocation of Symbolic Resources: An Analysis of the Linguistic and Ethnocultural Fields in Canada'. *Canadian Review of Sociology and Anthropology* 21, 2: 123-40.

British Columbia Claims Task Force

1991   *Report*. Vancouver, BC. 28 June.

Britsch-Devany, Susan

1988   'The Collaborative Development of a Language Renewal Program for Preschoolers'. *Human Organization* 47, 4: 297-301.

Brock, Kathy L.

1990   'Aboriginal Self-Government By Comparison'. Paper presented to the Indigenous Peoples and the Law Conference, Ottawa.

1991   'The Politics of Aboriginal Self-Government: A Paradox'. *Canadian Public Administration* 34, 2: 272-85.

Bryden, Joan

1991   'Recognition of Native Rights Must Come First'. *Kitchener-Waterloo Record*. 28 Oct.

Burger, Julian

1987   *Report From the Frontier: The State of the World's Indigenous Peoples*. New Jersey: Zed Books.

Burnaby, Barbara

1982   *Language and Education Among Canadian Native Peoples*. The Language and Literacy Series. Toronto: OISE Press.

1984   *Aboriginal Languages in Ontario*. Toronto: Ministry of Education.

Burnette, Robert, and John Koster

1974   *The Road to Wounded Knee*. New York: Bantam.

Burns, Peter T.

1991   'Delgamuukw v. BC: A Summary of the Judgement'. Conference proceedings, Delgamuukw and the Aboriginal Land Question. Victoria, BC. 10-11 Sept.

Burt, Larry W.

1982   *Tribalism in Crisis: Federal Indian Policy, 1953-1961*. Albuquerque: University of New Mexico Press.

Butterworth, G.V.

1989   *End of an Era: The Departments of Maori Affairs 1840-1989*. Wellington: Government Printer.

1990   *Maori Affairs*. Wellington: Government Printer.

Cabinet Social Equity Committee

1986   'Report on Seminar Held to Discuss Tribal Delivery Systems'. Unpublished paper. 8 July.

Calder, William
  1988   'The Provinces and Indian Self-Government in the Constitutional
         Forum'. Pp. 72-82 in Long and Boldt (1988).
Canada
  1982   *Outstanding Business: A Native Claims Policy*. Ottawa: Minister of
         Supply and Services.
  1991   *Aboriginal Peoples, Self-Government, and Constitutional Reform*.
         Ottawa: Minister of Supply and Services.
Canada's North: The Reference Manual
  1983   Ottawa: Communications Branch of Indian and Northern Affairs
         Canada.
Canadian Government
  1990   *Canadian Government Program and Services Reports*. Ottawa: CCH.
Cassidy, Frank
  1990   'Aboriginal Governments in Canada: An Emerging Field of Study'.
         Canadian Journal of Political Science 33, 1: 73-99.
  1991   'First Nations Can No Longer Be Rebuffed'. *Policy Options Poli-
         tiques*, May: 3-6.
Cassidy, Frank, and Norman Dale
  1988   *After Native Claims? The Implications of Comprehensive Claims Set-
         tlements for Natural Resources in British Columbia*. Halifax:
         Oolichan Books and Institute for Research on Public Policy.
Chapman, Robert
  1986   'Voting in the Maori Political Sub-System, 1935-1984'. Pp. B-
         83–B-108 in *Report of the Royal Commission on the Electoral
         System. 'Towards a Better Democracy'*. Wellington: Government
         Printer.
Chaudhuri, Joyotpaul
  1982   'American Indian Policy: An Overview of the Legal Complexities,
         Controversies and Dilemmas'. *The Social Science Journal* 19, 3
         (July): 9-21.
Clancy, P.
  1990   'Politics by Remote Control. Historical Perspectives on Devolution in
         Canada's North'. Pp. 13-42 in Dacks (1990).
Clark, Bruce
  1990   *Native Liberty, Crown Sovereignty: The Existing Aboriginal Right of
         Self-Government in Canada*. McGill-Queen's University Press.
Clark, Paul
  1975   *'Hauhau': The Pai Marire Search for Maori Identity*. Auckland:
         Auckland University Press/Oxford University Press.
Cleave, Peter
  1989   *The Sovereignty Game: Power, Knowledge, and Reading the Treaty*.
         Wellington: Institute of Policy Studies for the Victoria University Press.
Cleveland, Les
  1979   *The Politics of Utopia: New Zealand and Its Government*. Welling-
         ton: Methuen.
Cohen, Felix
  1982   *Handbook of Federal Indian Law*. Charlottesville, Va: Michie, Bobbs-
         Merrill.

Comeau, Pauline, and Aldo Santin
1990   *The First Canadians: A Profile of Canada's Native People Today.*
       Toronto: James Lorimer.
Committee for Aboriginal Electoral Reform
1991   'Report to the Royal Commission on Electoral Reform and Party
       Financing'. Unpublished. Ottawa.
Comprehensive Claims Branch
1991   'Comprehensive Claims in Canada'. Prepared by Claims and Histor-
       ical Research Centre. Native Affairs Program. Ottawa.
Coolican, Murray
1985   *Living Treaties: Lasting Agreements.* Report of the Task Force to
       Review Comprehensive Land Claims Policy. Ottawa: DIAND.
1990   In *Northern Perspectives* 18, 4 (Nov.-Dec.): 4.
Cornell, Stephen
1988   *The Return of the Native: American Indian Political Resurgence.*
       New York: Oxford.
Cox, Bob
1991   'Native Leaders Stand with Mercredi'. *Halifax Chronicle-Herald*, 8
       Oct. 1991: A9.
Cross Cultural Consulting Inc.
1989   'Canada's First Nations: An Overview of Select Historical and Con-
       temporary Perspectives'. Prepared for the Department of Indian
       Affairs and Northern Development.
Dacks, Gurston
1988   'The Aboriginal Peoples and the Government of the Northwest Ter-
       ritories'. In Long and Boldt (1988).
Dacks, Gurston, ed.
1990   *Devolution and Constitutional Development in the Canadian North.*
       Ottawa: Carleton University Press.
Dafoe, John
1991   'Manitoba's Inquiry Into Aboriginal Justice Merits Vastly More Than
       Wariness'. *Globe and Mail.* 7 Sept.
Dalziel, R.D.
1981   'The Politics of Settlement'. In W.H. Oliver and B.R. Williams, eds. *The
       Oxford History of New Zealand.* Wellington: Oxford University Press.
Daniell, S.
1983   'Reform of the New Zealand Political System: How Likely Is It? A
       Survey of the Attitudes of the Members of the New Zealand Parlia-
       ment to Reform Proposals'. *Political Science* 35: 151-89.
Daniels, Harry W.
1978   'Natives not a Disadvantaged Social Class but a Historical National
       Minority'. *The Native Perspective* 3, 2.
Davidson, Janet M.
1981   'The Polynesian Foundation'. Pp. 3-27 in W.H. Oliver and B.R.
       Williams, eds. *The Oxford History of New Zealand.* Wellington:
       Oxford University Press.
Davies, Maureen
1985a 'Aspects of Aboriginal Rights in International Law'. Pp. 16-47 in
       Morse (1985).

1985b   'Aboriginal Rights in International Law: Human Rights'. Pp. 745-94
         in Morse (1985).

Delacourt, Susan

1991   'Ottawa Agrees to New Territory'. *Globe and Mail.* 17 Dec.

Deloria Jr, Vine, and Clifford Lytle

1984   *The Nations Within: The Past and Future of American Indian
        Sovereignty.* New York: Pantheon.

Department of Inland Revenue

1990   'Te Urupare Rangapu Education Package, Te Tari Taake'. Unpub-
        lished internal document.

Department of Maori Affairs

1984   'Report of the Staffing and Management Requirements of the Com-
        munity Services Division, Department of Maori Affairs'. Wellington.

1987   'Initial Report to the Steering Group of Permanent Heads From the
        Task Force Group on Devolution'. Wellington. 5 June.

1988   'Report of the Department of Maori Affairs and the Board of Maori
        Affairs and Maori Trustee Office for the year ended 31 March 1988'.
        Wellington: Government Printer.

Department of Social Welfare

1986   'Puao-te-ata-tu'. 'Daybreak'. Ministerial Advisory Committee on the
        Maori Perspective for the Department of Social Welfare.

1989   'Devolution: Employment of Iwi Staff. The Path Ahead for Maori
        Development'. Implementing Puao-te-ata-tu. Series 5. Wellington:
        Government Printer.

Department of Statistics

1990   *The New Zealand Official 1990 Year Book.* Wellington: Government
        Printer.

Deputies Council

1991   'Towards Managing Diversity: A Study of Systemic Discrimination at
        DIAND'. Report of The Deputies' Council for change. Ottawa: Minister
        of Supply and Services.

Devolution Implementation Committee

1987   'Draft Discussion Paper'. Wellington. 13 Aug.

Dewes, Koro

1968   *The Place of Maori Language in the Education of the Maoris.*
        Paper presented to the 40th ANZAAS Congress. Christchurch, New
        Zealand.

1987   'Briefing Paper to the Cabinet Ad Hoc Committee on Maori Devel-
        opment'. Unpublished. Wellington. 25 Sept.

DIAND (Department of Indian Affairs and Northern Development)

n.d.   'A Review of Aboriginal Constitutional Reform'. *Information.*

1979   'A Demographic Profile of Registered Indian Women'. Research
        Branch. P.R.E. October.

1985   'Background Notes'. Prepared for the First Ministers Conference.
        Ottawa.

1986   *Communiqué.* 17 June.

1987   'Comprehensive Land Claims Policy'. Ottawa: Minister of Supply
        and Services.

1989a 'The Cree Naskapi (of Quebec) Act'. *Information* No. 11 (April).

1989b 'Alternative Funding Arrangements'. *Information* No. 7 (April).

1989c 'Minister's Position: New Relations With Indians'. *Transitions* 2, 10 (Oct.).

1989d 'A National Strategy for Aboriginal Economic Development'. Ottawa: Minister of Supply and Services.

1990a 'University Education and Economic Well-Being: Indian Achievement and Prospects'. Ottawa: Minister of Supply and Services.

1990b 'Canadian Aboriginal Economic Development Strategy'. Written by the Aboriginal Business Development Program. Ottawa: Minister of Supply and Services.

1990c 'Lands, Revenues, and Trust Review'. Phase 2 Report. Ottawa: Minister of Supply and Services.

1990d 'DIAND Programs and Services for Indians and Inuit'. *Information* No. 15 (March).

1990e 'Department of Indian Affairs and Northern Development. Land Claims Policy'. *Information* (July).

1990f 'Background Information on Oka'. 27 July.

1990g 'Prime Minister Commits Government to a Native Agenda'. *Transition* 3, 10 (Oct.).

1990h 'Community Self-Government Negotiations'. *Information* No. 35 (Nov.).

1991a 'Self-Government Sechelt Style'. *Information* No. 20 (Jan.).

1991b 'Comprehensive Claims'. *Information* No. 9 (Feb.).

1991c 'The Native Agenda'. *Information* No. 33 (March).

1991d 'Aboriginal Self-Government'. *Information* No. 3 (March).

1991e 'Band Support Funding'. *Information* No. 24 (June).

1991f 'Gwich'in Comprehensive Land Claim Agreement Initialled'. *Transition* 4, 9 (Sept.).

1991g 'Indian Residential Schools'. *Information* No. 46 (Sept.).

1991h *Communique* 1-916.

Dickason, Olive P.

1985 'From "One Nation" in the Northeast to "New Nation" in the Northwest: A Look at the Emergence of the Métis'. In Peterson and Brown (1985).

Dinnerstein, Leonard, et al.

1990 *Natives and Strangers: Blacks, Indians and Immigrants in America.* 2nd ed. New York: Oxford.

Dipple, Brian W.

1982 *The Vanishing American: White Attitudes and US Indian Policy.* Middleton, Conn: Wesleyen University Press.

DiTamasco, Nancy

1984 'Class and Politics in the Organization of Public Bureaucracy: The US Department of Labor'. Pp. 335-55 in Frank Fischer and Carmen Siriani, eds. *Critical Studies in Organizations and Bureaucracy.* Philadelphia: Temple University Press.

Diubaldo, Richard J.

1981 'The Absurd Little Mouse: When Eskimos Became Indians'. *Journal of Canadian Studies* 16, 2 (Summer).

Doherty, Phyllis, and Albert Currie
  1991   'Justice for Canada's Native Peoples: What and How Well Are Gov-
         ernments Doing? *Justice Research Notes* 2 (March): 3-8.
Dosman, Edgar
  1972   *Indians: The Urban Dilemma.* Toronto: McClelland and Stewart.
DRIE (Department of Regional and Industrial Expansion)
  1983   'Native Economic Development Fund'. News Release. 10 June 1983.
         Ottawa: DRIE.
DuCharme, Michele
  1986   'The Canadian Origins of South African Apartheid.' *Currents*
         (Summer): 2.
Dyck, Noel, ed.
  1980   'Indian, Métis, Native: Some Implications of Special Status'. *Cana-
         dian Ethnic Studies* 12, 1.
  1985   *Indigenous People and the Nation-State: Fourth World Politics
         in Canada, Australia, and Norway.* St John's, Nfld: Memorial
         University.
Economic Monitoring Group
  1989   *The Economy in Transition: Restructuring to 1989.* Wellington: New
         Zealand Planning Council.
Edelman, Murray
  1964   *The Symbolic Uses of Politics.* Urbana: University of Illinois Press.
Elliott, Jean Leonard
  1984   'Emerging Ethnic Nationalism in the Canadian Northwest Territo-
         ries'. *Canadian Review of Studies in Nationalism* 9, 2 (Fall).
Elliott, Jean Leonard, and Augie Fleras
  1991   *Unequal Relations: An Introduction to Race and Ethnic Dynamics in
         Canada.* Scarborough, Ont.: Prentice-Hall.
Erasmus, Georges
  1992   'Aboriginal Philosophy and Approaches to Governing'. Paper pre-
         sented to the Aboriginal Governments and Power-Sharing in Canada
         conference, organized by the Institute of Intergovernmental Rela-
         tions. Queen's University, Kingston, Ont. 17-18 Feb.
Farley, John E.
  1987   'The Status of Majority and Minority Groups in the United States
         Today'. In Menard and Moen (1987).
Feit, Harvey A.
  1989   'James Bay Cree Self-Governance and Land Management'. Pp. 68-98
         in Wilmsen (1989).
First Nations
  1990   'First Nations Submission on Claims'. 14 Dec. 1990. Ottawa.
Fisher, Robin
  1980   'The Impact of European Settlement on the Indigenous Peoples of
         Australia, New Zealand, and British Columbia: Some Comparative
         Dimensions'. *Canadian Ethnic Studies* 12, 1: 1-14.
Fitzgerald, Thomas K.
  1977   *Education and Identity: A Study of the New Zealand Maori Gradu-
         ate.* Wellington: New Zealand Council of Educational Research.

Fleras, Augie
 1981   'Maori Wardens and the Control of Liquor Among the Maori of New
        Zealand'. *Journal of Polynesian Society* 90, 4: 495-514.
 1983   *Te Kohanga Reo: Preparation for Life or Preparation for School?*
        Report on Maori Language Preschools. Wellington: Maori Affairs
        Department.
 1984   'From Social Welfare to Community Development: The Department of
        Maori Affairs in New Zealand'. *Community Development* 19, 1: 32-9.
 1985a 'Towards Tu Tangata: Historical Developments and Current Trends
        in Maori Policy and Administration'. *Political Science* 37: 18-39.
 1985b 'From Social Control to Political Self-Determination? Maori Seats
        and the Politics of Separate Maori Representation in New Zealand'.
        Canadian Journal of Political Science 18, 3: 551-76.
 1986   'The Politics of Maori Lobbying: The Case of the New Zealand Maori
        Council'. *Political Science* 38, 1: 39-52.
 1987a 'Aboriginality as a Language Issue: The Politicization of Te Reo
        Maori in New Zealand'. *Plural Societies* 17, 2: 25-51.
 1987b 'Redefining the Politics Over Aboriginal Language Renewal: Maori
        Language Preschools as Agents of Social Change'. *Canadian Journal
        of Native Studies* 7, 1: 1-40.
 1989a 'Inverting the Bureaucratic Pyramid: Reconciling Aboriginality and
        Bureaucracy in New Zealand'. *Human Organization* 48, 3: 214-25.
 1989b 'Te Kohanga Reo: A Maori Renewal Program'. *Canadian Journal of
        Native Education* 16, 2: 78-88.
 1990   'Race Relations as Collective Definition: Aboriginal-Government
        Relationships in Canada'. *Symbolic Interaction* 13, 1: 19-34.
 1991   'Tuku Rangatiratanga': Devolving Maori-Government Relations in
        New Zealand'. In Spoonley et al. (1991).
 1992   'Aboriginal Electoral Districts in Canada: Lessons from the New
        Zealand Experience'. *Report of the Royal Commission on Electoral
        Reform and Party Financing.* Book II. Ottawa.
 n.d.   'Maatua Whangai: A Community-Based Alternative in New Zealand
        Correctional Care'. Unpublished paper.
Foster, John E.
 1986   'The Plains Métis'. In Morrison and Wilson (1986).
Franks, C.E.S.
 1987   *Public Administration Questions Relating to Aboriginal Self-Gov-
        ernment.* Background Paper no. 12. Kingston, Ont.: Institute of Inter-
        governmental Relations.
Fraser, Graham
 1991   'Erasmus Appointed to Commission'. *Globe and Mail.* 28 Aug.
Frideres, James
 1988   *Native Peoples in Canada: Contemporary Conflicts.* 3rd ed. Scarbor-
        ough, Ont.: Prentice-Hall.
 1990   'Policies on Native Peoples in Canada'. In Peter S. Li, ed. *Race and
        Ethnic Relations in Canada.* Toronto: Oxford University Press.
 1991   'Introduction. Native Rights and the 21st Century: The Making of
        Red Power'. *Canadian Ethnic Studies* 22, 3: 1-7.

Fried, Morton H.
1975   *The Notion of Tribe*. Menlo Park, Ca.: Cummings.

Getches, David
1988   'Resolving Tensions between Tribal and State Governments: Learning from the American Experience'. Pp. 195-208 in Long and Boldt (1988).

Gibbins, Roger, and J. Rick Ponting
1986   'Faces and Interfaces of Indian Self-Government'. *Journal of Native Studies* 6: 43-62.

Gitksan-Wet'suwet'en
1987   Pamphlet published by the Gitskan-Wet'suwet'en Tribal Council. Hazelton, BC.

Globe and Mail
1990   '$4 Billion in Taxes: Where Does It Go?' 6 Sept.
1991a   'Aboriginal Affairs Commission Promised'. 24 April.
1991b   'Getting to the Heart of Aboriginal Rights Issues'. 27 May.
1991c   'A Place in the Mainstream'. 29 May.
1991d   'Status Indians Win Expanded Hunting Rights'. 29 May.
1991e   'Overhauled Process Urged for BC Native Land Claims'. 4 July.
1991f   'Oka Gave Voice to Aboriginals'. 10 July.
1991g   'A Real, Rare Opportunity'. 29 Aug.
1991h   'Self-Rule for Natives Tall Order, Panel Told'. 30 July.
1991i   'Native Self-Government Accepted by Premiers'. 27 Aug.
1991j   'Aboriginal Canadians and the Justice System'. Editorial. 31 Aug.
1991k   'Natives Need Own Courts, Justice Ministers Told'. 7 Sept.
1991l   'Natives Value Land Differently'. 9 Sept.
1991m   'Taking the Law into Their Own Hands'. 13 Sept.
1991n   '"Learn from Differences in Native Justice System," Professor Says'. 16 Sept.
1991o   'The Canada Question (III): Aboriginal Rights'. Editorial. 18 Sept.
1991p   'Mercredi Says Natives Seek Right to be Different'. 7 Nov.

Goar, Carol
1991   'Why Ottawa Plan Has Natives Angry'. *Toronto Star*. 28 Sept.

Grace, J.H.
1937   'Report on the Housing and Economic Survey of the Little River Settlement'. Report delivered to the Registrar of the Native Land Court in Wellington, NZ.

Graham, K.
1990   'Devolution and Local Government'. Pp. 195-224 in Dacks (1990).

Grant, Shelagh D.
1991   'A Case of Compounded Error: The Inuit Resettlement Project, 1953, and the Government Response, 1990'. *Northern Perspectives* 19, 1 (Spring).

Gray, Paul
1991   'The Trouble with Columbus'. *Time*. 7 Oct.: 52.

Greenland, Hauraki
1984   'Ethnicity as Ideology: The Critique of Pakeha Society'. Pp. 86-102 in Paul Spoonley et al., eds. *Tauiwi: Racism and Ethnicity in New Zealand*. Palmerston North, NZ.: Dunmore Press.

Griffins, Curt T. and Simon N. Verdun-Jones
  1989   'Native Indians and the Criminal Justice System'. Pp. 545-89 in Griffins and Verdun-Jones, eds. *Canadian Criminal Justice*. Toronto: Butterworths.
Guillemin, Jeanne
  1979   'American Indian Resistance and Protest'. In H. Graham and T. Gurr, eds. *Violence in America*. Beverly Hills: Sage.
Halifax Chronicle-Herald
  1991   'NS Micmacs Want Federal Indian Affairs Department Abolished'. 13 July.
Hall, Tony
  1986a 'The N'ungosuk Project: A Study in Aboriginal Language Renewal'. Unpublished paper.
  1986b 'Self-Government or Self-Delusion? Brian Mulroney and Aboriginal Rights'. *Journal of Native Studies* 6: 77-89.
  1990   'Canada's Bitter Legacy of Injustice'. *Globe and Mail*. 16 March.
  1991a 'Treating Native Activists Like Common Criminals'. *Globe and Mail*. 26 March.
  1991b 'Aboriginal Futures—Awakening our Imaginations'. *Canadian Dimension*, July/Aug.: 15-17.
Halligan, J.
  1980   'Continuity and Change in the New Zealand Parliament'. Unpublished doctoral dissertation. Wellington: Victoria University.
Handelman, Don, and Elliot Leyton, eds
  1978   *Bureaucracy and World View: Studies in the Logic of Official Interpretation*. Toronto: University of Toronto Press.
Hanson, Elizabeth
  1980   *The Politics of Social Security: The 1938 Act and Some Later Developments*. Auckland: Auckland/Oxford University Press.
Hawkes, David C., ed.
  1989   *Aboriginal Peoples and Government Responsibility: Exploring Federal and Provincial Roles*. Ottawa: Carleton University Press.
Heizer, Robert F., and Alan T. Almquist
  1971   *The Other Californians*. Berkeley: University of California Press.
Henton, Darcy
  1991   'Natives See Few Changes for the Better'. *Toronto Star*. 26 Dec.
Henton, Darcy, and William Walker
  1991   'Dene Indians Set to Fight Inuit Deal'. *Toronto Star*. 17 Dec.
Himona, Russ
  1989   'Government Policies: An Overview'. *He Putatara* 12: 4-5.
Horsman, Reginald
  1981   *Race and Manifest Destiny: The Origins of American Racial Anglo-Saxonism*. Cambridge: Harvard University Press.
Hughes, Ken (Chair)
  1991   *The Summer of 1990*. Fifth Report of the Standing Committee on Aboriginal Affairs. Ottawa.

Hui Rangatiratanga
  1990   Report of the Proceedings. 6-8 July. Rotorua, New Zealand.
Hunn, J.K., and J.M. Booth
  1962   'The Integration of Maori and Pakeha in New Zealand'. Study Paper
          No. 1. Wellington: Department of Maori Affairs.
Irwin, Colin
  1989   'Lords of the Arctic: Wards of the State'. *Northern Perspectives* 17, 1.
          Ottawa: Canadian Arctic Resources Committee.
Ittinuar, Peter
  1985   'The Inuit Perspective on Aboriginal Rights'. In Menno Boldt and
          J. Anthony Long (1985).
Iwi Transition Agency
  1990a   'Ko te Kaupapa Nui a Tira Ahu Iwi 1990/1991'. Corporate Plan of the
          Iwi Transition Agency. Wellington: Government Printer.
  1990b   'Nga Whetu Kapokapo—Navigation Points. Planning Guidelines for
          Iwi'. Unpublished paper.
Jackson, Moana
  1989   'The Crown, the Treaty, and the Usurpation of Maori Rights'. In con-
          ference proceedings, Aotearoa/New Zealand and Human Rights in
          the Pacific and Asia Region. 26-28 May.
Jackson, W.J.
  1973   *New Zealand: Politics of Change.* Wellington: A.W. and A.H. Reed.
Jackson, W.K., and G.A. Wood
  1964   'The New Zealand Parliament and Maori Representation'. *Historical
          Studies: Australia and New Zealand* 11: 383-96.
Jaimes, M. Annette
  1988   'Federal Indian Identification Policy: A Usurpation of Indigenous
          Sovereignty in North America'. *Policy Studies Journal* 16, 4
          (Summer): 778-99.
James, Colin
  1988   'New Zealand Maori Challenge'. *Far Eastern Economic Review* 141: 36-42.
Jesson, Bruce
  1988   'The Almost Uncontested Victory of the Libertarian Right'. *The
          Republican*, July: 7-14.
Jhappan, C. Radha
  1990   'Indian Symbolic Politics: The Double-Edged Sword of Publicity'.
          Canadian Ethnic Studies 22, 3: 19-39.
Johnson, Lyndon B.
  1968   'The Forgotten American: The President's Message to the Congress
          on Goals and Programs for the American Indian'. 6 March. Wash-
          ington, DC: US Government Printing Office.
Josephy Jr, Alvin M.
  1971   'The American Indian and the Bureau of Indian Affairs'. In Josephy,
          ed. *Red Power: The American Indians' Fight for Freedom.* Toronto:
          McGraw-Hill.
  1976   *The Patriot Chiefs: A Chronicle of American Indian Resistance.* New
          York: Penguin.

Jull, Peter
    1987   'Nunavut: Self Government and Arctic Sovereignty'. Background paper for the Nunavut Constitutional Forum, Ottawa.
    1991   'Redefining Aboriginal–White Relations: Canada's Inuit'. *International Journal of Canadian Studies* 3 (Spring): 11-25.

Kawharu, Hugh
    1989   *Waitangi: Maori and Pakeha Perspectives on the Treaty of Waitangi.* Auckland: Oxford University Press.

Kelly, Lawrence C.
    1983   *The Assault on Assimilation: John Collier and the Origins of Indian Policy Reform.* Albuquerque: University of New Mexico Press.

Kelsey, Jane
    1986   'Decolonization in the "First World": Indigenous Minorities Struggle for Justice and Self-Determination'. Pp. 102-41 in *Windsor Yearbook of Access to Justice.* Vol. 5. Windsor.
    1990   *A Question of Honour? Labour and the Treaty 1984-1989.* Wellington: Allen and Unwin.
    1991   'Treaty Justice in the 1980s'. Pp. 108-30 in Spoonley et al. (1991).

Kerr, Beatrice
    1987   'Te Kohanga Reo. He Kakano I Ruia Mai I Rangiatea'. Pp. 95-7 in Walter Hirsch, ed. *Living Languages: Bilingualism and Community Languages in New Zealand.* Auckland: Heinemann.

Kia Mohio, Kia Marama Trust
    1989   'Devolution: The Shadow and the Substance'. *Race, Gender, and Class* 9, 10: 57-73.

Kickingbird, Kirke, and Karen Ducheneaux
    1973   *One Hundred Million Acres.* New York: Macmillan.

Kilgour, David
    1988   *Uneasy Patriots: Western Canadians in Confederation.* Edmonton: Lone Pine.

Kitchener-Waterloo Record
    1991a 'First Nations Chief Suggests Natives Copy Quebec Moves'. 5 July.
    1991b 'Native Case Is Strong if Quebec Separates'. 10 July.
    1991c 'Ontario Recognizes Self-Rule for Natives'. 2 Aug.
    1991d 'Court Rules Against Native Land Claim in Temagami Area'. 15 Aug.
    1991e 'Indian Affairs Study Cites Discrimination'. 26 Oct.
    1991f 'Native Accord'. 7 Dec.

Kroeber, A.L.
    1955   'Nature of the Land-holding Group'. *Ethnology* 2, 4: 303-5.

Kymlicka, Will
    1991   'Cut the Hole to Fit the Peg'. *Globe and Mail.* 19 Feb.

Labour Government
    1988a 'He Tirohanga Rangapu—Partnership Perspectives'. Wellington: Government Printer.
    1988b 'Te Urupare Rangapu—Partnership Response'. Wellington: Government Printer.

1988c   Written submissions to the Discussion Paper 'Te Tirohanga Rangapu' (Partnership Perspectives). Vol. 1-4. Wellington.

Lacy, Michael G.
1982   'A Model of Cooptation Applied to the Political Relations of the United States and American Indians'. *The Social Science Journal* 19, 3 (July): 23-36.

Lange, David
1989   'Opening Address by the Prime Minister'. In conference proceedings, Aotearoa/New Zealand and Human Rights in the Pacific and Asia Region. Wellington: 26-28 May.

LaPrairie, Carol Pitcher
1988   'The Young Offenders Act and Aboriginal Youth'. Pp. 159-68 in Joe Hudson, Joseph P. Hornick, and Barbara A. Burrows, eds. *Justice and the Young Offender in Canada.* Toronto: Wall and Thompson.

LaRocque, Emma
1975   *Defeathering the Indian.* Agincourt, Ont.: Book Society of Canada.
1990   'Preface, or Here are Our Voices—Who Will Hear?' Pp. xv-xxx in Jeanne Perreault and Sylvia Vance, comp. and ed., *Writing the Circle: Native Women of Western Canada.* Edmonton: NeWest.

Lenihan, Donald
1991   'Getting Together on Native Claims'. *Globe and Mail.* 7 Nov.

Levine, S., and A. Robinson
1976   *The New Zealand Voter—A Survey of Public Opinion and Electoral Behaviour.* Wellington: Price Milburn.

Levine, Stephen, and Raj Vasil
1985   *Maori Political Perspectives: He Whakaaro Maori Mo Nga Tikanga Kawanatanga.* Auckland: Hutchinson.

Levine, Stuart, and Nancy O. Lurie, eds
1970   *The American Indian Today.* Baltimore: Penguin.

Li, Peter S.
1988   *Ethnic Inequality in a Class Society.* Toronto: Wall and Thompson.

Limerick, Patricia Nelson
1987   *The Legacy of Conquest.* New York: W.W. Norton.

Little Bear, L., Menno Boldt, and J. Anthony Long, eds
1984   *Pathways to Self-Determination: Canadian Indians and the Canadian State.* Toronto: University of Toronto Press.

London Free Press
1991   'Natives Press for Political Equality'. 11 May.

Long, J. Anthony, and Menno Boldt, eds
1988   *Governments in Conflict? Provinces and Indian Nations in Canada.* Toronto: University of Toronto Press.

Love, Ralph Ngatata
1977   'Policies of Frustration: The Growth of Maori Politics. The Ratana/Labour Era'. Unpublished doctoral dissertation. Wellington: Victoria University.

Lurie, Nancy O.
1970   'Historical Background'. In Levine and Lurie (1970).

McDonald, Geraldine
  1973   *Maori Mothers and Pre-school Education.* Wellington: New Zealand
          Council of Educational Research.
  1976   *Maori Family Education Association Project.* Report No. 1. Welling-
          ton: New Zealand Council of Educational Research.
MacDonald, Robert
  1990   *The Maori of Aotearoa-New Zealand.* Minority Rights Group report.
          Revised ed. London.
McHugh, P.G.
  1989   'Constitutional Theory and Maori Claims'. Pp. 25-63 in Kawharu
          (1989).
MacIntyre, Wendy
  1991   'DIAND is Changing says Deputy Minister'. *INTERCOM,* July-Aug.
Maclean's
  1990a   'Northern Agony'. 4 June.
  1990b   'Drumbeats of Anger'. 2 July.
  1991   'Promises to Keep'. 2 Sept.
McLeay, E.M.
  1980   'Political Arguments About Representation: The Case of the Maori
          Seats'. *Political Studies* 28: 43-62.
  1991   'Two Steps Forward, Two Steps Back: Maori Devolution, Maori
          Advisory Committees, and Maori Representation'. *Political
          Science* (NZ) 43, 1: 30-46.
McMillan, Alan D.
  1988   *Native Peoples and Cultures of Canada.* Vancouver/Toronto:
          Douglas and McIntyre.
McNickle, D'Arcy
  1973   *Native American Tribalism: Indian Survivals and Renewals.* New
          York: Oxford University Press.
McRobie, Alan
  1981   'Ethnic Representation: The New Zealand Experience'. Pp. 2-14 in
          Stokes (1981).
McTagget, Sue
  1986   Leaving the Nest. *Listener* [NZ]. 22 Nov.
Mahuta, Robert
  1981   'Maori Political Representation: A Case For Change'. In Stokes (1981).
Maidman, Frank
  1981   'Native People in Urban Settings: A Report on the Ontario Task Force
          on Native People in the Urban Setting'. N.p.
Manitoba
  1991   'Manitoba Aboriginal Justice Inquiry'. Conducted by Associate Chief
          Justice A.C. Hamilton and Associate Chief Judge Murray Sinclair.
Maori Synod
  1961   *A Maori View of the 'Hunn Report'.* Published for the Maori Synod
          of the Presbyterian Church of New Zealand.
Maracle, Lee
  1990   *Bobbie Lee: Indian Rebel.* Toronto: Women's Press.

Marchand, Len
  1990   'Aboriginal Electoral Reform'. Discussion paper.
Marger, Martin N.
  1991   *Race and Ethnic Relations*. 2nd ed. Belmont, Cal.: Wadsworth.
Marshall, James, Michael Peter, and Graham Smith
  1990   'The Business Round Table and the Privatisation of Education: Individualism and the Attack on Maori'. Paper presented at the NZARE Special Interest Conference. 6 July.
Martin, Fred V.
  1989   'Federal and Provincial Responsibility in the Metis Settlements of Alberta'. Pp. 173-242 in Hawkes (1989).
Martin, John
  1982   *State Papers*. Palmerston North, NZ: Massey University.
Martin, John, and Jim Harper
  1988   *Devolution and Accountability*. Studies in Public Administration. No. 34. Wellington: Government Printer.
Matthiasson, John S., and Carolyn J. Matthiasson
  1978   'A People Apart: Ethnicization of the Inuit in the Eastern Canadian Arctic'. In Leo Driedger, ed. *The Canadian Mosaic*. Toronto: McClelland and Stewart.
Matthiessen, Peter
  1983   *In the Spirit of Crazy Horse*. New York: Viking.
Maulson, Tom
  1991   'A People's Birthright: Not for Sale'. *Mother Jones*, Jan./Feb.
Mead, Hirini Moko
  1979   'A Pathway to the Future: He Ara Kite Aomarama'. Paper presented to the New Zealand Planning Council. Wellington.
Menard, S.W., and E.W. Moen, eds
  1987   *Perspectives on Population*. New York: Oxford University Press.
Merriam, Lewis, et al.
  1928   *The Problem of Indian Administration*. Baltimore: Johns Hopkins University Press.
Metge, A. Joan
  1976   *The Maori of New Zealand: Rautahi*. London: Routledge and Kegan Paul.
  1984   'Learning and Teaching: He Tikanga Maori'. Unpublished paper presented to the Department of Education, Maori and Pacific Island Division. Wellington.
Miller, J.R.
  1989   *Skyscrapers Hide the Heavens: A History of Indian-White Relations in Canada*. Toronto: University of Toronto Press.
Minister of Finance
  1986   'Maatua Whangai and Maori Delivery Structures'. Unpublished interdepartmental memo. 17 Oct.
Minister of State Services
  n.d.   Correspondence to the Devolution Implementation Committee.
Ministerial Committee of Inquiry
  1987   'Report of the Ministerial Committee of Inquiry into Violence'. Presented to the Minister of Justice. Wellington.

Ministerial Planning Group
1991   'Maori Social and Economic Status'. Unpublished paper. Wellington: Manatu Maori.
Ministerial Review
1985   'Ministerial Review Committee Report on the Department of Maori Affairs'. 3 Sept.
Mitchell, Robin
1990   *The Treaty and the Act*. Christchurch: Cadsonbury.
Mooney, James
1965   *Ghost-Dance Religion*. Chicago: University of Chicago Press.
Moran, Bridget
1988   *Stoney Creek Woman: Sai'k'uz Ts'eke: The Story of Mary John*. Vancouver: Tillacum Library.
Morris, C. Patrick
1988   'Termination by Accountants: The Reagan Indian Policy'. *Policy Studies Journal* 16, 4 (Summer): 731-50.
Morrison, R. Bruce, and C. Roderick Wilson, eds
1986   *Native Peoples: The Canadian Experience*. Toronto: McClelland and Stewart.
Morrisseau, Miles S.
1991   'Temagami Ruling Shows Supreme Court's Double Standard'. *Nativebeat* 1, 13 (Sept.).
Morse, Bradford W.
1985   *Aboriginal Peoples and the Law*. Ottawa: Carleton University Press.
1989   'Government Obligations, Aboriginal Peoples and Section 91(24)'. Pp. 59-92 in Hawkes (1989).
1991   'Inherent/Justiciable/Contingent/New: Defining the Right to Self-Government'. *Network*, Nov. - Dec.: 6-7.
Morton, A.S.
1978   'The New Nation'. In Antoine S. Lussier and D. Bruce Sealey, eds. *The Other Natives: The Métis*. Vol. 1, 1700-1885. Winnipeg: Manitoba Métis Federation.
Mulgan, Richard
1989   *Maori, Pakeha, and Democracy*. Auckland: Oxford University Press.
Mulroney, Brian
1985   'Statement by the Prime Minister of Canada to the Conference of First Ministers on the Rights of Aboriginal Peoples'. Pp. 148-56 in Boldt and Long (1985).
Nagel, Joane
1982   'The Political Mobilization of Native Americans'. *The Social Science Journal* 19, 3 (July): 37-45.
Nagle, Patrick
1991   'Perceptions of Injustice'. *Kitchener-Waterloo Record*. 11 Sept.
Native American Rights Fund
1986   'The Preservation of Tribal Existence'. In *Native American Rights Fund 1987 Annual Report*. Boulder, Col.: Native American Rights Fund.
Native Council of Canada
1978   'Policy Statement, March, 1978'. In Native Council (1979).

1979   *A Declaration of Métis and Indian Rights.* August. Ottawa: Native Council of Canada.

1992a   *The Challenge Before Us.* Book I. Ottawa.

1992b   *Towards a New Covenant.* Book II. Ottawa.

Newman, Peter C.

1990   'Haunted by History's Lively Ghosts'. *Maclean's.* 6 Aug.

1991   'Bourassa is Just as Distinct as Mercredi'. *Maclean's.* 9 Sept.

Nga Kauwae

1991   'Ko te Ahua o ka Awatea i Tenei Wa'. *Nga Kauwae* (Newsletter of Manatu Maori) 5 (May/June).

Ngati Porou

1986   'The Ngati Porou Report: A Preliminary Survey of Human and Natural Resources on the East Coast'. Centre for Maori Studies and Research. Hamilton: University of Waikato.

Norris, Mary Jane

1990   'The Demography of Aboriginal People in Canada'. Pp. 33-60 in Shiva S. Halli et al., eds. *Ethnic Demography.* Ottawa: Carleton University Press.

Norton, C.

1988   *New Zealand Parliamentary Election Results 1946-1987.* Wellington: Victoria University.

Nunavut Constitutional Forum

1983   'Building Nunavut: A Discussion Paper Containing Proposals for an Arctic Constitution'. Yellowknife: Government of the Northwest Territories.

Opekokew, S.

1987   *The Political and Legal Inequalities Among Aboriginal Peoples in Canada.* Kingston, Ont.: Institute of Intergovernmental Relations, Queen's University.

Orange, Claudia

1977   'A Kind of Equality: Labour and the Maori People 1935-1949'. MA thesis. History Department, University of Auckland.

1987   *The Treaty of Waitangi.* Wellington: Allan and Unwin.

Paine, Robert

1985   'Norwegians and Saami: Nation-State and the Fourth World'. Pp. 211-48 in Gerald Gold, ed. *Minorities and Mother Country Imagery.* St John's. Institute of Social and Economic Research. Memorial University.

Pangowish, Roland

1992   'Native Self-Government—I: Closing the Circle. *The New Federation*, Jan./Feb.: 20-3.

Panitch, Leo, ed.

1977   *The Canadian State: Political Economy and Political Power.* Toronto: University of Toronto Press.

Panui

1990   'Hui Whakakotahi'. By the Whakakotahi Task Force. 21 June.

Parsonson, Ann

1981   'The Pursuit of Mana'. Pp. 140-69 in W.H. Oliver and B.R. Williams, eds. *The Oxford History of New Zealand.* Wellington: Oxford University Press.

Patterson, E. Palmer
    1972   *The Canadian Indian: A History Since 1500*. Don Mills, Ont.: Collier-
            Macmillan.
Pearson, David
    1990   *A Dream Deferred: The Origins of Ethnic Conflict in New Zealand*.
            Wellington: Allen and Unwin/Port Nicholson Press.
    1991   'Biculturalism and Multiculturalism in Comparative Perspective'.
            Pp. 194-214 in Spoonley et al. (1991).
Penner, Keith
    1983   *Indian Self-Government in Canada*. Report of the Special Committee
            chaired by Keith Penner. Ottawa: Queens Printer.
Peters, Evelyn
    1989   'Federal and Provincial Responsibilities for the Cree, Naskapi and
            Inuit Under the James Bay and Northern Quebec, and Northeastern
            Quebec Agreements'. Pp. 243-96 in Hawkes (1989).
Peterson, Jacqueline
    1985   'Many Roads to Red River: Métis Genesis in the Great Lakes Region,
            1680-1815'. In Peterson and Brown (1985).
Peterson, J., and J.S.H. Brown, eds
    1985   *The New Peoples: Being and Becoming Métis in North America*.
            Winnipeg: University of Manitoba Press.
Petrella, Riccardo
    1980   'Nationalist and Regionalist Movements in Western Europe'. In
            Charles R. Foster, ed. *Nations Without a State: Ethnic Minorities in
            Western Europe*. New York: Praeger.
Petrone, Penny
    1990   *Native Literature in Canada: From the Oral Tradition to the Present*.
            Toronto: Oxford University Press.
Philp, Kenneth R.
    1977   *John Collier's Crusade for Indian Reform, 1920-1954*. Tucson: Uni-
            versity of Arizona Press.
Picard, André
    1991   'Hurdles Remain at Blockade Site'. *Globe and Mail*. 11 July.
Pitt-Rivers, George H.
    1927   *The Clash of Culture and the Contact of Races*. London: George Rout-
            ledge and Sons.
Platiel, Rudy
    1987   'An Uncertain Journey'. *Globe and Mail*. 21 March.
    1991a   'The Third Solitude'. *Globe and Mail*. 13 April.
    1991b   'An Inherent Problem'. *Globe and Mail*. 22 Oct.
    1991c   'Rethinking 1492: Who were the Savages and who were the Barbar-
            ians'. *Globe and Mail*. 27 Dec.
    1992a   'Aboriginal Rights'. *Globe and Mail*. 11 Jan.
    1992b   'Aboriginal Women Divided on Constitutional Protection'. *Globe
            and Mail*. 20 Jan.
Ponting, J. Rick, ed.
    1986   *Arduous Journey: Canadian Indians and Decolonization*. Toronto:
            McClelland and Stewart.

1988   'Public Opinion on Aboriginal Peoples' Issues in Canada'. *Canadian Social Trends* 11 (Winter).

1991   'Internationalization: Perspectives on an Emerging Direction in Aboriginal Affairs'. *Canadian Ethnic Studies* 22, 3: 85-109.

Ponting, J. Rick, and Roger Gibbins

1980   *Out of Irrelevance: A Socio-Political Introduction to Indian Affairs in Canada.* Toronto: Butterworths.

Porter III, Frank W.

1988   'Indians of North America: Conflict and Survival'. Pp. 7-11 in Barbara Graymont, ed. *The Iroquois.* New York: Chelsea.

Pratt, Alan

1989   'Federalism in the Era of Aboriginal Self-Government'. Pp. 19-58 in Hawkes (1989).

Presidential Commission on Indian Reservation Economies

1984   *Report and Recommendations to the President of the United States.* November. Washington, DC: US Government Printing Office.

Price, A. Grenfell

1972   *White Settlers and Native Peoples: An Historical Study of Racial Contact.* Westport, Conn.: Greenwood Press.

Prince, Michael, J.

1987   'How Ottawa Decides Social Policy: Recent Changes in Philosophy, Structure, and Process'. Pp. 247-73 in Jacqueline S. Ismael, ed. *The Canadian Welfare State: Evolution and Transition.* Edmonton: University of Alberta Press.

Puketapu, Kara

1981   'The Rogue'. Unpublished paper. Department of Maori Affairs.

1982   'Reform From Within'. Paper presented to Public Service Management Group. Wellington.

Puketapu, Kara, and P. Haber-Thomas

1977   'The Community Services'. Report of the State Services Commission on the Department of Maori Affairs. Wellington.

Purich, Donald

1986   *Our Land: Native Peoples in Canada.* Toronto: James Lorimer.

Rangihau, John

1984   Paper presented to the Kohanga Reo National Conference. Ngaruawahia Marae. January.

Raphals, Philip

1991   'Nations in Waiting'. *Canadian Forum* 10, 14.

Rawson, Bruce

1988   'Federal Perspectives on Indian-Provincial Relations'. Pp. 23-30 in Long and Boldt (1988).

RCMP

1989   *Policing for a Pluralistic Society '89 (Building a Network).* Prepared by International Briefing Associates. Ottawa. 28-31 March.

Reedy, Tamati

1982   *Fostering the Growth of Indigenous Languages.* Paper presented to the Second Indigenous Peoples International Conference. Honolulu.

1985   'Human Resource Management in Public Administration: A Maori

Dimension'. Talk presented to the New Zealand Institute of Public Administration. Auckland. 18 Sept.

1990   'Introduction'. Pp. 5-9 in Butterworth (1990).

Report

1981   'Maori Affairs Position Paper'. Unpublished report of the National Party on Maori Affairs. Research Unit 81/39.

1982   *Race Against Time*. Produced by the Race Relations Conciliator. Wellington: Human Rights Commission.

1983   'Te Kohanga Reo: A National Review'. Unpublished report by the Maori Affairs Department.

1984   'Hui Taumata: Maori Economic Development Strategy'. Wellington: Department of Maori Affairs.

1988   'Government Review of the Te Kohanga Reo'. Unpublished paper. Wellington: Department of Maori Affairs.

Responsiveness Unit

1989   *Towards Responsiveness: Objective Setting and Evaluation*. Prepared by the Responsiveness Unit of the State Services Commission. Wellington: Government Printer.

Reynolds, Ted

1990   'The Treaty—What Went Wrong and What Are We Doing About It?' *New Zealand Geographic* 5 (Jan.-March): 33-71.

Rice, Vernon, and Colin James

1987   'Old Treaty Gives Maori Cultural Renaissance a Political Dimension'. *International Herald Tribune*. 1 Dec.

Roberts, David, and Geoffrey York

1991   'Judges Urge Separate Native Justice System'. *Globe and Mail*. 30 Aug.

Royal Commission

1992   'The Right of Aboriginal Self-government and the Constitution'. Commentary by the Royal Commission on Aboriginal Peoples. Ottawa. 13 Feb.

Sanders, Douglas

1989   'Pre-Existing Rights: The Aboriginal Peoples of Canada'. In G.-A. Beaudoin and E. Ratushny, eds. *The Canadian Charter of Rights and Freedoms*. 2nd ed. Toronto: Carswell.

Sawchuk, Joe

1985   'The Métis, Non-Status Indians and the New Aboriginality: Government Influence on Native Political Alliances and Identity'. *Canadian Ethnic Studies* 17, 2.

Schermerhorn, R.A.

1970   *Comparative Ethnic Relations: A Framework for Theory and Research*. New York: Random House.

Schwartz, Bryan

1986   *First Principles, Second Thoughts: Aboriginal Peoples, Constitutional Reform and Canadian Statecraft*. Montreal: Institute for Research on Public Policy.

Senate Select Committee on Indian Affairs

1981   *Analysis of the Fiscal Year 1982 Budget Pertaining to Indian Affairs Programs*. Washington, DC: US Government Printing Office.

Sharp, Andrew
  1990   *Justice and the Maori: Maori Claims in New Zealand Political Argument in the 1980s.* Auckland: Oxford University Press.
  1991   'The Treaty of Waitangi: Reasoning and Social Justice in New Zealand'. Pp. 131-47 in Spoonley et al. (1991).
Sheppard, Robert
  1991   'More Distinct Societies on the Way'. *Globe and Mail,* 19 Dec.
Shkilnyk, Anastasia
  1985a *A Poison Stronger Than Love.* New Haven, Conn.: Yale University Press.
  1985b *Canada's Aboriginal Languages: An Overview of Current Activities in Language Retention.* Unpublished report for the Secretary of State.
  1986   *Progress Report—Aboriginal Language Policy Developments.* Unpublished manuscript prepared for the Assembly of First Nations in Canada.
Siddon, Tom
  1991   'Natives, Ottawa Are Building a New Relationship'. Letter to the editor. *Toronto Star.* 13 July.
Silman, Janet, ed.
  1987   *Enough is Enough: Aboriginal Women Speak Out.* Toronto: Women's Press.
Simpson, Alan
  1981   'Redistributing the Maori Vote'. Pp. 28-52 in Stokes (1981).
Simpson, Jeffrey
  1990   'Native Shares in Canada'. 11 May.
  1991a 'The Debate Over Aboriginal Rights: Inherent or Contingent on the Crown? *Globe and Mail.* 15 Aug.
  1991b 'The Telling Nature of the New Royal Commission on Aboriginal Affairs'. *Globe and Mail.* 30 Aug.
  1991c 'From the Cheap Seats, a Way to Handle Native Issues'. *Globe and Mail.* 21 Nov.
Sinclair, Keith
  1971   *A History of New Zealand.* Harmondsworth: Penguin.
Smith, Dan
  1986a 'Indian Affairs: Expectations and Excuses'. *Toronto Star.* 2 Nov.
  1986b 'New Land Claims Idea a Balm for Old Wounds'. *Toronto Star.* 20 Dec.
  1991   'The Native Peoples: The Struggle for Self-Rule'. *Toronto Star.* 15-18 Sept.
Smith, Graham Hingangaroa
  1987   'Akonga Maori: Preferred Maori Teaching and Learning Methodologies'. Unpublished discussion paper.
  1990   'Taha Maori: Pakeha Capture'. Pp. 183-97 in John Codd, Richard Harker, and Roy Nash, eds. *Education, Politics and Economic Crisis.* Palmerston North, NZ.: Dunmore Press.
Smith, Linda Tuhuwai, and Graham Hingangaroa Smith
  1990   'Ki te Whai Ao, Ki te Ao Marama: Crisis and Change in Maori Education'. Pp. 123-55 in Alison Jones, ed. *Myths and Realities: Schooling in New Zealand.* Palmerston North, NZ.: Dunmore Press.

Sorrenson, M.P.K.
    1986   'A History of Maori Representation in Parliament'. Pp. B-6–B-82 in
             Report of the Royal Commission on the Electoral System. 'Towards
             a Better Democracy'. Wellington: Government Printer.

Spicer, Edward H.
    1962   *Cycles of Conquest: The Impact of Spain, Mexico, and the United*
             States on the Indians of the Southwest. Tucson: University of
             Arizona Press.

Spoonley, Paul
    1988   *Racism and Ethnicity: Critical Issues in New Zealand.* Auckland:
             Oxford University Press.

Spoonley, Paul, et al., eds
    1991   *Nga Take: Ethnic Relations and Racism in Aotearoa/New Zealand.*
             Palmerston North, NZ: Dunmore Press.

Standing Committee
    1990   *Our Future Our Selves: Aboriginal and Torres Strait Islander Com-*
             munity Control Management and Resources. House of Representa-
             tives Standing Committee on Aboriginal Affairs. Canberra:
             Government Publishing Service.

State Services Commission
    1988   *Sharing Control: A Study of Responsiveness and Devolution in the*
             Statutory Social Services. Wellington: Government Printer.
    1989   'Partnership Dialogue: A Maori Consultation Process. He Korero
             Rangapu'. Unpublished document.

Stea, David, and Ben Wisner, eds
    1984   'The Fourth World: A Geography of Indigenous Struggles'.
             Antipodes: A Radical Journal of Geography 16, 2.

Steiner, Stan
    1968   *The New Indians.* New York: Delta.

Steinlien, Oystein
    1989   'The Sami Law: A Change of Norwegian Government Policy
             Toward the Sami Minority?' *Canadian Journal of Native Studies*
             9, 1: 1-14.

Stokes, Evelyn
    1981   *Maori Representation in Parliament.* Occasional Paper No. 14.
             Hamilton, NZ: Waikato University.

Sto:lo
    1984   *How Secure is Our Future? A Look at Historical and Current Devel-*
             opments within Sto:lo Territory. Special edition. March.

Sturtevant, William C.
    1983   'Tribe and State in the Sixteenth and Twentieth Centuries'. Pp. 3-16
             in Tooker (1983).

Sullivan, Ann
    1990   'Iwi Policies Questioned'. *New Zealand Herald.* 16 May.

Tabacoff, D.
    1975   'The Role of the Maori MP in Contemporary New Zealand Politics'.
             In S. Levine, ed. *New Zealand Politics: A Reader.* Melbourne:
             Cheshire.

Tainui Report
    1983   'A Survey of Human and Natural Resources'. Occasional Paper No.
            19 by K.N. Egan and Robert T. Mahuta. Centre for Maori Studies and
            Research. Waikato University, Hamilton, NZ.
Tauroa, Hiwi
    1989   *Healing the Breach: One Man's Perspective on the Treaty of Wai-
            tangi.* Auckland: Collins.
Taylor, Graham D.
    1980   *The New Deal and American Indian Tribalism: The Administration
            of the Indian Reorganization Act, 1934-1945.* Lincoln: University of
            Nebraska Press.
Taylor, John Leonard
    1983   'An Historical Introduction to Métis Claims in Canada'. *Canadian
            Journal of Native Studies* 3, 1.
Taylor, John P., and Gary Paget
    1989   'Federal/Provincial Responsibility and the Sechelt'. Pp. 297-348 in
            Hawkes (1989).
Teasdale, G.R., and A.J. Whitelaw
    1981   *The Early Childhood Education of Aboriginal Australians: A Review
            of Six Action-Research Projects.* Victoria: ACER.
Temm, Paul
    1990   *The Waitangi Tribunal: The Conscience of a Nation.* Auckland:
            Random Centre.
Tennant, Paul
    1985   'Aboriginal Rights and the Penner Report on Indian Self-Govern-
            ment'. Pp. 321-32 in Boldt and Long (1985).
    1990   *Aboriginal Peoples and Politics: The Indian Land Question in British
            Columbia, 1849-1989.* Vancouver: University of British Columbia Press.
Thornton, Russell
    1984   'Cherokee Population Losses during the Trail of Tears: A New Per-
            spective and a New Estimate'. *Ethnohistory* 31, 4: 289-300.
Tobias, John L.
    1976   'Protection, Civilization, and Assimilation: An Outline History of
            Canada's Indian Policy'. *Western Canadian Journal of Anthropology*
            6, 2: 13-30.
Tonkinson, Robert, and Michael Howard
    1990   *Going It Alone? Prospects for Aboriginal Autonomy.* Canberra: Abo-
            riginal Studies Press.
Tooker, Elisabeth, ed.
    1983   *The Development of Political Organization in Native North America.*
            Proceedings of the American Ethnological Society, 1979.
Toronto Star
    1990a   'Ottawa $2.5 Billion Black Hole Frustrates Natives, Bureaucrats'. 11
            Nov.
    1990b   'Oka Costs Natives Canada's Sympathy'. 27 Nov.
    1991a   'Natives Want Their Language to be Protected'. 22 Jan.
    1991b   'Natives Unwilling to Welcome Newcomer'. 28 April.

1991c 'Ontario Natives Take "Historic Step" Towards Self-Government'.
        4 June.
1991d 'District Society of Natives Vital to Reform, Clark Warns'. 8 July.
1991e 'One Year After Oka Crisis Hot Summer Looms Again'. 8 July.
1991f 'Native Rights Document May Lack Clout'. 11 Aug.
1991g 'Ottawa Launches Native Probe'. 28 Aug.
1991h 'Manitoba Findings on Native Justice Get Mixed Reaction'.
        31 Aug.
1991i 'Natives Call Great Whale Ruling a Big Victory'. 11 Sept.
1991j 'Natives Polled on Law System'. 14 Sept.
1991k 'Natives Deserve 12 Commons Seats, Panel Says'. 19 Sept.
1991l 'Angry Leaders Blast "Meech II"'. 25 Sept.
1991m 'Support for Natives Is Strong, Poll Finds'. 11 Nov.

Turpel, Mary Ellen
    1992   'Statement'. *Between The Lines*. TVOntario broadcast. 6 March.

US Congress
    1976   'Public Law 93-638: The Indian Self-Determination and Education
            Assistance Act'. *United States Statutes at Large*. Vol. 88, Part 2: 2203-4.

US Department of the Interior
    1986   'Bureau of Indian Affairs 1986 Budget Request Is $923.7 Million'.
            Release for 5 Feb. Washington, DC: US Government Printing Office.

Usher, Peter J.
    1991   'Some Implications of the Sparrow Judgement for Resource Conser-
            vation and Management'. *Alternatives* 18, 2: 20-1.

Vallee, Frank G.
    1971   'The Emerging Northern Mosaic'. In Richard J. Ossenberg, ed. *Cana-
            dian Society*. Scarborough, Ont.: Prentice-Hall.

van den Berghe, Pierre
    1981   'Protection of Ethnic Minorities: A Critical Appraisal'. Pp. 343-55 in
            R.G. Wirsing, ed. *Protection of Ethnic Minorities: A Comparative Per-
            spective*. New York: Pergamon.

Van Kirk, Sylvia
    1980   '*Many Tender Ties': Women in Fur Trade Society, 1670-1870*. Win-
            nipeg: Watson and Dwyer.

Van Loon, Richard
    1990   'The Federal Perspective'. *Northern Perspectives* 18, 4 (November-
            December): 8-9.

Vasil, Raj
    1988   *Biculturalism—Reconciling Aotearoa with New Zealand*. Welling-
            ton: Victoria University Press for the Institute of Policy Studies.
    1990   *What Do the Maori Want? New Maori Political Perspectives*. Auck-
            land: Random Century.

Vowles, Jack
    1991   'How Do We Treat The Treaty?' *Political Science* (N2) 43, 1: 68-80.

Wagner, Murray W.
    1991   'Footsteps along the Road: Indian Land Claims and Access to Natural
            Resources'. *Alternatives* 18, 2: 22-7.

Waitangi Tribunal

    1988   *Finding of the Waitangi Tribunal on the Manukau Claim*. Wellington: Government Printer.

Walker, Ranginui

    1979   'The Maori Minority and the Democratic Process'. Paper presented to the New Zealand Council. Wellington.

    1984   'The Genesis of Maori Activism'. *Journal of Polynesian Society* 93: 267-82.

    1987   'Maori Aspirations and Social Policy'. Preliminary review of submissions to the Royal Commission on Social Policy.

    1989   'The Maori People: Their Political Development'. Pp. 320-40 in Hyam Gold, ed. *New Zealand Politics and Perspectives*. Auckland: Longman Paul.

    1990   'The Tino Rangatiratanga Agenda'. *Listener and TV Times*, 19 July: 72.

Walsh, Pat, and Kurt Wetzel

    1990   'State Restructuring, Corporate Strategy and Industrial Relations: State-Owned Enterprise Management in New Zealand'. Paper presented to the 5th Biennial Conference of the Association of Industrial Relations Academics of Australia and New Zealand. Melbourne: University of Melbourne. 4-7 July.

Ward, Alan

    1974   *A Show of Injustice: Racial Amalgamation in Nineteenth Century New Zealand*. Canberra: Oxford University Press/Auckland University Press.

Washburn, Wilcomb E., ed.

    1973   *The American Indian and the United States: A Documentary History*. New York: Random House.

Watson, Graham

    1981   'The Reification of Ethnicity and Political Consequences in the North'. *Canadian Review of Sociology and Anthropology* 18, 4 (November).

Watt, Keith

    1990a 'Uneasy Partners'. *Report on Business Magazine*, December: 42-9.

    1990b 'NWT a Model for the World?' *Globe and Mail*. 31 Dec.

Weaver, Sally M.

    1981   *Making Canadian Indian Policy: The Hidden Agenda, 1968-1970*. Toronto: University of Toronto Press.

    1983   'Australian Aborigine Policy: Aboriginal Pressure Groups or Government Advisory Bodies?' *Oceania* 54: 1-22, 85-108.

    1984   'Struggles of the Nation-State to Define Aboriginal Ethnicity: Canada and Australia'. Pp. 182-210 in G. Gold, ed. *Minorities and Mother Country Imagery*. Institute of Social and Economic Research No. 13. St John's, Nfld: Memorial University Press.

    1985a 'Federal Policy-Making for Métis and Non-Status Indians in the Context of Native Policy'. *Canadian Ethnic Studies* 17, 2.

    1985b 'Federal Difficulties With Aboriginal Demands'. Pp. 139-47 in Boldt and Long (1985).

1990   'Self-Government for Indians 1980-1990: Political Transformations or Symbolic Gestures'. Paper presented to the UNESCO Conference on the Migration and the Transformation of Cultures in Canada.

1991   'A New Paradigm in Canadian Indian Policy for the 1990s'. *Canadian Ethnic Studies* 22, 3: 8-18.

Weber, Max
1947   *The Theory of Social and Economic Organization.* New York: Oxford University Press.

Webster, Peter
1979   *Rua and the Millenium.* Wellington: Victoria University Press.

Wetere, Koro
1987   'A Status Report on Maori Affairs'. Unpublished address by the Minister of Maori Affairs, 20 July.

Wilkinson, Charles F.
1987   *American Indians, Time and the Law: Native Societies in a Modern Constitutional Democracy.* New Haven: Yale University Press.

Williams, J.A.
1969   *Politics of the New Zealand Maori: Protest and Cooperation, 1891-1909.* London: Oxford University Press.

Williams, Joe
1989   'Indigenous Human Rights in New Zealand from an International Perspective'. In conference proceedings, the Aotearoa/New Zealand and Human Rights in the Pacific and Asia Region Conference. Wellington. 26-28 May.

Williams Jr, Robert A.
1990   *The American Indian in Western Legal Thought.* New York: Oxford University Press.

Wilmsen, Edwin N. (ed.)
1989   *We Are Here: Politics of Aboriginal Land Tenure.* Berkeley: University of California Press.

Witt, Shirley Hill
1965   'Nationalistic Trends among American Indians'. In Levine and Lurie (1970).

1984   'Native Women Today: Sexism and the Indian Woman'. Pp. 23-31 in Alison M. Jaggar and Paula S. Rothenberg, eds. *Feminist Frameworks: Alternative Theoretical Accounts of the Relations Between Women and Men.* 2nd ed. Toronto: McGraw-Hill.

Wohlfeld, Monika J., and Neil Nevitte
1990   'PostIndustrial Value Change and Support for Native Issues'. *Canadian Ethnic Studies* 22, 3: 56-68.

Working Party
1984   Unpublished Report of the Working Party Review of the Department of Maori Affairs Head Office. Wellington.

Worsley, Peter
1967   *The Trumpet Shall Sound.* London: MacGibbon.

Wright, Jr, J. Leitch
1986   *Creeks and Seminoles.* Lincoln: University of Nebraska Press.

York, Geoffrey

　　1986　'Crees Frustrated by Experiment in Self-Government'. *Globe and Mail*. 20 May.

　　1991　'The Troubled and Troubling Legacy of Wounded Knee'. *Globe and Mail*. 22 June.

INDEX

Abele, Frances, 49
aboriginal criminal justice, 120-4
(*see also* aboriginal peoples in
Canada); in BC, 123; in New
Zealand, 122; in the United
States, 123
aboriginal electoral districts, 11,
86-92; in Canada, 86-8, 90-2; in
New Zealand, 88-90 (*also* separate
aboriginal representation)
aboriginal peoples, as nations, 1-6,
129-30; definition of, 1; resistance
by, 3
aboriginal peoples in Canada, 8-38;
as distinct societies, 69, 118, 221;
as social 'problem', 39-42, 51, 79,
225; aspirations of, 21-38; citizenship and, 22; comparisons with
South Africa, 8, 76; criminal justice
system, 21-2, 27, 120-4; demographic features, 12-13; government
policy and, 39-54; government
response to, 225-6; Inuit as, 15;
language preservation, 22; legal
distinctions, 13-15; Métis as, 15;
multiculturalism and, 30; non-
status Indians as, 14-15; Quebec
and, 60-1; rights, 63; self-determination, 23-9; self-government,
23-9, 47-9, 55-72; urban, 18-19, 28;
women, 19-20; social context and,
12-38; socio-economic status of,
16-20
aboriginal protest, 84-6, 93-101
aboriginal rights, 29-31, 45; definition of, 29-30
aboriginality, principle of, 63, 221,
224; in New Zealand, 222; in the
United States, 222; *see also* aboriginal rights

aboriginal-state relations, 124-6,
230-1
acculturation, *see* assimilation
Ahenakew, David, 30
Akwesasne, 92, 93
Alberta, 15, 26, 28
Allen, Paula Gunn, 19, 84, 104
alternative funding arrangements,
48, 78, 79, 80
anglo-conformity, *see* assimilation
Angus, Murray, 8, 35, 49, 81, 223
Arctic, 109-10; *see also* Nunavut
Armstrong, M. Jocelyn, 180, 188,
189
Asch, Michael, 29, 59, 65-6, 119
Assembly of First Nations (AFN), 14,
63-4, 82, 85, 109
assimilation, 10, 17, 40-2, 50, 52,
53, 54, 77, 80, 144-5, 147, 148-9,
164, 165, 167, 176, 197, 198, 224-5
Australia, 172
Aucoin, Pierre, 204
Awatere, Donna, 178
Axworthy, Thomas, 44, 45

band councils, 74
Band Support Funding programs, 45
Berger, Thomas, 104
biculturalism, 188, 196, 217-18; *see
also* partnership
Bienvenue, Rita, 16
Bill C-31, 14, 19, 75
Blauner, Robert, 73
BNA (British North America) Act,
76; *see also* Constitution Act
Bodley, John, 3
Boldt, Menno, 42, 43, 50, 52, 54, 58
British Columbia, 36-8, 66-7; BC
Claims Task Force, 38
Britsch-Devany, Susan, 211, 213, 214